Ethics and Cyber Warfare

ETHICS AND CYBER WARFARE

The Quest for Responsible Security in the Age of Digital Warfare

George Lucas

OXFORD
UNIVERSITY PRESS

Oxford University Press is a department of the University of Oxford. It furthers
the University's objective of excellence in research, scholarship, and education
by publishing worldwide. Oxford is a registered trade mark of Oxford University
Press in the UK and certain other countries.

Published in the United States of America by Oxford University Press
198 Madison Avenue, New York, NY 10016, United States of America.

Library of Congress Cataloging-in-Publication Data
Names: Lucas, George R., author.
Title: Ethics and cyberwarfare: the quest for responsible security in the
age of digital warfare / George Lucas.
Description: New York, NY : Oxford University Press, 2017. |
Includes bibliographical references and index.
Identifiers: LCCN 2016009377 | ISBN 9780190276522 (hardcover : alk. paper)
Subjects: LCSH: Cyberspace operations (Military science) | National security. |
Hacktivism. | Computer crimes. | State crimes. | Information warfare—Moral and
ethical aspects. | Information technology—Moral and ethical aspects. | Just war doctrine.
Classification: LCC U167.5.C92 L83 2016 | DDC 172/.42—dc23
LC record available at https://lccn.loc.gov/2016009377

9 8 7 6 5 4 3 2 1
Printed by Sheridan Books, Inc., United States of America

For my girls: Jessica, Kimberly, and Theresa
With love from Dad

Where is the Wisdom
Made lost
In information?

                     —T. S. Eliot, *The Rock*, 1934

CONTENTS

PREFACE

One of the most astonishing features of cyber conflict is the rapidity with which any account of it becomes outmoded. In this work, I attribute that problem to a principle widely known in technology circles as "Moore's Law," holding generally that the pace of technological change—that is, the rate of change of the rate of technological change—doubles every two years. Recently, such estimates of the period of that exponential function have shrunk to eighteen months. It takes at least eighteen months for a manuscript to go from first draft to print edition, which virtually guarantees that any set of facts cited as evidence herein will quickly be overtaken by events.

I have allowed for this as much as possible, both by trying to update and revise my evidentiary accounts daily, even during production (for as long as the publisher could allow), and even more by trying to select evidence and cases that already enjoy broad familiarity and currency, and perhaps therefore also enjoy some staying power in the public consciousness. These include the Stuxnet/Olympic Games episode (ca. 2010) and, more recently, the revelations in July 2015 of the theft of twenty-two million personnel files from the US Office of Personnel Management during the preceding year. I can obviously not guarantee, however, that some series of cyber events—dramatic, tragic, or (like the Sony Pictures hack in late 2014) comic—will not transpire in the interim between my releasing the manuscript and the time of its publication that will render the entire treatment inaccurate, incomplete, or dated.

A second feature of cyber conflict, however, is even more problematic, and it is to this that the book is primarily addressed: the astonishing divergence in the interpretations of these cyber events. What I mean to highlight is the extraordinary diversity, not merely in the interpretive accounts of episodes such as Stuxnet, but even in what counts as evidence, as well as in what the "evidence" or relevant set of facts actually is on which those divergent interpretations might be based. Observers do not agree on exactly what happened, when, to whom, or (again, as in the case of Stuxnet) who first discovered the event or "figured it all out."

This divergence transcends mere differences of opinion. It is more to be compared to the conflicting journalistic reports pouring forth in the immediate aftermath of a tragedy (such as the Paris shootings in 2015): where did they occur; when did they take place exactly; how many people were involved, killed, injured, captured; and so forth. There is, in short, a kind of incipient hysteria in the accounts offered, even in the facts themselves, let alone in interpretations of past episodes of cyber conflict, even after the passage of months or years. I highlight several instances of these, including the continuing dispute over what exactly happened, who "did it," and how government officials and other principal actors reacted in the immediate aftermath of the series of distributed denial of service attacks in Estonia in 2007, the subsequent interpretations of which range from mere acts of vandalism by one or more dissidents inside Estonia itself, all the way to claims of a highly organized campaign of cyber warfare against Estonia carried out by agents or organizations affiliated with the Russian Federation. I not only document these divergent accounts but also disclose at least some instances of deliberate dissemblance and what I term "historical revisionism" by self-interested parties attempting to minimize the extent of their own confusion and uncertainty during the crisis.

This widespread ambiguity, uncertainty, and sharp disagreement on virtually everything relevant for consideration is indicative of what the eminent Scottish moral philosopher Alasdair MacIntyre once termed an "epistemological crisis." Such a crisis is not entirely unlike the kind of "paradigm collapse" that another eminent philosopher, Thomas Kuhn, had outlined as the harbinger of disruptive innovation and transformative change in the midst of a so-called scientific revolution. An epistemological crisis, however, is more widespread and pervasive, a more generalized phenomenon that (significantly) stems from the complete lack of a comprehensive conceptual foundation or adequate interpretive framework from which to gather data, determine which data count as relevant evidence, and finally assemble that data into a coherent narrative. That narrative must encompass all known data, all acknowledged anomalies in that data, and in particular sort out and make sense of rival interpretations and conflicting points of view regarding the significance and proper interpretation of that data. The successful narrative must further be able to explain how those disputes between rivals arise, what each opposing position is able to explain thoroughly, as well as what each is, by contrast, wholly inadequate to explain, *and why*.[1]

The kinds of chaos and confusion to which we are witness at present in the rival accounts of cyber conflicts, past and present, as well as in what to expect, what to fear, and what to protect ourselves against, is precisely what we should anticipate, according to MacIntyre, when we are mired in an epistemological crisis, and when we find ourselves utterly lacking a broad conceptual foundation and adequate interpretive framework from which to establish order out of chaos.

It is the aim of this book to provide such a foundation for future discussions of cyber conflict, one which may assist rivals and adversaries alike to determine what counts as evidence, how to make sense of that evidence, and where they might search for common ground in their efforts to ensure that pursuit of competing interests in the cyber domain does not result in collective catastrophe.

In engaging in this important enterprise, finally, ethics is not to be viewed as ancillary or of secondary importance, factored in at the end merely to guarantee that everyone involved can feel good about themselves, justify their individual positions, or remain "civilized" (whatever that may mean in this context). Instead, I follow the lead of political philosopher Michael Walzer in equating ethics with sound strategy. "Ethics" and "sound strategy" are alike in inquiring about the ultimate ends of our actions. Both demand that we prove willing to subordinate choices among tactics to the satisfactory achievement of those ends. Both invite us, further, to examine what ends are appropriate, meaningful, and ultimately worth pursuing.

Hence, talking about ethics in the midst of cyber conflict invites all concerned to reflect more deeply on who they are, what they think they are "about" in this new domain, what they hope to accomplish, as well as what they hope fervently to avoid. Discussion of ethics likewise invites us to engage in tactical discussions about the various means most suited to pursuit of the desired ends, without undermining or subverting those ends. Whenever important public figures advocate for "ethics and leadership," they have something like this sense of the connectivity of tactics, operations, and strategy—of worthy ends toward which to strive and of the means most appropriate to reaching those goals—at least vaguely in mind. Nothing could be more important for us to consider at the present moment, as these considerations shape our collective policies toward conflict in the cyber domain.

NOTE

1. See Alasdair MacIntyre, "Epistemological Crises, Dramatic Narrative, and the Philosophy of Science," *The Monist* 60, no. 4 (October 1977): 453–472. See also Thomas S. Kuhn, *The Structure of Scientific Revolutions* (Chicago: University of Chicago Press, 1963).

ACKNOWLEDGMENTS

I deeply appreciate the support of the John J. Reilly Center for Science, Technology, and Values at Notre Dame University for extending a long-term visiting research appointment that enabled the completion of this work immediately following my retirement from the U.S. Department of Defense. I benefitted earlier from several years of public presentations and discussion of the nascent ideas for this book with cadets and research faculty while serving as a research fellow at the Centre de Recherche des Écoles de Saint-Cyr Coëtquidan (CREC) in the French Military Academy (Saint-Cyr, Brittany). The final months of writing were supported with a fellowship from the Inamori Center for Ethics and Excellence at Case Western Reserve University (Cleveland OH).

I wish to thank my spouse, Professor Patricia Cook (Naval Postgraduate School, Monterey), and my editor, Peter Ohlin at Oxford, for patiently working through my often-tortured prose and helping to make the presentation of the central ideas clearer than they might otherwise have been. Emily Sacharin at Oxford, for her part, has kept this project on schedule, and moving forward from the beginning, and has been a terrific colleague with whom to collaborate on this and earlier publications. She will be missed, but has been ably succeeded by Andrew Ward, whom I also wish to thank, along with Ginny Faber, for her extremely helpful editorial advice. The index for this book was prepared meticulously by Joan C. Cook, whom I especially wish to thank.

Introduction

Crime or Warfare?

In a darkened room, in front of several hundred distinguished international legal scholars, moral philosophers, and public policy authorities gathered at the Center for Ethics and the Rule of Law at the University of Pennsylvania Law School in Philadelphia, the deputy director of the National Security Agency (NSA) displays a PowerPoint slide of an immense multicolored map of the world. Generated by the agency's powerful Internet mapping, exploration, and analysis program Treasure Map,[1] the slide shows thousands of locations across Eastern Europe and the Middle East from which crippling cyberattacks against virtually every major financial institution in the United States had apparently been launched in the fall of 2012 (see Figure Intro. 1). The audience is challenged with a question: were these cyberattacks simply crimes on a massive scale, or do they represent something different—perhaps *acts of war* in a new kind of warfare?

The speaker at the front of the room that day in November 2013 was Brigadier General Chris Inglis (PhD, USAF Reserve), invited by Professor Claire Finkelstein, director of the center. Inglis had been approved and dispatched on a round of public speaking by the NSA during the latter part of 2013. His appearances, including a *60 Minutes* interview and tour of NSA facilities in Ft. Meade, Maryland,[2] that had aired in October, were an essential component of the agency's attempts at damage control, offering a public account of its hitherto classified and secret data-collection and analysis activities in the wake of the revelations in June and July made by former NSA contractor Edward Snowden that the United States was conducting clandestine surveillance operations at home and abroad on a massive scale.

Figure Intro. 1
The National Security Agency's Treasure Map depiction of 2012 cyberattacks on US Financial Institutions.

During a brief period of employment in NSA's signals intelligence (SIGINT) station in Hawaii, Snowden had quietly and surreptitiously downloaded massive amounts of classified data documenting the agency's data-collection and analysis efforts and findings. He then fled with the stolen data, first to Hong Kong, and eventually to the Russian Federation, where he sought political asylum to avoid capture and arrest by the FBI. He released portions of this stolen information to the *The Guardian* newspaper in London and to other news media outlets, documenting the US intelligence agency's involvement in cyberespionage, big-data collection and analysis, and surveillance activities throughout the world that (he alleged) included extensive surveillance of American citizens. These revelations stimulated international outrage and concern, evoking images in the public mind of the former East Germany's feared secret police, the Stasi.

Was Snowden engaged in legitimate whistleblowing, seeking to inform and protect the American public against government overreach that threatened to infringe on their individual liberty and privacy, as he and his supporters maintain? Or was Snowden's release of classified government documents an act of treason, as his angry critics and detractors claim, at a time when the United States is engaged in an ongoing, proactive, and possibly new kind of preemptive war of national self-defense?

In the summer of 2010, a German industrial computer security expert, Ralph Langner, reported that a disturbing form of malware had burrowed its way into the supervisory control and data acquisitions systems (SCDASs) of large industries in many nations. An exhaustive investigation of this computer worm by the Internet security firm Symantec revealed that the malware was intended to disrupt the normal functioning of the programmable logic controllers that are the basic components of most computer-controlled industrial processes. While the worm (nicknamed "Stuxnet" after portions of Microsoft code that it disrupted) had been detected in systems all over the world, over 60 percent of the infected systems were in Iran. Langner and other security experts suggested that Stuxnet had been designed to disrupt only very specific targets, since it seemed to be dormant and harmless in the remaining systems it had infected—indeed, it had apparently been set to self-destruct in those systems by July 2012. Many IT security experts now support the theory that Stuxnet was developed jointly by the United States and Israel as a sophisticated cyber weapon for use in a large clandestine operation known as "Olympic Games."[3]

Stuxnet had been designed to affect the control systems of Siemens nuclear centrifuges—but only of a single array, consisting of precisely 984 of one particular model, which happened to be located in the top-secret Natanz nuclear power facility in Iran. International law prohibited Iran from acquiring this kind of embargoed equipment, which could be used to process fuel for a nuclear weapon. The Stuxnet computer malware disabled the centrifuges, causing them to spin out of control, causing serious damage to them, while simultaneously sending information to the Iranian nuclear technicians that the equipment was functioning normally.

The Stuxnet program was likely introduced into the otherwise-secured Iranian network via an infected USB thumb drive, whereupon it seriously degraded Iran's covert nuclear weapons program, setting it back, according to some estimates at the time, by as much as five years. Then, when an unwitting Iranian nuclear technician took his laptop home from the Natanz lab and logged onto the Internet, the malware escaped and infected other systems around the world, which eventually led to its discovery by Langner and other security experts. Arguably, Stuxnet was the first example of a virtual weapon in cyberspace causing physical damage in the real world. In this instance, however, there was no collateral damage to nonmilitary infrastructure or any accompanying injury or loss of life.[4] Despite the lack of excessive or unrelated harm to anything other than its intended military target, however, should we now regard—or for that matter, would the Iranian government itself have been justified at the time in regarding—this unmistakable act of military-industrial sabotage as also, in fact, *an act of war?*

Only three years earlier, in the late spring of 2007, the Baltic nation of Estonia had been the victim of a stream of massive distributed denial of service (DDoS) cyberattacks that had affected financial institutions, news organizations, and government agencies throughout the tiny NATO-member nation. DDoS attacks involve large networks of hijacked, compromised computers, termed "botnets,"[5] that can be ordered by hackers to generate and transmit an enormous barrage of messages or logon requests to a specific Internet address, overwhelming it and effectively shutting down whatever agency, organization, or financial service is associated with that address. The attacks appeared to have originated from multiple locations within the neighboring Russian Federation, as well as from some locations inside Estonia itself.[6]

Only days before the attacks commenced, the Estonian government had reached a controversial decision to move a prominent World War II Russian memorial statue from a central location in the capital city of Tallinn to a less-prestigious location in a nearby military cemetery. Ethnic Russians constitute a sizeable minority (nearly 40 percent) of Estonia's population, and a large majority of them had been outraged by the decision. Their subsequent street protests in Estonia were attended by formal diplomatic objections lodged by the Russian government. These were followed closely by the DDoS attacks, which, intermittently for three weeks in April and May, effectively cut the country off from the rest of the world, and its citizens from their government and financial institutions. The Estonian government, at the time, gave serious consideration to requesting military assistance from NATO under treaty provisions providing for defense and collective security. This would have required characterizing the cyberattacks as the equivalent of a conventional armed attack (a grave step that NATO command was unwilling to take).

Then, as suddenly as they had begun, the cyberattacks ceased. The Russian government has consistently disavowed any formal responsibility for the attacks, claiming they had no control over "patriotic dissidents" within their borders who might likewise have been outraged by the decision to move the memorial. Significantly, no personal injuries or loss of life accompanied the attacks. No physical damage was done to personal or public property or civilian infrastructure; nor were any thefts of financial resources or of personal information subsequently attributed to the attacks. Accordingly, are we to merely regard them as vigilante acts carried out by individuals and dissident groups both inside and outside Estonia to protest the government's actions? Or should we, in agreement with former

White House national security adviser and cyber expert Richard A. Clarke, among others, regard the Estonian incident in 2007 as *the first documented case of a genuine cyberwar?*[7]

In contrast, theft of personal information and identity (if not personal property or financial resources directly) was widely reported, and without any doubt was the direct result of the two massive cyberattacks in the United States.

In the summer of 2015, the director of the US Office of Personnel Management (OPM) abruptly resigned in the wake of a massive cyberattack on that agency that had resulted in the theft of detailed personal information (including highly confidential fingerprint files) on some twenty-two million current and former civilian federal civil service employees (including myself). Although the Chinese government has never publicly acknowledged responsibility for the attacks, the attacks have been attributed with a high degree of certainty to cyberespionage agents of the People's Liberation Army (PLA) in China. The intended use of this data and the motives behind the attack remain unclear at the time of this writing and are the source of much concern and speculation.[8]

But that the attack had been carried out by highly proficient Chinese military "cyber warriors" is not seriously doubted. Indeed, so accurate and reliable has the field of cyber forensics become in only a few short years that in 2014 the United States was able to indict five members of the PLA's now-infamous battalion of cyber warriors, known as Shanghai Unit 61384, on probable cause for having been responsible for massive cyberthefts of patents and trade secrets from US-based aerospace and defense industries over several years, including the theft from defense contractor Lockheed-Martin of detailed plans and specifications for the US military's controversial new strike fighter, the F-35. The indictments were not expected to result in the actual arrest and prosecution of the individuals named but were intended instead to send a message to the Chinese government that its disavowal or denial of state accountability for the crimes under international law was no longer plausible.[9]

Only a few months later, in a widely reported incident in November 2014, North Korean cyber warriors apparently hacked into the files of Sony Pictures, stealing personal information and emails, releasing some of them publicly and threatening to release others, an action known as "doxing."[10] Their goal was to blackmail Sony executives into canceling the upcoming release of the movie *The Interview*. The movie, a comedy, portrayed a bungling attempt to assassinate North Korea's leader Kim Jong-un. The incident itself seemed almost comic (never, it was frequently remarked with amusement at the time, had such a second-rate movie received such first-class publicity), save for the importance of what it signified: the interference by agents of a foreign government in the internal affairs of another sovereign nation, attempting to inhibit freedom of expression and violating personal privacy on a massive scale for political purposes. This kind of extortion and blackmail, and its impact on corporate and individual behavior in a sovereign country, was not at all amusing. The United States thus treated the incident as a serious criminal act in the context of a wider international conflict.[11] But should we regard this incident, and others like it, when they are carried out by state agents on behalf of their governments for political reasons, as the equivalent of military skirmishes in an ongoing cyberwar?

Under most circumstances, with the possible exception of Stuxnet, we would decidedly *not* regard any of these large-scale hacking incidents as akin to warfare, let alone as acts of armed conflict. Indeed, had they been undertaken by individuals or organizations, they would be classified straightforwardly as crimes, with the individuals involved subject to apprehension, extradition, arrest, indictment, trial, and possible imprisonment. The United States and other nations, especially those party to what is known as the CCC—the Convention on Cyber Crime, formulated by delegates in Bucharest, Romania, in 2001—now cooperate in combating cybercrime and cybercriminals today.[12]

Hacktivism is a recent term of art used to classify and describe the individuals and organizations that carry out criminal activities on the Internet or in other regions of the cyber domain for political purposes rather than personal or financial gain,[13] for example, to protest government or organizational actions, such as happened in Estonia.

In the real world, when nation-states and their agents engage in criminal activities on foreign soil for political benefit, we call it espionage.[14] Espionage is not covered explicitly under international law, although the individuals who engage in it are subject to arrest and prosecution as criminals, traitors, or enemy spies under the laws of the domestic legal jurisdiction where the activities occur. Perhaps, as some critics of the concept of cyber warfare say, we should regard all instances of cybercrime as espionage and resist confusing or conflating crime or espionage carried out in the virtual cyber domain with acts of war and armed conflict carried out in the real world.[15]

By contrast, we should reserve the term *cyber warfare* to describe a type of cyberattack like Stuxnet—that is, that causes physical damage to people and objects in the real world.[16] Richard Clarke and other counterterrorism experts have worried about a conceivable series of cyberattacks that could be launched against vital civilian infrastructure and military installations. Attacks on air- and ground-traffic-control systems could, for example, cause freight trains loaded with chemicals and flammable materials to derail, or planes to collide in mid-air or fall out of the sky. Electric power grids could be shut down, and hydroelectric generators could be made to spin out of control and explode (like the Stuxnet-controlled centrifuges), destroying dams and causing massive flooding. Chemical plants might begin to leak poisonous fumes into nearby cities. The resultant "cyber Pearl Harbor," or "cyber Armageddon," could lead to death and destruction on the scale of a thermonuclear war.[17] Perhaps most disturbingly, such writers sometimes suggest that these massive cyberattacks could be carried out not only by determined nation-state adversaries with the national resources to invest in the development of cyber weapons, but also by small terrorist cells with only two or three members, or even by our next-door neighbor's alienated fourteen-year-old, laboring in isolation and secrecy in his or her upstairs bedroom!

The term *cyber warfare* was coined in the 1990s by John Arquilla, who at the time was a renowned international and strategic studies expert at the Rand Corporation. He and an equally eminent computer scientist at Georgetown University, Dr. Dorothy Denning, also termed this new phenomenon "information warfare."[18] Their warnings about the threats this new capability posed, however, were met with skepticism at the time. Their fellow Rand Corporation scholar Martin C. Libicki has since offered some of the most detailed and plausible analyses of what the actual threat levels of such warfare are now, and might soon become, as well as how we might secure ourselves against such threats.[19]

Such anxiety-provoking predictions, then, have abounded for more than a decade. Yet again, with the possible exception of Stuxnet, the doomsday scenarios have not occurred, at least not yet. I myself have maintained that the threats posed by the teenage neighbor or the terrorist cell are exaggerated. To wage a genuine cyberwar, an individual must be more than a clever computer geek. He or she requires privileged access to a hydroelectric generator on which to design and test the software, and it can prove difficult to gain access to such equipment (let alone to wrestle it up the steps and into the third-floor terrorists' flat in, say, Hamburg, or into the neighbor's son's bedroom). Genuine cyber weapons consist solely of complex software that is designed to exploit vulnerabilities residing in other software, such as computer operating systems or ICAs (industrial control systems) that govern the operation of industrial devices and processes throughout the world.[20] Designing such weapons requires knowledge, not just of how to code software and write destructive virus programs, but also of how the intended "targets" (the vastly varied industrial machines and systems) actually operate. A software weapon may, for example, emulate the normal operation of an array of equipment at a factory or an energy company while it takes control of and destroys that equipment or disrupts the processes it controls, such as the flow of oil through a pipeline or of electricity across a power grid. All this requires a range of knowledge, experience, expertise, and physical resources on which to practice and test weapons designs that far exceed those of any typical individual or even the most dedicated and well-resourced criminal or terrorist group.

Contrary to the blanket dismissal of *all* such prospects by naysayers such as Thomas Rid, however, the hypothetical threat of determined adversary nations engaging in something like genuine warfare in the cyber domain remains a plausible one. Surely Stuxnet demonstrates that. *How seriously should we take this threat of genuine cyber warfare, and what should individuals, organizations, or states be permitted to do in response?*

That question—the price of cybersecurity—is a central topic in this book. To help answer it, the book examines what has actually been happening in the cyber domain—activities that many authorities have begun to describe as a new kind of warfare, sometimes called "soft" war, or "unarmed conflict."[21]

Indeed, if we set the interesting but unique case of Stuxnet aside for the moment, all of the other examples of conflict in the cyber domain— examples which Rid and I agree comprise crime, vandalism, vigilantism, and espionage—have trended in a very different direction than originally predicted by earlier cyber experts like Arquilla and Clarke. We have increasingly observed that instead of individuals or terrorist groups wreaking havoc in the cyber domain, states—for example, North Korea, China, and Russia, and perhaps the United States, the United Kingdom, Australia, and other US allies—are getting into the act.

As I will demonstrate, states are increasingly engaging in this "soft" or "unarmed" conflict that differs from the kind of low-intensity conflict traditionally associated with espionage. As in the Sony–North Korea case, states are behaving more and more like individual hackers, carrying out crimes of petty vandalism, theft, disruption, destruction, and even cyberbullying to advance their national political interests. Nations are also increasingly behaving like nonstate vigilante groups, such as the former LulzSec and Anonymous;[22] that is, they are randomly attacking the digital property, vital information, essential activities, or other valuable organizational resources of their adversaries, while also engaging in threats, extortion, and blackmail.[23]

What distinguishes these cybercrimes from other criminal activities is that these actions by states are not carried out for individual financial gain or other personal motives. Instead, even state-sponsored criminal activities carried out in cyberspace are explicitly intended (as Clausewitz described the intention of warfare itself) to *impose the cyber aggressor's political will upon its adversaries through nonpolitical means.*[24] These cyberattacks differ in scope and in kind from both conventional crime and conventional espionage. I call such activities *state-sponsored hacktivism*, and it—rather than the Stuxnet-like effects-based warfare carried out with sophisticated cyber weapons that was earlier predicted—seems to be the direction in which international relations and interstate conflict are trending. Indeed, it seems quite reasonable to regard state-sponsored hacktivism as constituting a revolutionary new kind of warfare, carried out without regard for existing international law or the customary norms of responsible state behavior.

If acts of terrorism and non-state-based insurgencies have come to be called "irregular warfare," state-sponsored hacktivism represents a novel irregular mode of engaging in conflict and domination: ongoing, "unrestricted" warfare—warfare without rules, "war of all against all"—and it is being carried out in a new cyber domain that increasingly resembles Thomas Hobbes's hypothetical state of nature, in which the rule of law has been actively repudiated and resisted by the citizens. The danger is that such warfare not only blurs the lines between war and "mere" criminal activities, but that such a state of war also becomes increasingly difficult to distinguish from peace. The prospect of cyber warfare on this understanding renders existing norms of ethical and legal conduct highly contested, and their practical application to situations of grave conflict extremely difficult.

How should we come to terms with this new development? How, in particular, does it affect our notions of warfare and state-sponsored conflict in general? And most especially, how does it affect (I would say "transform") the debate about whether there is now, or ever could be, a unique form of warfare properly called cyber warfare? These are among the important topics this book will address.

Let us return to the Treasure Map slide with which we began. Recall that the deputy director of NSA was engaging in public outreach and damage control in the aftermath of the Snowden leaks. What did this have to do with cyber warfare? Wasn't it about government misconduct and the potential erosion of individual rights and personal privacy? But the global interactive map (Figure Intro. 1) that NSA revealed in response appeared to illustrate a massive cyberattack originating from thousands of nodes or sites throughout Europe and the Middle East. That, in turn, suggested a massive criminal network engaged in financial theft or fraud, since US banks and financial institutions were the apparent targets.

But not so. It was all spoofed.[25] The attacks in the fall of 2012 originated from a single masked site, apparently inside Iran. The group that eventually claimed credit for the attacks described itself as the "Cyber Fighters of Izz ad-Din al-Qassam" (مقاتلون لسيراني عز الدين القسا).

Who *are* the Cyber Fighters of Izz al-Din al-Qassam? The group appears to have taken its name from a prominent early twentieth-century Muslim cleric and anticolonialist. In 2012, on the anniversary of the 9/11 attacks, this group claimed to have carried out the massive DDoS attacks on US financial institutions that Brigadier General Inglis had portrayed. They claimed responsibility in a Twitter post and said that the attacks had been launched in retaliation for the continued presence on YouTube of the American-made film *The Innocence of Muslims*, a scandalous piece of hate-mongering propaganda that portrays Islam and the prophet Mohammed in an unflattering light. The Cyber Fighters of Izz al-Din al-Qassam vowed to continue the attacks until the US president ordered the film removed from the Internet.

Two things stood out regarding what were seen at the time as the most serious and disruptive attacks on American financial institutions ever carried out. First, despite claiming to be an independent and unaffiliated organization, this Islamic group's attacks were not indiscriminately directed at all US financial institutions, but only at some. The institutions that were targeted were primarily those that had complied with the terms of the ongoing US economic sanctions against Iran, part of the international effort to halt the Iranian nuclear arms program. In particular, the group's demand that a film be censored on account of its political or religious content seemed hollow: its leaders had to know that it was beyond the power of a democratic government or its leaders anywhere in the world to grant such a demand, even were they willing in principle to comply.

The second oddity was that the anonymous Twitter account from which this group issued its September 2012 proclamation turned out to be the same one from which messages had flowed a few weeks earlier in the aftermath of a massive cyber attack on the internal computer network of Aramco, the Saudi Arabian oil giant. Those attacks, on August 15, 2012, allegedly carried out by an entirely different vigilante group, calling itself the "Cutting Sword of Justice" (قطع السيف العدل), erased data on all the affected computer drives, and inserted in their place the image of a burning American flag.[26]

US security officials seemed quite certain in the final analysis that both attacks were acts of retaliation by Iranian state agents rather than some anonymous Islamic vigilante group.[27] And they were direct responses to the damage done to Iran's nuclear and oil infrastructure by Stuxnet and the surveillance software Flame. Strike and counterstrike. Attack and retaliation. The NSA, it turns out, had been engaged in countering attacks against America's financial infrastructure by an enemy state, with which we were engaged in a de facto war. The tools of the so-called Enterprise Knowledge System that Snowden revealed to the public—including the much-ballyhooed "XKeyscore," that gargantuan "Mainway" database in Utah, PRiSM, and Treasure Map—*were all weapons of warfare*, deployed in a war of national self-defense against terrorists and hacktivists who were agents of enemy nations bent on conducting a new kind of warfare against the United States.[28]

This is state-sponsored hacktivism. It is the new face of warfare in the twenty-first century.

NOTES

1. Treasure Map is an interactive, real-time big-data collection and analysis tool capable, in principle, of tracking the activities of every router, registry, IP address, and physical device connected to the World Wide Web, or, as NSA operatives put it, "any device, anywhere, all the time." The program was developed by the NSA in cooperation with Cisco Systems and information technology experts at the University of California, San Diego. See https://firstlook.org/theintercept/document/2014/09/14/treasure-map-presentation/ (accessed July 10, 2015).

2. See John Miller, "Inside the NSA," *60 Minutes*, CBS News, December 15, 2013, http://www.cbsnews.com/videos/inside-the-nsa/; a script from the segment, entitled "NSA Speaks Out on Snowden Spying," is available at CBS news online, http://www.cbsnews.com/news/nsa-speaks-out-on-snowden-spying/.

3. For a detailed and authoritative account of Olympic Games, including the cyber weapons Stuxnet and Duqu (a similar virus believed to be spread via infected thumb drives), the malware Gauss, and the surveillance software Flame, see David E. Sanger, *Confront and Conceal: Obama's Secret Wars and Surprising Use of American Power* (New York: Crown Books, 2012), 188–225. For an account of what are sometimes labeled these "four amigos," see David Gilbert, *International Business Times*, August 9, 2012, http://www.ibtimes.co.uk/gauss-malware-discovered-virus-lebanon-flame-stuxnet-372025. For a brief time following the initial discovery of Stuxnet, these other malware programs, discovered independently, were thought to have been criminal knock-offs or copycat software produced for nonmilitary purposes by third parties.

4. See the account of this event and its subsequent analysis offered by Peter W. Singer and Allan Friedman in *Cybersecurity and Cyberwar: What Everyone Needs to Know* (New York: Oxford University Press, 2013), 114–120. Readers wanting more information on the background concepts invoked in my discussion will find Singer and Friedman's volume lively and informative.

5. *Bots* (from "robots") are another type of malicious software that automatically simulate communications with other network servers that would normally be

conducted by a human user. Bots can interact in so-called web crawl autonomously with instant messaging or dynamically with other websites. A bot can be designed, for example, to connect back to a central server that then acts as command and control center for an entire network of compromised devices (a *botnet*). A botnet allows attackers to launch broad-based, remote-controlled, flood-type attacks against a target, overwhelming the target system's ability to receive or generate responses to legitimate messages and effectively shutting it down. See Cisco Security Systems, "What Is the Difference: Viruses, Worms, Trojans and Bots?," http://www.cisco.com/web/about/security/intelligence/virus-worm-diffs.html (accessed 2/12/2016).

6. See chapter 3 for more discussion of the controversy surrounding the Estonian attacks. For a detailed and authoritative post facto account of the attacks, see Jason Richards, "Denial-of-Service: The Estonian Cyberwar and Its Implications for U.S. National Security," *International Affairs Review* online, http://www.iar-gwu.org/node/65. A comprehensive IT report was issued several years after the events, in 2013, by the *Arbor Networks IT Security Blog*. See Dan Holden, "Estonia Six Years Later," posted May 16, 2013, http://www.arbornetworks.com/asert/2013/05/estonia-six-years-later/ (accessed July 10, 2015). An excellent summary of the circumstances leading up to the attack on Estonia and its consequences can be found in "Technology: World War 2.0," episode 2, season 1, of the PBS program *Wired Science*, which aired shortly after the incident in 2007, now located on YouTube, https://www.youtube.com/watch?v=T9ZBrxJi0qs (accessed July 10, 2015). See also Charles Clover, "Kremlin-Backed Group behind Estonia Cyber Blitz," *Financial Times*, March 11, 2009, http://www.ft.com/cms/s/0/57536d5a-0ddc-11de-8ea3-0000779fd2ac.html#axzz3fWK3S3P5 (accessed July 10, 2015); and Tom Espiner, "Estonia's Cyberattacks: Lessons Learned a Year On," *ZD NET UK*, May 1, 2008, http://www.zdnet.com/article/estonias-cyberattacks-lessons-learned-a-year-on/ (accessed July 10, 2015).

7. See Richard A. Clarke and Robert K. Knake, *Cyber War: The Next Threat to National Security and What to Do about It* (New York: HarperCollins, 2010), 11–16. See also Joel Brenner, *America the Vulnerable* (New York: Penguin Press, 2011), 127–129. These relatively early accounts have since been extensively amended and their details disputed. As will be discussed in detail in chapter 2, no definitive and uncontroversial account has been offered or accepted, although a true "war" would have required multiple attacks back and forth between the adversaries, which did not occur. That was in part because the sort of virtual conflict that occurred in Estonia in 2007 was finally judged as not rising to the level of a genuine "armed attack" as envisioned in article 5 of the NATO Treaty, although it likely involved an extensive number of distinct botnets operating from numerous locations, exceeding the capacity of one individual, or even a few, to have launched alone.

8. One of the most challenging and exasperating features of attempting to offer a comprehensive analytical study of such phenomena is the astonishing rapidity and frequency with which events occur or are updated; interpretations of even the most recent past events are modified or challenged with equal rapidity, rendering it difficult to give a full, fair, and objective account. A cyber-forensics topic that was suddenly trending during the writing of this book concerned one typical operative, Ge Xing, a resident of Kunming and apparent member of PLA Unit 78020, who was allegedly posting misinformation about China's competitors in the South China Sea (Thailand, in particular). See Josh Chin, "Sleuths

Link Hacker to China's Military," *Wall Street Journal*, September 24, 2015, A1, A14.

9. Ellen Nakashima and William Wan, "U.S. Announces First Charges against Foreign Country in Connection with Cyber-Spying," *Washington Post*, May 19, 2014, https://www.washingtonpost.com/world/national-security/us-to-announce-first-criminal-charges-against-foreign-country-for-cyberspying/2014/05/19/586c9992-df45-11e3-810f-764fe508b82d_story.html (accessed May 19, 2016).

10. "Doxing," from the word "documents" (docx), is a cyberbullying tactic first practiced in the 1990s, when it was primarily directed against women, as a form of intimidation. The Sony attack was one of the first cases in which a state engaged in doxing for political purposes, although it was not entirely unlike covert espionage agents practicing conventional blackmail or extortion of key personnel to force them to collaborate with spies. CIA director John O. Brennan is a more recent victim of what security blogger Bruce Schneier terms "political" doxing. See "The Rise of Political Doxing," *Schneier on Security blog*, November 2, 2015, https://www.schneier.com/blog/archives/2015/11/the_rise_of_pol.html (accessed February 15, 2016).

11. See the summary account by Mark Hosenball and Jim Finkle, "U.S. Suspects North Korea Had Help Attacking Sony Pictures," Reuters News Service, December 29, 2014, http://www.reuters.com/article/2014/12/30/us-northkorea-cyberattack-idUSKBN0K71FK20141230 (accessed July 10, 2015).

12. See the International Convention on Cybercrime (Council of Europe, Convention on Cybercrime, Budapest, November 23, 2001), http://conventions.coe.int/Treaty/EN/Treaties/html/185.htm (accessed July 10, 2015).

13. Singer and Friedman, *Cybersecurity and Cyberwar*, 77–80.

14. I use the term *espionage* in its original and broadest sense as covering every kind of clandestine activity carried out in the service of the state, including intelligence, surveillance, kidnapping, "rendition" (the capture and transport of a subject outside US borders for the purpose of torture) and interrogation, targeted killing and assassination, sabotage, and other covert activities—by spies who are always agents of some nation-state. The term frequently has a more restricted use, limited to surveillance and intelligence-gathering, as opposed to the tasks of "covert operatives," who carry out the remainder of these activities. Those are recent bureaucratic distinctions, however, and not inherent in the original meaning of "espionage."

15. Foremost among such critics is a scholar in the Department of War Studies at King's College, University of London, Professor Thomas C. Rid. See, for example, "Cyber War Will Not Take Place," *Journal of Strategic Studies* 35, no. 1 (2011): 5–32, and his most recent book of the same title (Oxford: Oxford University Press, 2013).

16. See Singer and Friedman, *Cybersecurity and Cyberwar*, 120–121, for discussion of rival definitions of what constitutes cyber warfare. They argue for a more limited and focused definition than is usually employed in the public accounts, but one that is still slightly broader than the very specific and restricted concept I defend in this book.

17. Clarke and Knake, *Cyber War*, 64–68, give a dramatic portrayal of what such a conflict might be like. From an allied nation's perspective, see Alan Bentley, "Is Armageddon on the Cyber Horizon?," *The Guardian*, April 17, 2013, http://www.

theguardian.com/media-network/media-network-blog/2013/apr/17/cyber-attack-armageddon-protection (accessed July 10, 2015).

18. John Arquilla and David Ronfeldt, "Cyberwar Is Coming!," *Comparative Strategy* 12, no. 2 (1993): 141–165; John Arquilla, "Ethics and Information Warfare," in *The Changing Role of Information in Warfare*, ed. Z. Khalilzad, J. White, and A. Marshall (Santa Monica, CA: Rand Corporation, 1999), 379–401; John Arquilla, "Conflict, Security, and Computer Ethics," in *The Cambridge Handbook of Information and Computer Ethics*, ed. Luciano Floridi (New York: Cambridge University Press, 2010), 133–149. See also Dorothy E. Denning, *Information Warfare and Security* (Boston: Addison-Wesley, 1998).

19. Libicki has written several books on the subject. See *What Is Information Warfare?* (Washington, DC: National Defense University, Institute for National Strategic Studies, 1995); *Conquest in Cyberspace: National Security and Information Warfare* (New York: Cambridge University Press, 2007); and *Cyberdeterrence and Cyberwar* (Santa Monica, CA: Rand Corporation, 2009).

20. Neil C. Rowe, "The Ethics of Cyberweapons in Warfare," *International Journal of Technoethics* 1, no. 1 (2010): 20–31.

21. See Michael Gross and Tami Meisels, *Soft War: The Ethics of Unarmed Conflict* (Oxford: Oxford University Press, 2016).

22. See Singer and Friedman, *Cybersecurity and Cyberwar*, 80–84, for an account of the growth and composition of Anonymous.

23. Lest it seem that I am only labeling the cyber activities of adversary second- and third-world states as constituting this kind of warfare, the reader may wish to google several other incidents, including "Aurora," "Red October," "DarkHotel," and "Regin," which also appear to be acts of state-sponsored hacktivism, presumably launched by Britain and the United States.

24. Technically, of course, states cannot "commit crimes"; only individuals can do so. But states can break the law or order their agents to engage in criminal acts. It is when such acts are commanded by states and carried by individuals for the sake of the political objectives of their state that I have here in mind.

25. "Spoofing" is a widely used term with several meanings in various contexts, all involving the disguising of the true source of a message or program or masquerading as someone or something else. In this instance, Iranian agents initially masquaraded the true source of their attacks on US financial institutions, making it appear as if they were emanating from multiple sites in eastern Europe and Asia.

26. A dramatic and detailed account of both attacks and the theories of their origin and significance is offered by journalist Shane Harris in his well-researched and cleverly titled history of cyber warfare: *@War: The Rise of the Military-Internet Complex* (New York: Houghton Mifflin Harcourt, 2014), 187–197. The current NSA director, Admiral Michael Rogers, testified more recently that the Iranian attacks appear to have abated in the aftermath of the nuclear arms control agreement negotiated with the United States, Europe, China, and Russia. See Damian Paletta, "NSA Chief: Iran Cyberattacks Have Slowed," *Wall Street Journal*, September 11, 2015, A4.

27. Further evidence has since come to light that the same group of hackers was at the time also attempting to infiltrate the control system of a small dam used for flood control in Rye, New York, just twenty miles north of New York City, in what proved to be a technically infeasible attempt to duplicate the success of Stuxnet, and do genuine real-world damage. This problem of intention versus

capability in governing the tactics of state-sponsored hacktivists (and leading to the ascendancy of this tactic over "effects-based" initiatives, is taken up in subsequent chapters. For the account of this unsuccessful Iranian "effects-based" cyberattack, see Danny Yadron, "Iranian Hacking Threat Emerges," *Wall Street Journal*, December 21, 2015, A1, 16.

28. In the immediate aftermath of the Snowden leaks, I offered a nonclassified summary account of the Enterprise Knowledge System in "NSA Management Directive 424: Secrecy and Privacy in the Aftermath of Snowden," *Ethics and International Affairs* 28, no. 1 (2014): 29–38. Readers can get an idea of how XKeyscore, in particular, works by reading about its nonclassified civilian spinoff, Synthesy, available commercially from Digital Reasoning Systems, Inc. Synthesy is used on Wall Street to track down rogue traders and bad financial actors in pretty much the same manner that NSA and the CIA used it to track down terrorists. See Bradley Hope, "Spy Tools Come to Wall Street," *Wall Street Journal*, August 3, 2015), C1, 6.

CHAPTER 1

Cyber (In)security

Threat Assessment in the Cyber Domain

A t first glance, as the philosopher and cyber expert Randall Dipert observes,[1] the cyber domain is a strange place, utterly unlike the more
familiar "real-world" domains of land, sea, air, and space.

Cyber itself is a new term, derived from an ancient Greek noun referring
to a "space" or a "domain." The word *cyberspace* is therefore a redundancy.
It was coined by science-fiction writer William Gibson in a short story written in 1982, and later described in his 1984 novel *Neuromancer* as "clusters
and constellations" of data and their interconnections drawn from every
computer in the universe.

The term *cyber warfare* first appeared in a Rand Corporation report written in 1992 by John Arquilla and David Ronfelt, who used it to describe a
new form of conflict perpetrated through the disruption of the flow of critical data managed across networked computer information systems. The
threat of this new form of conflict, which they also termed "information
warfare,"[2] was not taken seriously at first. Concerns about the prospects
of cyber conflict quickly grew, however, especially in the first decade of the
twenty-first century, in response to exponential growth in Internet crime,
vandalism, and corporate and state espionage.

WHAT, WHEN, AND WHERE?

Accurately assessing the gravity of the threat posed by largely hypothetical forms of virtual conflict, however, has proven to be quite difficult. This

stems in part from the problem of accurately conceptualizing just what the cyber domain is.

The cyber domain is, as we have seen, often labeled a "fifth" domain of experience, alongside our more familiar and conventional four domains of land, sea, air, and space. The other four domains "contain" or consist of "things" or "entities" (objects) and "events," which are largely occurences among and between the things in that particular domain. In a nutshell, "what" cyberspace is, by comparison, is a unique environment in which electrons and photons, through interactions determined by binary bits of computer code, dictate the form and structure of "objects" and "events." Cyberspace bears some resemblance to the near-earth plasma environment, that region of space closest to our own planet. Both consist largely of electromagnetic phenomena with extraordinarily fast response times over extremely large distances. But even this comparison is far from exact. The analogy does, however, highlight one notable feature regarding the "when" of cyber events: they are continuous and virtually instantaneous. Likewise, as in a plasma field, the "where" of discrete cyber objects is difficult to pinpoint, since they are almost entirely nonlocalized. These features are common to all quantized energy fields, but they are without precedent in the remaining three more conventional domains of land, sea, and air.

Finally, cyberspace is often understood as identical to, even taken to be a synonym for, the Internet or the World Wide Web. But the cyber domain, as Dipert also points out, is in fact far more extensive.[3] It also includes hardware, such as portable thumb drives, which connect to the Internet via other hardware devices, such as printers and laptops and television sets and streaming devices, which are likewise connected to the Internet via cables or wireless networks. Cyberspace also includes cell phone networks, which operate on different frequencies from the bandwidth devoted to Internet traffic. It includes satellite communications and the Global Positioning System (GPS), and conventional objects that are increasingly becoming networked into these distinct but intertwined systems of communication, such as an automobile's navigation system or on-board monitoring and safety systems on aircraft or the devices in the home that people can now monitor and control from their smartphones.

This emerging cyber network, often called the Internet of Things (IOT), increasingly also includes drones and other remotely piloted, unmanned military systems and the hardware and software that control them, communicating across command centers, and indeed, monitoring and governing the Internet itself. All these characteristics of the IOT, as the editors of *The Economist* recently pointed out, make it "a hacker's paradise." Yet security is often still the farthest thing from the minds of designers and users.[4]

HOW?

In cyberspace, a relatively simple phenomenon or transaction, such as sending an email message, making a cell phone call, or paying a bill online, consists of an "object" (e.g., the email message itself) and its attendant "event" (e.g., sending and receiving the message). These all have component parts that interact at many different points around the globe, spanning many countries and continents simultaneously. This provides enormous opportunities for mischief. Consider this simple example (which I often rely on to describe the workings of cyberspace and the problems encountered in it).

Suppose I place a normal phone call from my home, near Washington, DC, to my brother in Tampa, Florida. That phone call travels as a fairly conventional electromagnetic transmission for about a thousand miles over a series of trunk lines, which are simply large copper wires or coaxial cables (or, increasingly, fiber-optic cables) that stretch along a physical route, in a more or less straight line, from my city to my brother's.

If I decide to email my brother instead, my message will be disassembled into a swarm of discrete data packets, after which the Internet Protocol addressing system will label each packet and search for the quickest and least-congested Internet pathway to transmit them to their destination. As a result, these discrete data packets will almost assuredly travel around the world at speeds approaching that of light, perhaps more than once, and through the communication infrastructures of many countries, before they are finally reassembled at their destination. Owing to the historical evolution of the Internet from its origins in the 1960s as a US Department of Defense system for vital military command and control in the event of a nuclear war, moreover, the design and dissemination of the physical infrastructure supporting Internet communications entails that virtually all these discrete data packets, no matter where they start out or end up, will at some point pass through the original portions of the Internet's physical infrastructure (its "backbone"), which are located within the continental United States.

Verifying the identity and authenticity of Internet communications, as a result, can be quite tricky. When I get a conventional telephone call from my brother, I can usually tell who it is very quickly from the unique sound of his voice. But when I receive an email containing his name and return address, it may seem to come from him, but it may be fraudulent. The digital identity of the data packets may have been spoofed to fool me into thinking the message is from him, when in reality, the email is part of what is termed a "spear phishing" scam. Clever cybercriminals (say, somewhere in Uzbekistan) can fake my brother's and many other users' digital identities and send us phony emails, hoping we will innocently open them.

If I do open the email, it may contain a virus that will destroy or steal my data. Or, the email might contain a "worm"—a sinister software program that will download onto my computer and begin transmitting my sensitive private information to the original sender, while replicating itself and "crawling" through my personal network and email connections to affect the hardware of many other users' systems in the same manner. The generic term of art for all of these software programs is *malware*, and there is an amazing variety of malware that, when maliciously introduced into our personal computer operating systems, can steal our credentials, identities, or credit card information, which will then be sold to criminal gangs in Russia or Azerbaijan, who will, in turn, use it to drain our bank accounts or to charge merchandise to our credit cards, among many other nefarious uses.

Is this what the Chinese plan to do with the twenty-two million confidential personnel files that they apparently hacked from the OPM? If that seems like unlikely behavior for state agents (unless a few of them have decided to pursue criminal activities on the side), the troubling fact remains that the Chinese government could do so if it saw some advantage to be gained—and the results would be catastrophic for millions of Americans. In fact, no one yet has the slightest idea why the Chinese government stole these records—indeed, technically, we still don't know with absolute certainty it was they who did so.[5] But clearly, they should not have been able to do so, and would not have been able had the OPM's internal cybersecurity measures and those of the cybersecurity contractor it employed been more competent and robust.

WHY?

Let's pause for a brief history of malevolent misbehavior in the cyber domain. Not so long ago, cyber activism was limited to pranks, practical jokes, and random acts of vandalism on the Internet carried out by individuals or small groups. Pranksters attached software viruses to emails that, when opened, quickly began to damage the infected individual's computer, or spread through an organization's internal network, posting goofy messages and perhaps even erasing valuable data or software stored on hard drives. Cyber vandals posted offensive messages or unwanted photos, or otherwise defaced an organization's website, often for no apparent reason other than their own amusement or to gain bragging rights with fellow computer hackers. About the only crimes committed in those early days were trespassing (invading an individual's PC or a private company network) and destruction of property. Apart from mean-spirit-edness or a warped sense of humor, however, about the only reasons given at the time by hackers for such malicious activities were complaints about the monopolistic practices of, and the mediocre software distributed by, the Microsoft Corporation.

It was not long before sophisticated individuals and criminal gangs began exploiting the same software vulnerabilities as the pranksters for the purpose of stealing bank deposits, credit card numbers, or even victims' personal identities. At the same time, cyber activism was evolving into ever more sophisticated acts of political sabotage: defacing or even temporarily shutting down government or commercial websites with DDoS attacks, or dispatching those dreaded software worms that traveled "peer-to-peer" (computer to computer), penetrating firewalls and antivirus software in order to gain control over each PC or laptop, transforming it into a "zombie." These "zombies"—individual compromised machines—could then be remotely networked with others to form a massive botnet controlled by political dissidents or criminal organizations, who, in turn, used them to launch DDoS attacks to shut down banks and financial institutions (like stock markets) or to hack into individual users' accounts and divert the victims' funds to the criminals' own accounts.[6] This seems to be what happened in Estonia, *except for the last part*—the diversion of funds and draining of personal bank accounts did not take place. Why?

When the Stuxnet worm was introduced into the SCDA system that controlled the centrifuges in Iran, it did exactly what conventional weapons launched by states usually do: it targeted and destroyed military hardware that posed a grave threat of harm to others. Stealing random personal bank deposits at from ordinary citizens, in comparison, does not seem to be the sort of thing that a state would do. In fact, the typical criminal activities that usually follow personal data theft were not observed in Estonia, which strongly suggests that a state or its agents, not random individuals (or "patriots," as Russian Federation officials blandly asserted at the time), had carried out the attacks.[7]

"Hacktivism" is the new term being used to classify acts of malevolence and mischief in the cyber domain, from straightforward crime and vandalism to the many forms of political protest that are now carried out on the Internet. Technically, the "hacktivist" is one who engages in vandalism and even in criminal activities in pursuit of political goals or objectives rather than personal satisfaction or financial gain. Well-known individuals, such as Julian Assange of WikiLeaks, and loosely organized groups, such as Anonymous, the now-defunct LulzSec, and Cyberwarriors for Freedom, resorted to Internet malevolence in order to publicize their concerns, which can range from defending personal privacy, liberty, and freedom of expression on the Internet itself all the way to expressing their opposition to oppressive political regimes like those of Syria or Egypt.

THREE WAYS OF BEING A HACKTIVIST

There are many ways of carrying out hacktivism. I find it useful to focus on the hacktivist's political goals. These political goals can be categorized as *transparency, whistleblowing,* and *vigilantism.* WikiLeaks purports, for example, to provide greater transparency by exposing the covert activities of governments and large corporations. Whistleblowers, such as US Army private Chelsea Manning (the former Bradley Manning) and former NSA contractor Edward Snowden, aim to expose what they take to be grave specific acts of wrongdoing or injustice, in Manning's and Snowden's cases, on the part of the US military and government, respectively.

Vigilante groups, such as Anonymous or the former LulzSec, are a bit harder to pin down, since the individual members may espouse a variety of disparate political causes. The organizational response to the group's chosen cause, however, involves its members taking the law (or, in its absence, morality) into their own hands; that is, based on the group's shared judgment regarding immoral or illegal behavior, it launches attacks against targets that might range from the Syrian government of Bashir al Assad, for its massive human rights violations, to ordinary business and commercial organizations, law-abiding individuals, and security and defense or constabulary organizations, such as the FBI, to whose practices the organization objects.

This is vigilantism. And (as the name Anonymous suggests) the members of these groups cannot easily be identified, traced, or otherwise held accountable for their actions. (The ringleader of LulzSec, known as "Sabu," may have been an exception; he was tracked down, arrested, and turned into an FBI informant and then took part in a sting operation against Anonymous.[8]) As in conventional vigilantism, the vigilante's judgment as to what constitutes a legal or moral offense is subjective and often inconsistent or otherwise open to question.

Importantly, in all cases involving transparency, whistleblowing, and vigilantism, the burden of proof is on those who deliberately violate their fiduciary duties and contractual agreements or flout or disobey the law in order to expose or to protest activities they have deemed to be even more egregious than their own. This comparative judgment by the protester or whistleblower invokes what is called "the principle of proportionality," which holds that the degree of harm that results from the vigilante's actions must be *demonstrably less* than the harm being done by those whom the vigilante opposes. The problem is that this comparative judgment is notoriously difficult to make. Vigilantes often exaggerate or misrepresent the harm caused by the actions against which they protest and underestimate the destructive effect of their own activities on the public welfare.

Another difficulty with vigilantism is that there is no independent or adversarial review of these decisions. According to the "principle of publicity," or the "principle of legitimate authority," the final authority to evaluate the legitimacy of a protester's or dissident's actions does not rest with that individual or organization but with the public, in whose collective interests the individual or organization claims to act. So, in all these cases, it must be possible in principle to bring the dissident's actions and intentions before an impartial court of public opinion for independent review. This criterion is the one most frequently ignored and, consequently, the one both vigilantes and whistleblowers, and would-be whistleblowers, most often fail to meet. Both are prone to suffer from an abundance of self-righteousness.

The generic term *hacktivism* covers many sins, some more justifiable (or, at least, understandable and sometimes excusable) than others. I doubt, for example, that most readers would take exception to Anonymous defacing the government website of Bashir al Assad or exposing the online behavior of child pornographers. More worrisome are attacks on legitimate government, military, or corporate websites that result in harm to innocent bystanders. But that is the very nature of vigilantism. Anonymous and other cyber vigilantes have engaged in all these activities indiscriminately. Anonymous apparently lacks any kind of command or control center to reign in extremism or to deliberate on the appropriateness or suitability (let alone the moral justification) of the actions of its members. It functions instead like a loose-knit confederation of anarchists—what a professor at New York University went so far as to characterize as "a cyber lynch mob."[9]

But none of this social activism in cyberspace, no matter how well- or ill-advised, constitutes warfare, let alone rises to the level of a use of force or an armed attack. So, what has the phenomenon of hacktivism to do with the concerns of this book?

CONVENTIONAL WARFARE

Up to this point, we have been discussing the problem of whether or not any form of cyber conflict rises to the level of warfare or, more accurately, proves to be the equivalent of armed force. I have relied on readers' intuitive understanding of what conventional war is, without having given it a more precise definition. What follows is a definition of both conventional warfare and "irregular warfare," a different kind of conflict that followed, or "disrupted," it.

Conventional war is defined as a form of political conflict between adversaries that is generally undertaken only when other modes of conflict resolution—such as diplomacy, negotiation, sanctions, and compromise—have failed. The resort to armed force is made to compel an otherwise implacable or recalcitrant adversary to comply with the more powerful nation's will or political ambitions.[10] The nineteenth-century Prussian military strategist Carl von Clausewitz provided the classic summative assessment of war as just such a "continuation of State policy by other means." The goal of armed conflict in pursuit of a nation's political objectives, he argued, is to defeat the enemy's armies, occupy his cities, and most significantly, *break his will to fight or resist.*[11]

This conventional, or "classical," understanding of warfare is heavily dependent on the underlying paradigm of the nation-state and of international relations as a kind of "perpetual anarchy" of the competing interests of nation-states (e.g., in acquiring territory or natural resources, providing for national security, or expanding profitable trade relations). And while the policies of an individual nation-state may represent a perfectly rational or logical course of action for *that particular nation* (or coalition of allies), the multiplicity of such interests virtually guarantees conflict between rival sets of interests and policy objectives. That is to say, the occasional resort to armed force to resolve at least some of these conflicts is all but inevitable.[12]

The very last conventional armed conflict, or war, however, may well have occurred more than two decades ago, in early 1991, when the army of Iraqi leader Saddam Hussein confronted a similarly trained and equipped UN coalition military force led by the United States in the deserts of Kuwait and southeastern Iraq. The apparent technological symmetry in that instance, as we realize in hindsight, turned out to be illusory. Since then, the conventional use of armed force has been combined with, or even supplanted by, "asymmetric" or "irregular" warfare. A striking feature of unconventional or irregular warfare is that adversaries and insurgent interest groups, frustrated by the radical asymmetries in military power stacked in favor in conventional forces, adopt new tactics for disrupting social systems and attacking the weak links in logistical supply chains through the use of, for example, suicide bombers and improvised explosive devices (IEDs), or of cyberattacks that can throw conventional military forces seriously off balance. Subsequently, new technologies owned initially by the besieged conventional forces become the optimal response. Drone attacks, for example, are "systemic" in precisely the same way IEDs and suicide bombers are: they disrupt the insurgent's command structure, relentlessly hunting him out where he lives and hides, demoralizing him, and hopefully breaking his ability and will to fight.

Similarly, cyber surveillance involving big-data collection on a previously unimaginable scale holds the promise of turning the tables and frustrating even the cleverest and most determined attackers, by carrying the cyber fight back to its source.[13] Here is yet another sense in which the lessons learned from the disruptive innovation brought about by the transition from conventional to irregular warfare during the past decade offer some useful comparisons with cyber warfare.

UNRESTRICTED WARFARE

In 1999, only a few years after the stunning defeat of Saddam's conventional army by the United States in Kuwait, two air-force colonels in the Chinese PLA published an extensive study of the United States' ability to project military power in the foreseeable future.[14] Their monograph, entitled *Unrestricted Warfare*, acknowledged that no one could any longer stand toe-to-toe with the US military in a conventional war, and recommended that the only way forward for China was to develop offensive and defensive capabilities in other areas, *including cyberspace*, where the United States was both highly vulnerable and by no means dominant, and to be willing to use those capabilities relentlessly in the pursuit of national interests.

Indeed, cyber- and national-security expert Richard Clarke links China's development of its now considerable offensive cyber capability with the doctrine espoused by these two theorists. That doctrine, he explains, is termed *shashou-jian*, and is meant to employ new kinds of weapons that are outside the traditional military spectrum and that capitalize on the vulnerabilities in an adversary's otherwise-advanced capacities: in the American case, its advanced capabilities and heavy reliance on cyberspace technology, both domestic and that of its allies, such as the technologically sophisticated nation of Estonia.[15]

These reflections by the Chinese military theorists led directly to state-sponsored campaigns allegedly carried out by two top-secret branches of the PLA—Unit 61398, based in Shanghai, and the even more sinister Unit 78020, in Kunming—both heavily engaged in cyberespionage and covert actions, such as the alleged planting of "trapdoors" and "logic bombs" in vital civilian infrastructure,[16] as well as the massive theft of industrial and classified military technologies, which the United States only began to acknowledge and publicly denounce in 2013. These developments lie at the heart of the threat assessment for the kind of cyber warfare feared by Clarke, Brenner, Harris, and many other experts in the field of cyber conflict and cybersecurity. Cyber conflict is thus considered to be a major, if not the main, weapon in the arsenal of weapons and tactics assembled to conduct "unrestricted warfare."

Global acts of cybercrime stand side by side with relentless and ongoing commercial and military espionage and the theft of industrial and state secrets that threaten the security and fundamental economic welfare of individuals and nations. Yet efforts to counter these activities are strongly opposed in many rights-respecting and reasonably democratic societies as constituting unacceptable infringements of liberty and privacy. Indeed, efforts to impose the kinds of controls and constraints that would provide greater security are among the proposed security measures that Internet vigilantes like Anonymous protest. Meanwhile Clarke, Brenner, and other security experts worried about our vulnerabilities on this score lament the present impasse and predict that the obsession with privacy, anonymity, and unrestricted freedom of action in the cyber domain will not be overcome short of a horrendous cyber Armageddon, on the magnitude of the attack on Pearl Harbor or the 9/11 attacks.

Some of the more extreme scenarios, as noted previously, may be exaggerated. The threat of terrorists or of your neighbor's alienated teenage son causing planes filled with helpless passengers to collide in mid-air or passenger trains to crash or derail or hydroelectric dams to burst and flood tens of thousands of hectares (ruining crops and drowning thousands of victims), or shutting down electrical power grids, while simultaneously releasing poisonous gases from chemical factories to destroy the populations of nearby cities—all seem highly unlikely. To date, the greatest threat by far to American and European security remains Internet crime, and this has been a focus of coordinated international law enforcement efforts. As of July 2015, for example, twenty countries that had been collaborating for several years with the FBI in Operation Shrouded Horizon finally succeeded in arresting the chief perpetrators of and taking down a cyber operation known as Darkode.com, a "dark web" forum that US Department of Justice officials described as "the world's most sophisticated English-language Internet Forum for criminal hackers" trafficking in malware.[17]

So we are left with the question, do any of the other forms of cyber conflict about which we read, or sometimes experience ourselves, ever constitute genuine cyber warfare? Or, more precisely, when, if ever, does non-criminal cyberactivity rise to a level equivalent to an armed attack by one (or more) state(s) against another sovereign state, as discussed in the UN Charter?[18]

Much of the confusion over this important question arises from the unwillingness of cyber pundits to distinguish between activities on a broad spectrum of cyber conflict—ranging, as we now see, from practical jokes, vandalism, and politically motivated hacktivism to serious cybercrimes (mostly robbery and financial schemes involving deception and identity theft) to commercial and industrial and state-sponsored cyberespionage (as the NSA was found to be doing) to physical sabotage (like Stuxnet). One critical feature of cyber conflict is that it has blurred the distinctions between what were once quite different kinds of conflict.

Another important difference is that the pursuit of cyber strategies and tactics and the use of cyber weapons by states have been largely under the control of intelligence agencies and personnel, whose rules of engagement are very different from those of conventional military combatants. Spies and espionage agents are generally engaged in activities that do not rise to the level of a "threat or use of force" under international law, let alone of armed conflict between states, but that do constitute criminal acts in the domestic jurisdiction within which they take place. Conventional war occurs in zones of combat in which the customary rule of law has broken down, and to which the international law of armed conflict therefore applies. This legal regime is, in general, far more lenient than is most domestic law regarding the permission to pursue conflict with deadly force. Even so, there *are* certain rules in international law that restrict the use of deadly force in conventional war (such as noncombatant immunity, military necessity, and proportionality) that do not apply to the pursuit of espionage.

In my opinion, this fundamental distinction regarding what are generally termed "standing orders and rules of engagement" within the different cultures involved in this new form of unrestricted warfare has not been sufficiently acknowledged, let alone understood. Cyberwar is "unrestricted" warfare carried out by spies and espionage agents who do not think themselves bound by legal restraints, unlike conventional combatants who are trained in the international law of armed conflict. "Unrestricted warfare" is not legally permissible or morally justifiable according to the rules and laws governing conventional armed conflict, but it is nevertheless routine practice among agents of espionage. Many cyber weapons and tactics are designed to attack civilians and civilian (noncombatant) targets, a feature that is illegal, and decidedly immoral, in the conventional case.[19]

If there is any bright spot to be found in all this, it is that, as noted, it takes vast resources, expertise, access, and practice time to build effective cyber weapons with genuine destructive capacity. These resources are accessible only to nation-states or, at the very least, to large, well-staffed, highly organized criminal organizations. That may be scant comfort, but nations and even large criminal organizations (unlike terrorists or troubled fourteen-year-olds) usually have clear-cut goals, purposes, and political or economic interests to which other governing authorities can appeal. Representatives of adversarial nations can communicate and, by appealing to those conflicting interests, negotiate a compromise. And they can also credibly threaten one another with punishment and retaliation, which could serve to deter malicious activities.

In the meantime, however, the need for individuals, organizations, and nations to protect their privacy, property, commercial and defense innovations, and overall safety and welfare through enhanced cybersecurity, especially with respect to highly vulnerable civil infrastructure, is urgent and still largely unaddressed.

STATE-SPONSORED HACKTIVISM AS A NEW FORM OF WARFARE

A genuine cyber Armageddon—an effects-based equivalent of a large-scale conventional war or even a nuclear war, carried out with software weapons deployed in the cyber domain—is thus far the dominant threat posited by the advocates of enhanced cybersecurity, though for the present at least, the possibility of something like this happening appears to remain highly remote. Critics of this extreme threat assessment have claimed that the fearmongers deliberately engage in confusion, obfuscation, and equivocation: they may simply be confused about what really constitutes authentic warfare, or, perhaps unconsciously, they use the term *cyber warfare* metaphorically, similar to our describing the *war* on drugs, a *war* on crime, the *war* on poverty, or, importantly, the *global war on terror*.

Whatever the case, the current discussion of the threat of cyber warfare rests on a misuse of important terminology. Again, critics of the Armageddon scenario accuse its advocates of using the discussion as a tactic to gain public attention, garner scarce resources for their own preferred programs, or, more ominously, frighten the public into sacrificing their individuality, liberty, and privacy (and Internet anonymity) in favor of ever-increasing government intrusion and control. Conspiracy theorists, alongside Internet anarchists, would have us all believe that the cybersecurity community (largely consisting of government and security forces) is, at bottom, out to subvert and suppress freedom of expression, anonymity, liberty, and personal privacy by exaggerating the threat of cyber warfare.

What neither side in this debate explains, however, is that extreme, effects-based cyber conflict is only *one form* of cyber warfare. Neither side has yet paid sufficient attention to the alternative of state-sponsored hacktivism emphasized in this book—that is, they have failed to grasp the significance of the increasing tendency of states to pursue practices once thought to be the purview of individuals and nonstate organizations, including criminal organizations. I believe that this recent trend in state behavior has still not sparked sufficient concern. Professor Thomas Rid, a well-known security studies scholar at King's College, University of London, who vociferously opposes all uses of the term "cyber warfare," for example, has not examined this alternative conception of what cyber conflict at the state level actually is. He and his supporters dismiss cyber warfare as merely a new, inflated form of espionage.

I am frankly not at all sure that state-sponsored hacktivism can be so easily classified or dismissed. To be certain, it entails activities similar to the domestic crimes that agents of espionage routinely commit. But, as described earlier, it also entails a good deal more. One would be hard pressed to find a historical equivalent to or precedent for the North Korean hack of Sony Pictures in the world of conventional espionage. Likewise, we cannot cite a previous historical instance in which enemy spies attempted to steal the confidential personal data of *millions* of ordinary citizens (rather than the personal data on a select number of high-value targets, perhaps singled out for rendition or assassination). As discussed earlier, we don't even know with 100 percent certainty that enemy *nations* carried out these operations through their state agents, nor do we have a clear idea of what their intentions might have been if they did. The attacks are unsettling nonetheless. And *unlike the threat of the prospect of cyber Armageddon, this is really happening.*

To be sure, the aforementioned critics of the idea of genuine cyber warfare might reply that state-sponsored hacktivism is merely "espionage on steroids"—that is, new and novel forms of the usual kinds of activities that spies have always engaged in but on a scale of magnitude only recently made possible through the medium of the cyber domain. *Perhaps.* But, just as with conventional armed conflict itself, scale and magnitude matter. So does persistence. Yes, enemy spies routinely try to steal state secrets or plans for new weapons systems or economically important industrial secrets. This happens all the time. But when it occurs on the scale of magnitude we have seen over the past few years or persists despite well-aimed threats to "cease and desist," it is not implausible to claim that cyber conflict has now supplanted conventional armed conflict in its ability to harm state interests, as well as to force weakened and vulnerable adversaries to their knees.

Such domination, such imposition of the political will of the adversary upon its victim, has, according to Clausewitz, always been the principal purpose and vocation of warfare as an instrument of the state. State-sponsored hacktivism itself is one principal component of what political philosopher Michael Gross has termed "soft war," a conception that envisions a wide range of nonkinetic alternatives to conventional war.[20] Under the broad heading of "unrestricted warfare," these alternative forms of unarmed conflict are, finally, what the military theorists and strategists in the PLA in China were proposing in 1999 as an alternative means of conducting hostilities and resolving conflicts without resort to conventional armed conflict. And in their account, cyber conflict was only the most prominent form of this new mode of warfare. "Soft" war in the cyber domain relies on craft, cleverness, and ingenuity in lieu of conventional kinetic force.[21] Yet our experience of this novel new form of "unarmed" warfare promises to do unlimited harm of its own if not fully understood and appropriately governed.

NOTES

1. Randall Dipert, "The Essential Features for an Ontology for Cyberwarfare," *Conflict and Cooperation in Cyberspace*, ed. P. A. Yannakogeorgos and A. B. Lowther (Boca Raton, FL: CRC Press, 2013), 35–48.
2. The subsequent Rand Corporation anthology compiled by Arquilla and Ronfeldt a decade later documents this initial skepticism amid the exponential increase in the kinds of events they had predicted. See John Arquilla and David Ronfeldt, *Networks and Netwars: The Future of Terror, Crime, and Militancy* (Santa Monica, CA: Rand Corporation, 2001).
3. See Randall Dipert, "Other Than Internet (OTI) Cyber Warfare: Challenges for Ethics, Law, and Policy," *Journal of Military Ethics* 12, no. 1 (2013): 34–53. See also my response and augmented account of OTI objects in cyberspace in George R. Lucas, Jr., "Ethics and Cyber Conflict: A Review of Recent Work," *Journal of Military Ethics* 13, no. 1 (2014): 20–31.
4. *The Economist* 416, no. 8947, July 18–24, 2015, 10, 65. More recently, economist Robert J. Samuelson has written anxiously about our playing "internet routlette" in our headlong rush toward an ever-expanding "internet of things." *Washington Post*, August 24, 2015, A13. The CBS News television magazine, *60 Minutes*, recently featured a segment on "DARPA-Dan" Kaufman, a security expert and game designer recruited by the Defense Advanced Research Projects Agency (DARPA) to determine vulnerabilities in a range of increasingly networked devices, from refrigerators to cars, and to develop enhanced security for such objects against cyberattack. Leslie Stahl, "Nobody's Safe on the Internet," February 8, 2015, http://www.cbsnews.com/news/darpa-dan-kaufman-internet-security-60-minutes/. Meanwhile, in a manner directly relevant to the concerns of this book with state involvement in hacking for political purposes, the US Department of Transportation has begun worrying that America's key urban

traffic-control systems are increasingly vulnerable to cyberattack, with surprisingly dangerous implications. "Is More Gridlock Just a Hack Away?," *Washington Post*, August 9, 2015, C1, C2.

5. I increasingly suspect that this massive OPM security breach was intended to demonstrate China's superior cyber power and our nation's vulnerability. In effect, this is "cyber bullying" at the state level, and it will come to be viewed as another example of what I term state-sponsored hacktivism.

6. Reporter Mark Bowden authored a detailed account of "Confikker," a worm of unknown provenance first detected in 2008 as resident on millions of computers throughout the world, capable of creating what Singer and Friedman term "the Holy Grail of a botnet." We remain unaware at the present time of who developed and transmitted this malware or for what purpose. See Mark Bowdon, *Worm: The First Digital World War* (New York: Atlantic Monthly Press, 2011); Singer and Friedman, *Cybersecurity and Cyberwar: What Everyone Needs to Know* (New York: Oxford University Press 2014), 72. Since Confikker has now quietly resided on the global Internet for several years with no detectable malevolent activity, my own best surmise is that this an "Internet failsafe switch," a security program designed presumably by agents of the United States or its allies to shut down the Internet, or regain total control of it, should an adversary or rogue state attempt to carry out massive acts of industrial or state sabotage as an act of war.

7. Controversy continues to swirl around the nature of this attack, and no definitive account has yet been produced. See, for example, Ian Traynor, "Russia Accused of Unleashing Cyberwar to Disable Estonia," *The Guardian*, May 16, 2007, http://www.theguardian.com/world/2007/may/17/topstories3.russia. Traynor initially reported the allegations of state-sponsored cyber warfare carried out by Russia against Estonia that Richard Clarke and others had espoused. But only a year later, *The Guardian* seemed to publish a retraction in which the attack was described as the work of a lone Estonian youngster of Russian descent, carried out from inside Estonia's borders. See Charles Arthur, "That Cyberwarfare by Russia on Estonia? It Was One Kind in Estonia!," *The Guardian*, January 25, 2008, http://www.theguardian.com/technology/blog/2008/jan/25/thatcyberwarfarebyrussiaon.

8. See the account of this episode regarding hacktivist Hector Savier Monsegur ("Sabu") in Shane Harris, *@War: The Rise of the Military-Internet Complex* (New York: Houghton Mifflin Harcourt, 2014), 131–135.

9. Gabriella Coleman, "Anonymous: From the Lulz to Collective Action," *New Everyday*, April 6, 2011, http://mediacommons.futureofthebook.org/tne/pieces/anonymous-lulz-collective-action (accessed July 19, 2015).

10. See Brian Orend, "War," *Stanford Encyclopedia of Philosophy*, Edward N. Zalta, http://plato.stanford.edu/archives/fall2008/entries/war/. Orend gives a more extensive description and analysis of conventional warfare in *The Morality of War*, 2nd ed. (Petersboro, ON: Broadview Press, 2013).

11. Carl von Clausewitz, *On War*, ed. and trans. by Michael Howard and Peter Paret (Princeton, NJ: Princeton University Press, 1976), bk. 1, chaps. 1–2. First published in 1830.

12. See my article "War," in the *The Bloomsbury Companion to Political Philosophy*, ed. Andrew Fiala (London: Bloomsbury, 2015), 109–126.

13. I offer descriptive accounts of these new developments, also termed "hybrid" warfare (because of the combining of the new tactics with older conventional

tactics and munitions) in "Postmodern War," *Journal of Military Ethics* 9, no. 4 (2010): 289–298; and in an address on the occasion of NATO's sixtieth anniversary, "'This Is Not Your Father's War': Confronting the Moral Challenges of 'Unconventional' War," *Journal of National Security Law and Policy* 3, no. 2: 331–342.

14. Qiao Liang and Wang Xiangsui, *Unrestricted Warfare*, U.S. Central Intelligence Agency translation (Beijing, China: People's Liberation Army Literature and Arts Publishing House, 1999). The CIA version is available on the web at http://www.c4i.org/unrestricted.pdf. The subtitle of the original Chinese edition, published in Beijing by the PLA Literature and Arts Publishing House in 1999, translates literally as "warfare without borders." When the Pan American Publishing Company published the book in English, it substituted the provocative and misleading "China's Master Plan to Destroy the U.S." The significance of this book, the extent to which it reflects actual government or military policies in China, and what bearing it had on the subsequent rise of cyber conflict are disputed matters. The account I offer here is intended as the most plausible and objective reconciliation of those contending interpretations.

15. See the extended discussion of this theory in Clarke and Knake, *Cyber War*, 47–54.

16. *Trapdoors* (also referred to as "backdoors") are bits of code embedded surreptitiously in operating systems that enable hackers to bypass security firewalls or encryption to gain access and take control of a software-controlled device or industrial system at a later time. A *logic bomb* is a small malware program that begins to operate (or "explode") when initiated by some kind of trigger or "fuse," such as a specific date or time. Once initiated, the program begins to damage the system within which it is embedded. See Stephen Northcutt, "Trap Doors, Trojan Horses, and Logic Bombs," SANS Technology Institute Security Laboratory website, May 2, 2007, http://www.sans.edu/research/security-laboratory/article/log-bmb-trp-door (accessed May 20, 2016).

    The most famous instance of an alleged military/security/intelligence use of a logic bomb was the destruction of a Soviet-era oil pipeline in Siberia, whose massive explosion in 1982 was attributed to a logic bomb allegedly planted by the CIA. See Thomas Reed, *At the Abyss: An Insider's History of the Cold War* (New York: Random House, 2007). Reed is a former US National Security Council aide. This account is widely regarded as apocryphal, and is dismissed by most experts. Agents of the former Soviet Union deny the account. That is fortunate, if true, because if such an event had occurred, it would have represented the effort of astonishing blockheads—a pointless, cruel, environmentally destructive attack on civilian infrastructure that could well have triggered a serious international incident at the time, or even war. Even if it is apocryphal, it would therefore not be an achievement to celebrate, so much as an example of the kind of reckless and stupid behavior that we will want to discourage.

17. As its name suggests, the "dark web" is a specific heavily encrypted region of the Internet that is not easily accessible to most users. "Darkode.com" was a criminal forum hosted in this region of the web and used primarily to traffic in stolen data. See "Major Computing Hacking Forum Dismantled" (press release, US Department of Justice, Office of Public Affairs, Washington DC, July 15, 2015), http://www.justice.gov/opa/pr/major-computer-hacking-forum-dismantled.

18. See Natasha T. Balendra, "Defining Armed Conflict," *Cardoza Law Review* 29, no. 6 (2008): 2461–2516. The term "armed attack," which has replaced the terms

"war" and "warfare" in the formal terminology of international law, is nowhere officially defined, not even in the Charter of the United Nations. Instead, its meaning is presumed to be obvious: a use of force involving lethal weapons and destructive armaments. Article 2 (4) of the Charter prohibits the use of force or the threat of the use of force by any nation against any other nation without prior United Nations authorization. The Security Council reviews disputes and threats and authorizes the use of force under UN jurisdiction for the purposes of the collective security of member nations. There is only one exception to this prohibition: when one or more nations is the victim of armed aggression or an armed attack. The victim-nation may use force in the form of armed conflict to defend itself; other nations may come to its aid in repelling the armed attack. This leaves a number of essential questions unaddressed, for example, (1) if these provisions leave so much to the imagination regarding what constitutes a conventional armed attack, armed conflict, and the use of force, how in our present case are we exactly to determine when other means or methods of aggression or "domination" in the cyber realm rise to its equivalent?, and (2) if international law itself consists of what nations do or tolerate being done, they appear to both do and tolerate much wider uses of force for conflict resolution than the written or "black-letter" law formally sanctions. Some legal philosophers therefore argue that international law is merely rhetorical, and has little or no normative force. But even if this is so, it is a form of rhetoric that is extremely powerful and persuasive in moderating state behavior, even if it is not successful in completely eliminating or adequately punishing illegal behavior. We will return to these important questions in chapter 3.

19. Neil C. Rowe, "War Crimes from Cyber Weapons," *Journal of Information Warfare* 6, no. 3 (2007): 15–25. As Michael Schmitt observes, moreover, article 36 of the 1997 Additional Protocol to the 1949 Geneva Conventions prohibits any state from seeking to develop or acquire any "new weapon, method, or means of warfare" that might be reasonably be found to violate existing laws of armed conflict—whence the development, let alone use of cyber weapons that deliberately targeted "civilians or civilian objects" would, perforce, be prohibited under existing international law. See his introduction to *Cyberwar: Law and Ethics for Virtual Conflicts*, ed. Jens David Ohlin, Kevin Govern, and Claire Finkelstein (New York: Oxford University Press, 2015), v.

20. Gross, a very well-respected political philosopher, first advanced this notion in the concluding chapter in *The Ethics of Insurgency: A Critical Guide to Just Guerilla Warfare* (New York: Cambridge University Press, 2014). The concept of "soft war" as unarmed conflict and its current and future role in international relations have been examined by several scholars. See Michael Gross and Tami Meisels, eds. *Soft War: The Ethics of Unarmed Conflict* (New York: Oxford University Press, 2016).

21. Specifically, this kind of "warfare" relies upon what cybersecurity expert Winn Schwartau several years ago cleverly termed "weapons of mass disruption." See Winn Schwartau, *Cybershock* (New York: Thunder's Mouth Press, 2000).

CHAPTER 2

Is There a Role for Ethics or Law in Cyber Conflict?

As we have just seen, there is no widespread agreement on whether a distinct phenomenon that can be termed *cyber warfare* even exists, let alone of what it might consist. Despite that lack of clarity, I propose that Stuxnet represents what one conception of true cyber warfare might be like—that is, "effects-based" cyber conflict equivalent to conventional warfare but carried out with cyber weapons.

IRREGULAR WAR AND CYBERWAR

In chapter 1, I proposed an alternative kind of cyber warfare—"state-sponsored hacktivism"—that is distinct from the kind of cyber conflict envisioned by previous analysts. One important characteristic of state-sponsored hacktivism is that it is the *cyber equivalent of irregular or unconventional warfare* in the real world, a kind of armed conflict that has currently all but displaced notions of conventional warfare as Carl von Clausewitz envisioned it.

Irregular or unconventional warfare blurs the conventional distinctions and sows uncertainty and confusion regarding strategic goals, proper military tactics, and legal constraints on combat operations. Its practitioners were constantly forced to ask whether they were conducting combat, resisting insurgencies, providing security and police protection, engaging in a humanitarian military intervention, making or keeping the peace, or "building" nations—which in turn raised questions concerning the appropriate rules of engagement and legal regimes applicable to their various operations, including sometimes whether the old rules could be said to still apply.[1] The strategic, moral, and legal landscape of irregular warfare was further obscured by the emergence and increased use of exotic new military technologies, such as robotics and remotely piloted systems, each raising additional questions regarding appropriate use, governance, and cultural impact on the beliefs and behaviors of military forces. Drone pilots, for example, alongside Special Forces units, gradually supplanted and increasingly even replaced the activities of conventional air and ground forces.[2]

Much can be learned about the impact of cyber warfare from earlier examinations of the internal transformation of military professionalism and combat leadership during the initial years of irregular warfare, beginning as early as the Vietnam War. For one thing, we immediately notice that a very similar cultural transformation is currently underway with respect to cyber warfare. Virtual cyber conflict has blurred and confused once-essential distinctions between conventional low-intensity conflict such as espionage and the kinetic, high-intensity, conflict of conventional war. Even more significantly, cyber conflict has also *inverted the command and power structures involved in waging war*—indeed, has turned them topsy-turvy. Once upon a time, intelligence and espionage organizations served the broader strategic purposes of the conventional war command structure to which they were wholly subordinate. Now, it is the leaders of both the military and civilian intelligence and espionage communities who call the shots, determine the strategy, and establish the parameters of conduct for cyber conflict. Conventional warriors threaten to be shouldered aside by a new generation of cyber warriors, just as special forces and drone pilots now occupy center stage in unconventional combat. New questions of law, morality, and the appropriateness of governance under the norms of professional military ethics have similarly been raised.[3]

The most significant new feature peculiar to cyber conflict stems from a deep-seated distinction between "warriors" and "spies."[4] Conventional combatants (warriors) are required to be familiar with the customary professional ethical (internal) and legal (external) constraints on their conduct, even if those are on occasion violated, ignored, or held in contempt. By contrast, there *are* no external constraints to hold in contempt in the world of spying, where intelligence gathering and analysis routinely target civilians as well as military personnel in activities that, regardless, almost always, as noted earlier, constitute criminal behavior in the jurisdictions in which the activities take place. This invariably leads to the inaccurate belief that spies can do whatever they want to whomever they wish, if circumstances and national interests so dictate.[5]

There are somewhat poorly understood personal and professional constraints that constitute the nascent field of "intelligence ethics" concerning, for example, duties of loyalty owed to assets and allies in foreign
countries, limitations on the types of deception that can be practiced in a
given set of circumstances, respect for the privacy and property of ordinary
citizens, and so forth.[6] And intelligence organizations in most democratic
countries, in fact, answer to a domestic legal regime of accountability and
oversight, and there is an established organizational hierarchy governing
covert operations. (The robustness and effectiveness of these oversight and
accountability structures received intense scrutiny in the aftermath of the
Snowden affair in the United States.)

But whatever those internal constraints on professional espionage
agents are, or how well or poorly they are understood, they are substantially
different from the customary constraints placed on conventional military
and combat personnel. There is not, as yet, a "code of the cyberwarrior"[7] or
"law of armed conflict" in cyberspace. How might this difference come into
play when formulating a national security strategy in the cyber domain?[8]

ETHICS AND "FOLK MORALITY"

A second problem we face is that even if we can argue plausibly that there
is such a thing as cyber warfare, it is not a given that ethics could come to
play a significant role in cyber conflict. Doesn't the very concept of "unrestricted warfare" entail a war without rules, constraints, or restrictions?
And indeed, hasn't irregular warfare, alongside insurgency, terrorism, and
counterterrorism, presented us with a similar dilemma of constituting war
without rules pursued by adversaries who seem to ignore or deliberately
violate all of the existing international laws and rules of engagement?

Third and finally: were it not enough that cyber conflict, and cyberwar
specifically, is an inchoate concept subject to variety of interpretations,
ethics is even more so. Just as with cyber warfare, there is no widespread,
let alone universal, agreement on what constitutes ethics or morality. Any
hope of achieving sufficient consensus to develop a moral framework for
discussing cyber warfare would, moreover, have to confront and overcome
a set of widely held views about morality itself. I propose to define those
views collectively as constituting *folk morality*. This term, folk, itself merely
designates the aggregation of popular or widely held beliefs about any important topic, very much as psychologists often use the term *folk psychology*
to designate views about mind, consciousness, and intentionality and "the
self," which are also widely believed. The problem with these popular or

widely held beliefs is that many simply prove to be false or erroneous, while others are gravely misleading or wholly incompatible with each other. Here are some examples in the case of folk morality.

On one hand, a great many people claim to worry about "morality" (complaining about its perceived erosion in social life, for example) and strive to practice what they believe to be ethical behavior. Yet some of the very same people simultaneously believe (quite correctly) that understandings of what moral principles are and of what consistutes moral behavior vary among individuals and cultures, as well as in different practices or professions, such as business, healthcare, or the military, or are rooted in religious beliefs that also vary among individuals and cultures. From this diversity of moral beliefs and opinions, however, they derive the conclusion that there are, finally, no "universal" moral principles according to which we all should try to live.

But if the latter conclusion, sometimes called "moral relativism," is strictly true, then there could be no "erosion" of moral principles in any culture about which to worry or complain—there would merely be these widely differing moral beliefs. It would then become hard to hold moral convictions, such as a commitment to justice or human rights, if moral relativism were true. This is because claims about "justice" or human rights are precisely intended to be universal and cross-cultural, and independent of cultural practices or religious beliefs that might encourage behaviors inimical to both. We might conclude in this instance that a person who took his or her own ethical behavior seriously, while adhering to some version of moral relativism, was perhaps confused: either meaning also to uphold another universal principle (namely, a principle of tolerance toward others), or else that, in the end, his or her own commitment to the importance of morality in everyday life was strangely limited or insincere.

This first element of folk morality—a deeply ingrained cultural and legal relativism—proves to be inadequate to address the new and unfamiliar moral and legal challenges arising in the cyber domain, where notions of "privacy" and "liberty" are often advanced as universal claims, demanding the respect of all citizens and governments. Meanwhile, these purportedly universal claims about privacy and liberty in cyberspace have, we will discover, become intertwined with much more problematic claims regarding an alleged universal "right" to anonymity. The latter right is not, like the former two, merely a demand to be left alone, but, in addition, a demand to escape all consequences and accountability for what one does on the Internet. In the cyber domain, the prevailing belief system often appears to be "each cyber citizen should be free to do whatever she or he pleases, without fear of consequences."

Now it is quite possible that all three of these "rights-claims" are valid. It is also possible, however, that the first two are valid, while the third is false or invalid. If the one fundamental element of folk morality we have thus far identified (moral relativism) is true, however, then *none of these alleged rights can be upheld*, nor could we hope to discriminate between those (like privacy and liberty) that may turn out to be vitally important, and others (like the "right" to anonymity) that might prove false. Our widespread popular beliefs that constitute folk morality, that is to say, prove hopelessly deficient when it comes time to address these largely unprecedented claims regarding Internet anonymity.

Relativism is not the only fundamental tenet or element of "folk morality." Many people, despite their personal moral convictions, also believe that ethics has no place in international relations—as Machiavelli and Clausewitz seemed to argue—and certainly not when it comes to war and armed conflict, since these involve illegal and apparently immoral actions like killing people and breaking things. But this view, termed "realism," is likewise hard to reconcile with our other beliefs about morality, even during wartime. How, for one thing, can we express moral outrage over the beheadings of helpless civilian prisoners by "soldiers" of the Islamic State (ISIL/ISIS) if, in the end, those personnel are simply behaving in accordance with the claims of realism that there are no moral principles applicable during wartime? If we think we are correct in believing such behavior to be morally wrong, or if we defend the validity of basic tenets of international human rights law that prohibit such actions, then realism (and our beliefs about it) cannot also be true (although it can be descriptively true that these beheadings are examples of the unfortunate ways in which people behave when the rule of law breaks down). Which is it? We cannot have it all ways at once, and yet having and holding false or inconsistent views "all at once" is a fundamental property of folk morality. In my own professional academic field of philosophy, we often lament that attempting to address this sensitive and formidable problem is what got Socrates killed—and it has only gotten worse ever since! In any event, this makes it quite a formidable challenge to attempt to apply "ethics" (on whatever confused definition) to the dilemmas of cyber war and conflict.

Perhaps this is why no one has yet attempted to write a book about the ethics of cyber warfare. To be sure, there are plenty of books devoted to the description, analysis, and policy implications of cyber conflict and information warfare. Some of these—for example, a superb insider take on the historical evolution of cyber warfare by Shane Harris and an earlier account by Jeffrey Carr; a first-rate comprehensive survey by Peter Singer and Allan Friedman; and the now-classic accounts by Clarke, Brenner, Arquilla, and

Libicki cited in chapter 1—do invoke ethical and legal concerns alongside policy considerations.[9]

Likewise, a good deal of attention has been paid to ethics and cyber conflict by a number of accomplished scholars—for example, Randall Dipert, in moral philosophy, and Michael Schmitt, in the field of the international law of armed conflict—whose work appears in peer-reviewed academic journals and in anthologies devoted wholly or in part to the topic of ethics in cyber conflict. And a constellation of bright new stars has arisen on the horizon: thoughtful young scholars and policy analysts such as Patrick Lin, Adam Henschke, Heather Roff, Fritz Allhoff, Ryan Jenkins, and B. J. Strawser, to name only a few, who have published important essays, organized international symposia, and edited anthologies devoted to the ethics of cyber warfare. Certainly, it would be difficult for any one individual to pretend to possess expertise in all the fields of information technology, computer science, political science, international relations, or international law that would be necessary to write an original treatise on this topic. A synoptic view of the field, however, would at least attempt to systematically draw together the various multidisciplinary threads of discussion, and to recognize and carefully synthesize the ideas of the leading international scholars who are contributing to it. This is especially urgent, as we will discover, on account of the wildly disparate accounts even of the largely indisputable facts surrounding cyber conflict, let alone of their proper interpretation.[10]

The most substantial discussions of the governance of cyber conflict to date have taken place in the field of international law. Almost immediately following the advent of cyber conflict, and with special urgency after the Estonian cyberattacks of July 2007, leading figures in international law from around the world—Michael Schmitt, Scott Shackelford, Duncan Hollister, David Graham, Major General Charles Dunlap (US Air Force, retired), to name only a few of the most prominent—offered significant interpretations of existing international law, both criminal law and the law of armed conflict, or "humanitarian" law, in an attempt to understand both the law's reach and its potential for jurisdictional authority in the cyber domain. The most important document arising from this international collaboration of leading legal scholars is the *Tallinn Manual on the International Law Applicable to Cyber Warfare*, published in 2012.[11] It is an attempt to interpret and extrapolate existing international law to the governance of the new forms of cyber conflict. This was a significant effort indeed, since there appears to be little appetite within the international community for writing new black-letter legislation or treaties to govern the cyber domain.

Accordingly, in the following chapter I will consider the manual's contributions to an enhanced understanding of the rule of law arising from this impressive collaboration. To the extent that the *Tallin Manual* has thus far failed to gain wide acceptance, however, I will also look at some of the reasons why this is so, raising questions about the relevance, adequacy, and applicability of those results, and more generally, of relying solely on existing international law to address all the morally salient features of cyber conflict, whether above or below the threshold deemed equivalent to an armed attack.

Specifically, there is the question of jurisdiction: for example, can the laws and legal conceptions concerning conventional armed conflict be legitimately interpreted to cover kinds of conflict that they were never explicitly intended by their framers to address? This is especially problematic when we are discussing low-intensity conflict, such as espionage, which has been traditionally understood to lie beyond the reach of international law. It continues to be problematic in light of the proposal by an International Group of Experts convened by Professor Schmitt as part of the overall Tallinn process to extend their discussions to other regimes of international law, such as the law of the sea, outer space, and international telecommunications, as well as human rights law and the law of state responsibility, as these might be found to have jurisdiction over forms of cyber conflict that are not the equivalent of armed conflict. Questions of jurisdiction, in turn, raise concerns about what philosophers term *normativity*, specifically about the *normative force* of the law itself, and call attention to a fundamental equivocation within international law regarding the kinds of entities that are the proper subjects of its governance.[12]

The issue of the normative force of law pertains to the power that the law has to influence behavior persuasively and, if necessary, coercively. International legal scholars frequently sidestep or equivocate on this important conception. On one hand, they describe international law as reflecting what states either do or tolerate being done. This conception is often referred to as *ius gentium*, "customary law," and it possesses little in the way of normative force if states choose to override it or tolerate others doing so. On the other hand, legal scholars (like most of us) also believe that the law defines *and prohibits* certain forms of conduct, such as genocide and other violations of basic human rights, in a manner that generates a binding obligation to comply with such legislation. The justification for this, in turn, is that legislation prohibiting such conduct is founded on fundamental inviolable principles (e.g., the sovereignty and territorial integrity of the state) that are not to be transgressed, no matter what states themselves do or tolerate. It is difficult to hold or reconcile these contrasting views coherently and consistently.[13]

Finally, we will see that there were also political flaws in what I labeled the Tallinn process, that is, in how the International Group of Experts was constituted and its findings formulated, adopted, and promulgated. In chapter 3, I will conclude by showing that the underlying methodology used by the authors was insufficiently inter disciplinary and insufficiently inclusive from a global political standpoint. In particular, the collaborators were not adequately familiar with the practices and the interests of the practitioners (including adversary nations) whose cyber conduct the law seeks to govern. In this, they *presupposed* what they were convened to demonstrate and justify: that international law properly has jurisdiction in these affairs. Many nations, including China, sharply disagree.[14]

In this important political sense, the Tallinn process failed to recognize the most basic and salient features of what in jurisprudence is termed *good governance*.[15] As a result, the *Tallinn Manual* has unfortunately thus far failed to attain acceptance within the international community beyond the immediate NATO constituency from which its expertise was drawn.[16]

ETHICS AND THE LAW

Ethics and the law are *not* identical topics, despite the tendency in folk morality to collapse one into the other or, even more mistakenly, to hold that law in itself is the bedrock concept pertaining to the appropriate norms of human behavior. Quite the contrary, when law fails to address important new conflicts and conundrums explicitly, it is necessary to resort to ethics to sort things out: to discern, for example, underlying principles of law and jurisprudence that might be invoked (in the absence of bright-line statutes, treaties, or precedent) to guide our insights and intuitions on how best to confront the controversy in question.[17]

All that said, with just a few exceptions, considerations of the ethics of cyber warfare entered the discussion relatively late in the evolution of cyber conflict. The preliminary ruminations on information warfare by early writers, such as Arquilla, Ronfelt, and Denning, did cite ethical concerns. But they were scientists, not moral philosphers, and thus tended to presume the authority and invoke the summary findings of moral frameworks (such as the classical and historical conceptions of just war doctrine), somewhat uncritically, leaving open the question, for example, of why individuals or governments that are contemptuous of just war doctrine should take those concerns or prescriptions seriously.

The first bona fide moral philosopher to take on the subject of cyber-domain ethics was Professor Randall Dipert, of the University at Buffalo—a philosopher, game theorist, mathematician, and technical cyber expert—in his pathbreaking article "The Ethics of Cyber Warfare."[18] Dipert's work has been enlightening and highly influential. I take issue with only one of his underlying observations—namely, his contention that objects and events in the cyber domain are so unique, and so utterly dis-analogous to anything we encounter in the everyday physical world, as to obviate both the relevance and applicability of both international law and the ethical precepts expressed in the just war tradition and just war theory. Neither, Dipert claims, has the ability to adjudicate conflict in the cyber domain.

This claim that just war theory, just war tradition, and the law of armed conflict are irrelevant to cyberwar and weapons has been made frequently over the past decade as well as in the early days of irregular warfare, including the humanitarian military interventions of the 1990s (in Somalia, Rwanda, Bosnia, and elsewhere). The new practice of irregular war convinced everyone that it was a game-changer, and that all bets were off concerning the adequacy of existing law or traditional forms of moral or legal reasoning to cope with this new regime. This, however, proved to be largely unfounded.

Rather, the question (already addressed by the Cooperative Cyber Defence Centre of Excellence [CCD COE] scholars in reference to the law) is not *whether* but *how* the law of armed conflict, as well as international criminal law and other legal regimes, such as space law or law of the sea, can be interpreted to apply. This is also the present challenge confronting just war theory in ethics: just war theory must likewise be able to demonstrate its continuing relevance and applicability to conflict in the cyber domain.[19] The ethics challenge is an important one to address, should it turn out (as I averred earlier) that there may yet be elements of cyber conflict that fall through the cracks of international law, on any reinterpretation. Whatever the relationship between them proves to be, we will likely discover an urgent need for the normative insights of both sources of guidance and governance of conduct in the cyber domain. But we need to know more: not simply whether existing legal or moral norms can be made to apply to cyber conflict, but also *what that means*. In other words, we should also be asking whether the existing laws and conventional moral principles are the *best, most effective* way to protect international peace and security in light of these new cyber capabilities.

The initial problem for just war theory as a form of ethics or moral discourse addressing war and armed conflict, however, is every bit as acute and perplexing as that posed earlier for international law—namely, if there is no such thing as cyber warfare—or, if what we tend to call warfare in the cyber domain is something else altogether—then how can the historical tradition of moral reasoning pertaining to conventional warfare be thought to address it? David Rodin, an internationally renowned political philosophy scholar at Oxford University, recently leveled the same objection regarding the use of just war *reasoning* (as I prefer to call it) in the case of humanitarian intervention, simply because military intervention for humanitarian reasons is not war, and treating it as if it were "deforms[s] key aspects of humanitarian intervention."[20]

This characterization presumes that everyone understands and agrees on what just war theory and just war tradition are, and, in particular, that their purpose is only to offer criteria for determining whether the use of armed force is morally justified in a given instance. This is analytically (circularly, or by definition) true, of course, since the tradition of discourse about the moral justification of war arose historically in response to the ongoing and seemingly endless practice of declaring and waging conventional wars. And, of course, in that limited historical sense, Rodin is correct to wonder whether it can now be fruitfully extrapolated to humanitarian military intervention—that is, to something that is not war.

In the case of another activity that is not, or may not be, war—that is, cyber conflict—we need to consider an argument first suggested by one of Professor Dipert's critics, Colonel James Cook (US Air Force Academy). Cook offers the view that, as in the early days of aviation, we are still unfamiliar with how to behave in this new cyber domain and relatively unfamiliar with its forms of conflict, and that this is what yields such pessimistic assessments of the relevance of law or moral philosophy in the cyber domain.[21] These anxieties, he says, will fade as we become more familiar with the new technology and practices.

Cook thus agrees on this one important point with a far more strident assessment offered by Michael Schmitt in the foreword to *Cyberwar: Law and Ethics for Virtual Conflicts*, a thoughtful and constructive collection of essays on cyberwar edited by Jens David Ohlin, Kevin Govern, and Claire Finkelstein.[22] Schmitt asserts that "all experts agree" that contemporary *jus ad bellum* (justified resort to) and *jus in bello* (proper conduct of) warfare can be made to apply unambiguously to all dimensions of cyber conflict. This is so, he argues, whether these conflicts take the form of war and military weapons or "under-the-threshold" activities like espionage. He further claims that this has been acknowledged by all relevant subsidiary organs of the UN and the International Committee of the Red Cross, whence this apparent consensus is "quite frankly, indisputable."

Schmidtt's confidence that there is such consensus is, however, less apparent in the other contributions to the anthology. Jens David Ohlin opines in his chapter, for example, that cyber conflict and the so-called "problem of attribution,"[23] as well as that of intent, muddy the legal waters considerably. International law of armed conflict has, he objects, paid insufficient attention to a principle that is paramount in domestic criminal law: that of causation. Agents, he argues, are normally held legally liable for actions of which they themselves are the cause, with intent and foreknowledge or premeditation, determining the degree of liability and of punishment. In light of structural problems, such as the diffusion of "control" and causation in cyber space, international law needs to be amended to address this issue more explicitly.[24] Jim Cook, in his chapter of Ohlin and colleagues' *Cyberwar*, allows that in important respects, "cyber weapons [remain] morally different from other tools of war."[25]

Schmitt himself subsequently acknowledges disputed legal interpretations, such as whether the damage caused by interference with functionality, such as was experienced during the DDoS attacks in Estonia, is on par with physical damage or injury, and if so, how much interference is required to exceed that threshold. He likewise worries that the exercise of applying international legal norms to the cyber domain will uncover lacunae in the law that will need to be addressed. Schmitt's evident exasperation in the foreword to *Cyberwar* is mostly with moral philosophers or ethicists, who, he charges, carelessly conflate moral and legal norms, and in so doing "badly mangle the law."[26]

I believe, somewhat in contrast, that lawyers and philosophers are (or should be) allies, not enemies, in this common endeavor. Otherwise, I find little cause to doubt Schmitt's complaint, having been guilty on occasion of engaging in this "mangling" myself. Conflation and confusion are perhaps inevitable in discussing a topic as diverse and complex as cyber conflict. To be fair, "lawyers do it, too!"[27] Spokesmen from the legal staff of the International Committee of the Red Cross, for example, sometimes refer to the fundamental tenets of international humanitarian law, which they summarize as *distinction, proportionality, military necessity*, and also variously *command responsibility*, and "humanity," including the *prohibition of superfluous injury and unnecessary suffering*.[28] On one hand, it is certainly convenient to summarize the substantive content of international humanitarian law in this fashion since these important legal norms are indeed all embodied in various ways in specific legal statutes; but on the other hand, legal experts know full well that none of these legal norms constitute written legislation or black-letter law. Rather, they inform the *eventual* codification of specific statutes in black-letter law. The history and origins of those legal norms, in turn, lie in the moral discourse of the just war tradition.

There is too much remaining to be done in the cyber realm to allow the conversation to be derailed by such petty inter disciplinary squabbles, although Schmitt's implicit demand for rigor and clarity, as well as caution and care in respecting important distinctions, is well advised. The historical origins of international law within a broader moral discourse pertaining to war and armed conflict in the Western world are well established and reasonably well understood.[29] So, for that matter, are the historical origins and basic contents of the just war tradition itself.

What is less well understood is the underlying nature of just war reasoning: not where it arises but *what it is* and what gives it jurisdictional authority—that is, its normativity or normative force. Why, that is to say, should anyone—and especially those nations and peoples outside the traditional boundaries portrayed in the history of just war theory—pay any attention to it?

There have been many recent important attempts to "revise" just war theory by challenging some of its most cherished concepts, such as proportionality; the question of whether national self-defense is a just cause for war; and, especially, whether a norm known as "the moral equality of soldiers" deserves its current privileged status in the law of armed conflict.[30] Surprisingly, however, the underlying question about just war theory's nature and source of normative authority remains unaddressed. Just war theory continues to be portrayed mainly in historical and cultural terms as an artifact of the Christian West. That being the case, it has little or no authority or obvious applicability to cultures and civilizations in other historical eras or in other parts of the world today.

At the same time, the historical just war tradition is the basis of all of the legal norms that now infuse and inform international law, which claims universal jurisdiction. Hence, either we must conclude that the entire body of international law is *grounded in little more than cultural bias* (which constituted the Chinese and Russian objections to the *Tallinn Manual*), or else we must demonstrate that the moral and legal norms that underlie it have a much broader purchase than their history and even the respect accorded some of their most venerable figures—such as Hugo Grotius, Emer de Vattel, Francisco de Vitoria, and St. Thomas Aquinas—can explain.

We need to probe beyond the petty squabbling between lawyers and moral philosophers regarding jurisdiction over cyber conflict, and make a case instead for the importance of the moral and legal norms that both disciplines seek to preserve in the cyber domain. To accomplish that objective, however, it is necessary to address the underlying lacunae in the nature and authority of just war theory itself. In subsequent chapters, I will attempt to develop a *new theory of just war theory*—one that grounds both the law of armed conflict and just war theory in a broader type of moral discourse—a genus of which both are distinct species.

It is difficult to know what precise label to use for this more general type of moral discourse. It could well be called "the morality of exceptions" or "the ethics of exigencies," or even (in a sense quite different than originally intended by J. L. Austin[31]) "a plea for excuses" or a "request for exemptions." In particular, such reasoning, and the list of necessary conditions for granting the excuse or exemption (or for acknowledging the exception or exigency at hand), is found in many other species of moral and legal discourse as well: that concerning civil disobedience, for example, and killing when undertaken in self-defense or in the defense of others from attack. Its structure is discerned in the family resemblances between those resulting lists of necessary conditions, as encountered ubiquitously in moral discussions regarding the rare occasions when lying or the forfeiture of contracts or the breaking of solemn promises or the forsaking of individual or group loyalties—all things that are more or less universally deemed prima facie impermissible—are nonetheless found in extreme circumstances to be permissible, and sometimes even morally obligatory. Indeed, a hint of how this all works is also found in the controversial and contested just war discussion of "supreme emergency."[32]

In all such instances of moral reasoning, and in all such species of this genus of moral and legal discourse, one finds, for example, demands for an overriding reason or just cause, alongside some form of requirement for "peer review"[33] or publicity as finally constituting the sole form of legitimate authority to grant the exemption. One also invariably finds the demand that any exemption from strict adherence to the prevailing norms of conduct in these realms be granted or acted on *only as a last resort.* There are also requirements or constraints imposed on how the exemption can be exercised when it is approved—for example, with respect to the harm that will be done relative to the overarching goal to be accomplished (proportionality), frequently coupled with a demand to limit any resultant harm to morally relevant agents (discrimination or distinction). Agents empowered to exercise a grave exemption from prevailing norms are also required to ensure that this "collateral damage" (a term, contrary to convention, that is obviously *not* related to war alone) will be deemed permissible only in pursuit of tactical objectives that promise to be absolutely essential to accomplishing the original justified strategic goal (i.e., "necessity" of the means used in pursuit of the just cause). Such forms of moral and legal reasoning are, accordingly, hardly limited to war and its conduct—although wars and armed conflicts are among the most important of the cases that elicit such deliberation.

In order to explore the significance of this feature of moral discourse for cyber warfare, we are ultimately led to explore its impact on the emergence and formation of appropriate norms of moral and legal conduct. This is a crucial and, indeed, hopeful development in the cyber domain, as information technology expert Pano Yannakogeorgos at the US Air Force Research Institute in Maxwell, Alabama, has pointed out.[34] The concept of "emergent norms" is well established in the fields of political science and international relations[35] but is viewed with deep suspicion and skepticism in moral philosophy, where norms as moral principles are thought to be distinct from practice (otherwise, how could they legitimately be said to govern practice?). Indeed, to attempt to derive norms—that is, "best practices" or ideals of how individuals and nations ought to behave—from descriptions of current practices (i.e., deriving *ought* from *is*) is thought to constitute a fundamental logical fallacy, often labeled "the naturalistic fallacy."[36]

How can norms of practice legitimately *emerge* from practices themselves? And what prospect does this larger conception in international relations and state behavior hold for cyber conflict?

Clearly, in an important sense, norms as a fundamental feature of both law and morality, particularly in regard to state behavior, are underconceptualized. That is, despite numerous accounts of *how norms function* in interstate conflict and of *which norms are currently recognized and respected*, it remains something of a mystery where those norms come from and, particularly, how they can even be said to emerge from practice, apart from peculiar accidents of history and custom. And history and custom, by themselves, are utterly lacking in normative force. Hence, I am obliged to demonstrate (see chapters 4 and 5) that norms of behavior governing new or novel situations always arise from reflection on better and worse reasons for engaging in otherwise-proscribed behavior, as well as on better and worse forms of subsequent conduct when doing so.

This is a particularly formidable problem to tackle, and I rely on important contributions to political theory and international relations by such philosophers as Jürgen Habermas and John Rawls. That discussion, in turn, is grounded in the thought of Immanuel Kant, on whose treatment of the duties of justice and of virtue, particularly in the *Metaphysics of Ethics* (1795), these eminent modern philosophers based their treatments of moral reasoning and the authority of resulting norms and principles. The examination of emergent norms also leans heavily on the thought of Aristotle and of Alasdair MacIntyre, the latter of whom is usually taken to be a harsh critic of abstract and decontextualized moral reasoning after the fashion of Kant. Even so, it turns out to be MacIntyre's account of how moral norms arise from practice, *and from ensuing reflections upon practice*, that helps to explain what sorts of norms are worthy of universal jurisdiction (one of the chief problems also addressed by Habermas and in the later work of Rawls).[37] MacIntyre's account of Aristotle provides, as I hope to demonstrate, the conceptual framework that clarifies *how* governing principles, which are finally orthogonal to practice, can and do nonetheless *arise from, and in the midst of,* practice. This occurs through a peculiar kind of reflection on practice that is notably different from the "reflective equilibrium" described by Rawls. MacIntyre's methodology is grounded in practical reasoning (*phronesis*), particularly as guided by experienced, mature, and rationally informed judgment (*sophrosyne*). MacIntyre argues that this method is exemplified by Aristotle first in his important works on moral and political philosophy (as well as on the physical and biological sciences), and only subsequently conceptualized as the formal methodology most appropriate to these "imperfect" or "incomplete sciences" in his great work of logical method, the *Posterior Analytics*.

That Aristotle and Kant, the most important ancient and modern figures for understanding morality and law, play an important role in a book about ethics is hardly surprising. This book, however, is devoted to bringing order out of the chaos that is conflict in the cyber domain and is thus intended for a wider audience than scholars interested in moral philosophy or jurisprudence. Hence, while I invoke these classical sources when necessary, I have done my best to avoid technical discussions that would likely not be of interest to more than a very few readers.

But it is only through an examination (however cursory or incomplete) of the ancient sources of moral and legal authority and jurisdiction that we can answer the questions at the forefront of our inquiry concerning both what laws and moral principles should be invoked in the cyber domain and, even more importantly, *why* these might finally be said to have normative force in that domain—or, for that matter, in any domain in which they are currently applied.

This tedious but necessary technical slogging will lead us to a consideration of when and how to engage in activities that are normally prohibited, such as lying, deception, betrayal of trust (disloyalty), the breaking or voiding of contracts, and the violation of oaths.

Edward Snowden did all of those things when he chose to violate both the law and the regulations of the government agency to which he had pledged allegiance, and then proceeded to steal that agency's highly classified data and to take it public. He justified his actions by claiming that he was engaged in whistleblowing.

As we saw in chapter 1, whistleblowing is a form of civil disobedience within an organizational or social setting that generally involves breaking the law. It also typically involves violating regulations of the society, company, or organization to which one has previously assented, by voluntarily swearing an oath, making a promise, or signing a contract. More than anything else, whistleblowing is thus an act of betrayal and disloyalty to one's group. This is why it is so dangerous, poorly received, and imperfectly understood by the victimized group, and why it is widely thought to be a form of exceptional activity for which, as with war itself, the "reasoning about exceptions" is most urgently required. To blow the whistle on your organization's activities inaccurately is similar to going to war unjustly: it is a grave moral error. If one is mistaken in one's accusations, it is a serious mistake that may have damaging consequences for which one is morally culpable. And it goes without saying that the same is true for other misguided acts of civil disobedience, lying, or the use of force in self-defense.

The whistleblower therefore must accept responsibility for his or her actions, including the opprobrium with which the organization and public are likely to initially respond, before they have had an opportunity to evaluate both the evidence and the reasoning on which he or she has relied. Importantly, therefore, the whistleblower must undertake this extreme activity only as a last resort, when lesser measures have been tried and have failed. The harm that will be done by the act of whistleblowing itself must, in addition, prove to be significantly less than the good achieved (or, alternatively, found to be proportionately less than the degree of wrongdoing and harm by the organization it exposes).

Whistleblowing is thus always a component of what Habermas terms "the public sphere," and is never simply an individual "private" act. In chapter 7, I argue that Snowden, finally, failed the implied test of publicity. He formulated and proceeded to act based on his own, entirely private, personal, and wholly unvetted conceptions of the meaning of individual privacy against what he took to be manifold violations of privacy by the NSA. He appears to have done this without due deliberation or any wider public discussion, though he seems to have had a sincere belief in the justice of his cause. Snowden's premeditated actions were those of a comparatively young and insufficiently oriented newcomer to the NSA. They were decidedly *not* the result of sober judgments, reluctantly reached by a seasoned, experienced, thoughtful, and reflective organizational veteran. Snowden's example should therefore be contrasted with the sort of whistleblower Daniel Ellsberg, decades earlier, had proven to be within the Department of Defense when he gave the *New York Times* top-secret classified documents showing that the government had for years been lying to the American public about the progress and winnability of the Vietnam War.

Having failed to comprehend, let alone fulfill, the responsibilities incumbent upon the whistleblower, Snowden, I will argue, erred in equating a well-intentioned (if paternalistic) program of preemptive self-defense in which he and his organization turned out to be deeply engaged, with a much different, malevolent program of unauthorized and unsupervised surveillance, government overreach, and oppression, which he and others at the time equated with the practices of the East German *Stasi*. In acting so precipitously on what turned out to be erroneous reasoning, finally, he did and continues to do irreparable harm to the security of the United States, Europe, and their allies.

Despite these grave moral errors, Snowden's actions undoubtedly served a larger purpose in framing the question with which we ourselves must conclude. The Snowden affair is relevant to this book on ethics and cyber warfare because it lies at the heart of considerations rightly laid before the public, regarding the price they are willing to pay in terms of their privacy and liberty for the sake of security and national self-defense against aggression.

What level of insecurity is the public willing to shoulder in order to maintain, not simply their own personal privacy, but also the continuing *anonymity* of actors in the cyber realm—anonymity that currently allows malevolent cyber actors to do whatever they please without accountability? This concluding question is a question at least as old as that posed by Thomas Hobbes, who forcefully argued that in an imperfect world, individuals must be willing surrender a measure of their natural rights for the sake of peace, order, security, and the rule of law. Such a political compromise thus far, however, seems beyond reach in the cyber domain, at least for the time being.

NOTES

1. These transformations are the topic of the essays found in *New Wars and New Soldiers*, ed. Paolo Tripodi and Jessica Wolfendale (London: Ashgate, 2011). See also four essays by G. R. Lucas, Jr.: "New Rules for New Wars: International Law and Just War Doctrine for Irregular War," *Case Western Reserve Journal of International Law* 43, no. 3 (2011): 677–705; "Revisiting Armed Humanitarian Intervention: A 25-Year Retrospective," in *Ethics of Armed Humanitarian Intervention*, ed. Don Scheid (Cambridge: Cambridge University Press, 2014), 26–45; "Postmodern War," *Journal of Military Ethics* 9, no. 4 (2010): 289–298; "'This Is Not Your Father's War': Confronting the Moral Challenges of 'Unconventional' War," *Journal of National Security Law and Policy*, 3, no. 2 (2009): 331–342.
2. As described in three essays by G. R. Lucas, Jr.: "Automated Warfare," *Stanford Law and Policy Review* 25, no. 2 (2014): 317–339; "Legal and Ethical Principles Governing Emerging Military Technologies: Research and Use," *Amsterdam Law Forum* 6, no. 1 (2014): 23–34; "Engineering, Ethics, and Industry: The Moral Challenges of Lethal Autonomy," *Killing by Remote Control*, ed. B. J. Strawser (New York: Oxford University Press, 2013), 211–228.
3. These are discussed in G. R. Lucas, Jr.: "Permissible Preventive Cyber Warfare," *The Ethics of Information Warfare*, ed. Luciano Floridi and Mariarosaria Taddeo (Frankfurt: Springer, 2014), 73–82; and G. R. Lucas, Jr., and David Whetham, "The Relevance of the Just War Tradition to Cyber Warfare," in *Cyber Warfare: A Multidisciplinary Analysis*, ed. James A. Green (London: Routledge, 2015), 160–173.
4. See G. R. Lucas, Jr., "Can There Be an 'Ethical' Cyberwar?," *Conflict and Cooperation in Cyberspace: The Challenge to National Security*, ed. P. A. Yannakogeorgos and A. B. Lowther (Boca Raton, FL: Taylor & Francis, 2014), 195–210; and G. R. Lucas, Jr., "Privacy, Anonymity and Cyber Security," *Amsterdam Law Forum* 5, no. 2 (2013): 107–114.
5. Discussed, for example, in G. R. Lucas, Jr., "Military Anthropology and the Ethics of Espionage," *International Journal of Intelligence Ethics* 1, no. 2 (2010): 3–31.
6. See, for example, Jan Goldman, ed., *The Ethics of Spying: A Reader for Intelligence Professionals*, vol. 2 (Lanham, MD: Scarecrow Press, 2009); and Goldman's earlier pathbreaking collection in vol. 1 (2005). See also David Perry, *Partly Cloudy: Ethics in War, Espionage, Covert Action, and Interrogation* (Lanham, MD: Scarecrow Press); and James M. Olson, *Fair Play: The Moral Dilemmas of Spying* (Washington, DC: Potomac Books, 2006). Goldman is also founder and editor of the *International Journal of Intelligence Ethics*, a peer-reviewed journal now in its fourth volume. None of these works or past issues of the journal have as of the time of this writing addressed such topics as ethics for cyber warriors or the fallout from the Snowden affair, but will inevitably do so in due course.
7. For the warrior's code for conventional conflict in a variety of cultures, see Shannon E. French, *The Code of the Warrior: Exploring Warrior Values Past and Present* (Lanham, MD: Rowman and Littlefield, 2004). I discuss this conventional code of professional military ethics and its possible applicability to cyber warfare in George Lucas, *Military Ethics: What Everyone Needs to Know* (New York: Oxford University Press, 2015). The concept of ethics for cyber warriors (including its alleged disadvantages as well as advantages) is discussed by several contributors to Fritz Allhoff, Adam Henscke, and Bradley J. Strawser, eds.,

Binary Bullets: The Ethics of Cyber Warfare (Oxford: Oxford University Press, 2016).

8. This interesting and problematic "cultural inversion" is discussed in clear layperson's terminology in *The Economist*, where similar points are made concerning the ascendancy over, and the impact of the accompanying transformation of espionage with respect to, conventional armed conflict. See "A New Age of Espionage," *The Economist*, August 2015, 53–54, preceded by the provocative note on "What Laws in the Jungle?" (13).

9. So closely did the design and deployment patterns of Stuxnet follow the ethical principles for cyber conflict laid out more than a decade ago by John Arquilla that when the worm and its mode of operation were finally made public, I said to him that its designers must have read his work! See George R. Lucas, Jr., "Just War Doctrine and Cyber Conflict," 12th Annual Stutt Ethics Lecture, US Naval Academy, March 21, 2012, http://www.youtube.com/watch?v=hCj2ra6yzl0. The transcript of the lecture can be found on the US Naval Academy website, http://www.usna.edu/Ethics/_files/documents/Just%20War%20and%20Cyber%20War%20GR%20Lucas.pdf.

10. Shane Harris's otherwise detailed account of the intricacies of cyber conflict from the standpoint of national security, for example, contains almost no treatment of the ethical issues involved in the security considerations, other than a cursory nod to a few of the legal concerns involved. It is fairly typical of the attitude of otherwise gifted authors and experts on cyber conflict that they seem to avoid the ethical issues like the plague. And no wonder, given some of the stubborn and astonishingly uninformed views of ethics with which they have to contend.

11. *Tallinn Manual on the International Law Applicable to Cyber Warfare*, ed. Michael Schmitt (Tallinn, ES: NATO Cooperative Cyber Defense Center of Excellence, 2012), https://ccdcoe.org/research.html. A print edition was published by Cambridge University Press in 2013. A second manual, "Tallinn 2.0" is anticipated in 2016, that will more fully address cyber operations that fall below the threshold of armed conflict.

12. There is a vast literature on normativity, ranging from what it means to recognize oneself as categorically obligated to fulfill a duty to believing there *are* such things as categorical obligations or duties (normative realism), and specifically to the degree that law or specific laws embody such categorical obligations, over and above stipulating actions (or prohibitions) of certain sorts. See, for example, Christine Korsgaard, *The Sources of Normativity* (Cambridge: Cambridge University Press, 1996); Thomas M. Scanlon, *Being Realistic about Reasons* (Oxford: Oxford University Press, 2014); and Allan Gibbard, *Thinking How to Live* (Cambridge, MA: Harvard University Press, 2003). David Copp discussed the problem of the law's normativity in his presidential address to the American Philosophical Association on April 3, 2015. See David Copp, "Explaining Normativity," *Proceedings and Addresses of the American Philosophical Association* 89 (November 2015): 48–73. Torben Spaak of Stockholm University devotes considerable attention to the normative force of law from the standpoint of legal positivism, in which morality and law are conceptually distinct. See Torben Spaak, "Legal Positivism, Law's Normativity, and the Normative Force of Legal Justification," *Ratio Juris* 16, no. 4 (2003): 469–485. His more extensive discussion of this problem can be found in an extended symposium on this topic at the University of Freiburg, "The Normativity of Law" (2006),

https://www.google.com/?gws_rd=ssl#q=normative+force+of+law (accessed 13 February 2016).

13. Inconsistency in behavior with respect to the law, however, is not by itself evidence of lack of normative force. For example, one might look for evidence of states acknowledging the *validity* of a norm, regardless of whether they actually obey it. An example of this, suggested to me by Elena Finckh, an international law scholar at the UN Disarmament Information and Research Institute (UNIDIR) in Geneva, would be the International Court of Justice case pertaining to France's nuclear tests: *Australia and New Zealand v. France* (known as the *Nuclear Tests Case*), http://www.casebriefs.com/blog/law/international-law/international-law-keyed-to-damrosche/chapter-4/nuclear-tests-case-australia-new-zealand-v-france/ (accessed May 20, 2016).

14. James T. Arredy, "China Aims to Rewrite Rules of Global Web," *Wall Street Journal*, July 29, 2015, A1, A10.

15. Canons of good governance as applied to control of emerging military technologies generally (including cyber conflict) are discussed at length by an experienced international lawyer and legal scholar at Rutgers University, Brigadier General Richard M. O'Meara, PhD (US Army, retired), in a fascinating and lively study. See Richard M. O'Meara, *Governing Military Technologies in the 21st Century: Ethics and Operations* (New York: Palgrave Macmillan, 2014). O'Meara, a former Army inspector general and Vietnam combat veteran, led the strenuous opposition by military lawyers in 2004 against the US government's approval of torture and prisoner abuse as acceptable forms of "enhanced interrogation." It is his account of what he terms "the canons of good governance" on which my treatment relies in this book. He writes, for example:

    Successful systems of "good governance" involve clearly defined and articulated expectations: that is, they identify the precise problems to be solved, changes to be made, or goals to be sought through governance in straightforward terms. The solutions proposed to these problems, moreover, are realistic: that is, they do not attempt to articulate ideal norms of what ought to be, but rather provide feasible norms describing what can, in fact, be accomplished, under existing political, cultural and legal constraints. Successful systems of governance, moreover, are holistic and inclusive, in the sense that all stakeholders are identified and involved in some fashion in making the rules. Finally, they issue rules or principles that are subject to assessment: that is, the results are capable of measurement and evaluation of effectiveness, in a manner that allows for subsequent amendment and improvement of the requirements when appropriate.

    Also enlightening is Jan Klabbers and Tuoko Piiparinin, "Normative Pluralism," *Normative Pluralism and International Law: Exploring Global Governance*, ed. Jan Klabbers and Tuoko Piiparinin (Cambridge: Cambridge University Press, 2014), 1–33. The editors explore the topic of morality and law.

16. I first encountered this sweeping characterization of its impact as, in the words of one senior staff person, "a spectacular failure," emanating from UN and ICRC experts meeting at ICRC headquarters in Geneva in May of 2013. This came as a stunning surprise and disappointment. I had assumed without question that the findings of the *Tallinn Manual* would prove definitive and authoritative, as I discuss at greater length in chapter 3.

17. On the point of applying law and morality to the governance of cyber conflict, for example, Ms. Elena Finckh writes:

The comparison [of cyber conflict] to "irregular warfare" . . . draws attention to a few well known problematics, namely, the fact that these fall "outside" most legal norms that have been developed for conventional inter-state conflicts. When states engage more and more in "hacktivism," moreover, attribution becomes extremely difficult, and hence, [so does] enforcement of the law (even if it were clear). . . . The relationship between law and morals is indeed a very entangled one. Both are conceptually distinct frameworks of investigation—and depending on what kind of question one seeks to answer admitting or denying a relation might be appropriate. The connection between law and morals, however, can never simply be affirmed or denied in absolute terms as it always depends on what it is you are trying to argue. For example, if one seeks to authoritatively answer whether certain acts in cyberspace are "wrong" one can do so by either moral or legal standards. Because law aspires to be in harmony with the values of its subjects' community, one will ideally find the "same" answer. One can, however, not determine whether something *is* legal, by providing moral or ethical arguments— even though one can invoke such arguments in order to determine whether something *should* be illegal (i.e. arguing for the development of new rules). Technological innovation in general enhances human capability and makes things possible that weren't before. For this reason it may appear that existing rules and regulation may no longer appropriately govern, i.e. outlaw undesirable behavior. In order to identify what "undesirable" behavior is, it is no longer sufficient to turn to the law, but one may answer this question in relation to the values which the law claims to protect, but apparently no longer does. (pers. comm., July 24 and August 2, 2015)

18. See Randall R. Dipert, *Journal of Military Ethics* 9, no. 4 (2010): 384–410. Dipert is, without question, the leading authority in this field and one of the few to possess nearly all the qualifications I cited as requisite for writing a book like this. What he has done instead is publish widely in scholarly and academic journals on this topic, as well as contribute to each of the recent important anthologies on ethics and cyber warfare.

19. Just war theory, also called the "just war tradition," is the name conventionally given to a centuries-long discussion in Western moral philosophy, stretching from Plato, Cicero, St. Augustine, and St. Thomas Aquinas all the way to Kant, Mill, and such modern political philosophers as Michael Walzer and John Rawls, regarding when, if ever, the resort to force is justified and what the proper conduct of the resulting armed conflict should be in international relations. We will return to this topic in great detail later.

20. See David Rodin, "Re-thinking the Responsibility to Protect: The Case for Human Sovereignty," in *The Ethics of Armed Humanitarian Intervention*, ed. Don E. Scheid (New York: Cambridge University Press, 2014), 243–260.

21. Jim Cook's thoughtful and somewhat reassuring views on the future of cyber conflict are well expressed in three essays: first, the aforementioned "'Cyberation' and Just War Doctrine: A Response to Randall Dipert," in the *Journal of Military Ethics* 9, no. 4 (2010): 411–423; "Is There Anything Morally Special about Cyberwar?," in *Cyberwar: Law and Ethics for Virtual Conflicts*, ed. Jens David Ohlin, Kevin Govern, and Claire Finkelstein (New York: Oxford University Press, 2015); and most recently, the unusual and imaginatively titled, "Just War under CyberGaia," *The Routledge Handbook of Military Ethics*, ed. George Lucas (London: Routledge Press, 2015), 421–431.

22. Ohlin, Govern, and Finkelstein, *Cyberwar*, v–viii.
23. The "problem of attribution" is the name now assigned to the dilemmas we discussed in an earlier chapter—namely: Did the Russians really attack Estonia, or did someone else; did the PLA really steal the OPM personnel records, or are their denials to be believed? In short, it is another name for the problem of agency: Who did it, what exactly did they do, when, and (most importantly) why? For a brief analysis, see Singer and Friedman, *Cybersecurity and Cyberwar*, 72–76. We will return to this problem, and the extent to which it can be solved, later.
24. In Jens David Ohlin, "Cyber Causation," in Ohlin, Govern, and Finkelstein, *Cyberwar: Law and Ethics*, 37–54.
25. Ibid., 36.
26. Ibid., vii.
27. Indeed, many hold that the distinction on which Schmitt insists cannot be categorically made, owing to the intertwining of moral and legal considerations. For example, one of Europe's leading arms control experts, Professor Harald Müller, at Goëthe University Frankfurt, argues, in the case of the tension between other new norms (like the responsibility to protect) and the prevailing norm of "nonintervention" that

> it would be wrong to see this as the collision between the legal and the moral [since] non-intervention is a norm meant to prevent war [and] this has a deep moral content, because war . . . inevitably has immoral consequences, even if fought for justifiable reasons. *Thus, it is of little use to maintain a categorical distinction between legal and moral norms*; rather we must think of all [state] behavior under the logic of appropriateness as *unequivocally having a moral component*, whether legally codified or not. (Harald Müller, introduction to *Norm Dynamics in Multilateral Arms Control: Interests, Conflicts, and Justice*, ed. Harald Müller and Carmen Wunderlich (Athens: University of Georgia Press, 2013), 5; my emphases.

28. The prohibition against weapons that inflict superfluous injury and unnecessary suffering is also known as "Rule 70" in the ICRC Handbook of Customary International Humanitarian Law. See: https://www.icrc.org/customary-ihl/eng/docs/v1_rul_rule70 [accessed 12 July 2016]. ICRC staff frequently refer to these as the "five pillars" or foundational principles of IHL. However, there is no specific reference that documents either the exact number or specific listing. Like the basic tenets of just war theory described in this chapter, however, the basic conception is consistent, despite variations of formulation and precise number of entries. See, for example, https://www.diakonia.se/en/ihl/the-law/international-humanitarian-law-1/introduction-to-ihl/principles-of-international-law/ (accessed May 24, 2016).
29. The references for this history are too numerous to cite here, but are cited at length in a summary discussion of that history and reciprocal relationship in George Lucas, *Military Ethics: What Everyone Needs to Know* (New York: Oxford University Press, 2015), chap. 2, "Ethics and International Law."
30. The pioneering work of David Rodin, *War and Self Defense* (Oxford: Oxford University Press, 2002), and of Jeff McMahan, *Killing in War* (New York: Oxford University Press, 2009), occupy center stage in this important discussion, to which numerous thoughtful critics and scholars have made substantive additional contributions as so-called revisionists. Many also credit Thomas Hurka's widely cited "Proportionality in the Morality of War," *Philosophy and Public*

Affairs 33, no. 1 (2005): 34–66, with having helped to launch the revisionist just war theory movement. Yet for all its lengthy and disjointed rambling, this poorly edited and thinly argued article fails even to note the use of proportionality routinely in numerous similar contexts of moral discourse involving making a justified exception to prevailing norms and moral principles. Other important figures and works in this movement include Cecile Fabre, *Cosmopolitan War* (Oxford: Oxford University Press, 2012); Cecile Fabre and Seth Lazar, eds., *The Morality of Defensive War* (Oxford: Oxford University Press, 2014); David Rodin and Henry Shue, eds., *Just and Unjust Warriors: The Moral and Legal Status of Soldiers* (Oxford: Oxford University Press, 2008). This is only a small sample of the extensive literature on this topic.

31. J. L. Austin, "A Plea for Excuses," *Proceedings of the Aristotelian Society* 57 (1956): 1–30. This famous article merely sought to call attention to important distinctions encapsulated in ordinary language, for example, between "mistakes" and "accidents" that might attend a request to be excused from blame for one's actions. This, unfortunately, is typical of the thin gruel that constituted (analytic) philosophy during this epoch. I have something a bit more significant in mind.

32. The concept of a "supreme emergency" during wartime that constitutes a case for making an exemption from normal moral and legal constraints was first raised by Michael Walzer, as a possible justification for Winston Churchill's decision to bomb civilian targets during WWII. See Michael Walzer, *Just and Unjust Wars* (New York: Basic Books, 1977), chap. 16. This "supreme emergency" concept has been much critiqued since, for example, Martin L. Cook, "Michael Walzer's Concept of Supreme Emergency," *Journal of Military Ethics* 6, no. 2 (2007): 138–151). But Stephen Coleman at the Australian Defence Force Academy was the first to recognize that the pattern of justification applied in supreme emergencies mirrored that of just war theory itself, during a presentation on "supreme emergency" at the second annual conference of the European chapter of the International Society for Military Ethics (Euro-ISME). See Stephen Coleman, "Even Dirtier Hands in War: Considering Walzer's Supreme Emergency Argument," *Research in Ethical Issues in Organizations* 13 (2015): 61–73, http://www.emeraldinsight.com/doi/abs/10.1108/S1529-209620150000013004 (accessed May 24, 2016).

33. Public questions about the quality and appropriately adversarial stance of the secretive peer-review procedure and oversight of clandestine activities by US Foreign Intelligence Surveillance (FISA) courts came to occupy center stage in the debates about Snowden and the NSA programs, for example.

34. Panayotis A. Yannakogeorgos, "The Prospects for Cyber Deterrence: American Sponsorship of Global Norms," in *Conflict and Cooperation in Cyberspace: The Challenge to National Security*, ed. Panayotis A. Yannakogeorgos and Adam B. Lowther (Boca Raton, FL: Taylor & Francis, 2013).

35. See Martha Finnemore and Kathryn Sikkink, "International Norm Dynamics and Political Change," *International Organization* 52, no. 4 (1998): 887–917; Richard Price, "Moral Limit and Possibility in World Politics," *International Organization* 62, no. 2 (2008): 191–220; and the essays in *Implementation in World Politics: How International Norms Change Practice*, ed. Alexander Betts and Phillip Orchard (Oxford: Oxford University Press, 2014). See also Müller and Wunderlich, *Norm Dynamics*. This important literature from political science and international relations, however, is primarily directed as a polemic against

realists and functional realist critics, by attempting to offer an empirical account of how "ideational" (moral) norms affect state policy and political change. My own efforts in this book are directed differently: toward providing *a conceptual foundation* for the historical and descriptive accounts of "norm dynamics" offered by social scientists. In particular, I seek to demonstrate how norms "emerge" and why, as a result, they are able exert the normative influence on state behavior empirically attributed to them by these other scholars.

36. The original formation of the naturalistic fallacy stems from the work of Scottish Enlightenment philosopher David Hume in his *Treatise on Human Nature* (section 3.1.1, "Moral Distinctions Not Derived from Reason"), in which the formidable skeptic complains of the prevalence of a widespread but unexplained transition in "vulgar systems of moral philosophy" from discussions of "what is or is not" a matter of fact or reason to what "ought or ought not" to be permitted as a condition of morality. Whether or not this is taken as a legitimate formal logical fallacy (it is often found in standard logic texts classified merely as an "informal fallacy"), it was finally redressed in the work of Richard M. Hare in 1952, who carefully defined the formal conditions under which an obligation (ought) could be derived from statements of fact (what is or is not), when the specific obligation was derived from a "practical syllogism" whose major premise was some broadly recognized principle guiding or constraining conduct in the general case. See Richard Hare, *The Language of Morals* (Oxford: Clarendon, 1952). The origins of this fallacy are often erroneously attributed, however, to G. E. Moore, who formulated a quite distinct version of a naturalistic fallacy. Moore's version did not address Hume's problem of the relations between descriptive facts and moral obligations; instead Moore denied that the Good was a natural kind or that it could itself be derived from purely naturalistic considerations, as utilitarians from Bentham to Sedgwick had routinely attempted to do. Moore's version, originating in his doctoral dissertation on Plato, stemmed from his unwavering conviction that "the Good" (whether in morals or aesthetics) was itself a primordial and indefinable conception from which all else derived.

37. MacIntyre's alternative account of normativity and binding moral precepts is found in "Intractable Moral Disagreements," in *Intractable Disputes about the Natural Law: Alasdair MacIntyre and Critics*, ed. Lawrence Cunningham (Notre Dame, IN: University of Notre Dame Press, 2009), 1–52.

CHAPTER 3

The *Tallinn Manual*

International Law in the Aftermath of Estonia

I have thus far proposed two forms of cyber conflict for consideration as legitimate forms of warfare.

1) The "effects-based cyber conflict" alternative is based on the Stuxnet attack on Iranian military infrastructure, in which a weapon designed entirely of software code was able to produce concrete *physical effects* comparable to those of an armed attack carried out with conventional weapons.

2) The second alternative is based on the *political effects* of the tactic that I label "state-sponsored hacktivism." Ought we to regard this kind of state activity as a new kind of warfare, distinguished in any meaningful sense from routine state-sponsored espionage and covert action or from crime?

Thus far, effects-based cyberattacks have monopolized the discussion of when cyberattacks might be said to constitute acts of war. In this chapter, we ask: What is the current status of both kinds of cyber conflict in international law? For the purposes of governance, how effectively can we subsume the dimensions of current cyber conflict within the boundaries and jurisdictions of existing regimes of domestic and international law? And most importantly, to what extent does either or both of these forms of cyber conflict qualify as examples of authentic warfare?

The answer for the most part seems straightforward. On the one hand, if, as Thomas Rid contends,[1] neither alternative results in genuine warfare, then we need only subsume various cyber phenomena under the appropriate bodies of either domestic or international law appropriate to crime (and thus, indirectly, to specific acts of espionage as well). To that end, the current Council of Europe's International Convention on Cybercrime of 2001[2] has pointed the way toward both enforcing domestic law on perpetrators of crime within one's own legal jurisdiction, and promoting cooperation among national law enforcement agencies in bringing international perpetrators of cybercrimes to justice.

There have been numerous instances of international cooperation among national law enforcement officials, agencies, and personnel in combating cybercrime since the widespread adoption of the Convention. As noted in chapter 1, a promising recent example of such cooperation was Operation Shrouded Horizon,[3] a consortium of twenty nations, whose activities were coordinated by the FBI, which in the summer of 2015, after years of effort, succeeded in shutting down Darkode.com, one of the largest and most sinister international criminal forums on the Internet. More than seventy of its principal administrators have since been arrested in the cooperating countries.

On the other hand, if effects-based use of cyber weapons or state-sponsored hacktivism can be said to be the equivalent of a use of force or armed conflict, then a different, but clear-cut, legal pathway lies before us—one that dispels the concerns of cyber experts who doubt the relevance of international law in responding to cyber conflict. We begin with Stuxnet.

INTERNATIONAL LAW APPLICABLE TO STUXNET

Stuxnet was unquestionably a weapon of some sort. The details of its composition and the kind of ontological oddity to which Dipert and others call attention[4]—namely, that being composed entirely of computer code, it was "non-physical"—are certainly intriguing but, as Ryan Jenkins observes, finally irrelevant to an effects-based account of what any weapon accomplishes in the physical world.[5]

Weapons by definition kill people and destroy things. The use of weapons by states falls under the jurisdiction of international humanitarian law (the law of armed conflict), which, as we have seen, dictates what weapons are permissible and when, how, and against whom they may be used. Article 36 of the 1977 Additional Protocol, as Michael Schmitt reminds us,[6] extends the reach of specific legislation and weapons prohibitions (such as "Rule 70" of customary IHL prohibiting the use of poison gas, hollow exploding bullets, or blinding lasers) to any other sort of weapon that might be found to violate the basic humanitarian principles informing these prohibitions; namely, such weapons must not prove to be inherently indiscriminate or disproportionate in the damage they inflict, and must not be found to cause superfluous injuries or unnecessary suffering.

Stuxnet, as we noted earlier, complied with every one of these humanitarian constraints in international law. Indeed, it appeared to have been designed to do so: it targeted only military hardware; it killed and injured no one; and it resulted in no discernible collateral damage to unrelated persons or property. Many experts have since hailed Stuxnet as perhaps the most ethical weapon of war ever developed.[7]

To be sure, not everyone agreed, including Ralph Langner, one of the original discoverers of Stuxnet "in the wild." Langner's initial concern was that, following its "escape" from the Natanz laboratory to the outside world via an infected laptop, Stuxnet violated the legal regulations regarding proportionality and discrimination, by infecting unrelated and vulnerable industrial systems far removed from its original military target.[8]

But that eventuality, too, had been anticipated. The worm had been programmed to lie dormant and harmless on the other systems it had accidentally infected and eventually to self-destruct without a trace. Langer had a further concern, however, shared by many others, that in the interim between infection and self-destruction, Stuxnet could have been downloaded from the infected sites by criminals, terrorists, or even rogue nations and then reverse engineered and replicated for indiscriminate uses against civilian targets.

This fear, however, betrays a fundamental misconception regarding a key feature of cyber weapons: they are not physical objects, as are nuclear or conventional weapons, which can sit around in storage until they are needed and thus might be stolen "off the shelf" for full-capacity use by an adversary. There is no inventory of Stuxnets sitting in an armory waiting to be used. Because cyber weapons are computer programs that operate by stealth and deception, once one is discovered, the programming innovations it employs quickly become ineffective. Thieves or rogue information technologists might study Stuxnet and learn something about generic cyber-weapon design, or how to recognize vulnerabilities in widely used software platforms in other widely disbursed civilian infrastracture that they can then target. But by the time they learn these peculiarities, security patches will have been installed in the most vulnerable software. Indeed, the nature of the deception will have become apparent to information technologists, so that all security teams and operators will be on the lookout for it. After the Stuxnet attack was discovered, many experts, somewhat hysterically, predicted an onslaught of Stuxnet-like attacks on legitimate industrial control systems; but to date, *not a single attack* attributed to a Stuxnet clone has ultimately been verifiable.[9] Cyber weapons are by and large "one and done" when it comes to their effectiveness.[10] This feature actually works in their favor in terms of their potential for compliance with international law pertaining to weapons design and attendant risks.[11]

As to any other effects-based cyber weapons systems that might be on the drawing board, among the conclusions arrived at by the authors of the *Tallinn Manual* are the following: if they are designed by states for use in conventional warfare, then they are subject to governance under the terms of the current international law of armed conflict, regardless of their physical makeup or material structure (their ontology).[12] By the same token, if such weapons are designed and used by, or fall into the hands of, nonstate agents such as terrorists and vigilantes, their use is never, under any circumstances, legally authorized and will always constitute a crime. The only difficulty, from a legal perspective, would be in determining the jurisdiction of any prosecution, and perhaps also the regime or regimes of domestic and international law that might be found to apply: for example, the customary law of the sea, telecommunications law, space law, or international human rights law, among others.

Readers might well ask, to what extent will such findings regarding the adequacy of legal jurisdiction deter the behavior of states, nonstate actors, organizations that are subject to current law? That, however, is an altogether different question, and one that is quite difficult to answer. We will take up the problem of submitting to the requirements of law and morality in later chapters. But for the present, our ever-dubious prospects of altering the behavior of contemptuous scofflaws was not, we should remember, the question originally posed by Dipert and other critics of the relevance of international law to the cyber domain. Their question was never whether or not criminals, espionage agents, or rogue states could ever be gotten to comply with international law when engaging in cyber conflict. Our original question was solely whether or not current international law or appropriate existing regimes of domestic legislation plausibly governs these allegedly new and unprecedented phenomena. The answer affirmed by the *Tallinn Manual*'s authors with respect to the use of effects-based cyber weapons appears to be an unequivocal "yes," regardless of whether or not these technically qualify as acts of war,[13] and regardless of whether adversaries will or will not comply with the law.

In this instance I agree entirely with the Tallinn findings. Stuxnet *was* a weapon, and its use in an act of military sabotage was as much an act of war as a conventional bombing attack by one state against an enemy state. Stuxnet was therefore subject to jurisdiction under the UN Charter, meaning that it was not authorized under the terms of the charter, save possibly as an act of preemptive (anticipatory) self-defense.[14] It was subject as well to jurisdiction under the law of armed conflict—with which, by contrast, it complied perfectly, like no weapon in the history of warfare ever has before.[15]

In similar fashion, cyber weapons currently being developed, or that are already available for (one-time) use in the arsenals of adversary nations, are finally subject to the same restrictions as conventional weapons. This establishment of jurisdiction is important, especially if, as Neil Rowe claims, the designers of cyber weapons tend unreflectively to assume that they are free to target civilians and civilian infrastructure, simply because these (as opposed to military targets) are more vulnerable to cyberattacks.[16] Cyber weapons are equally subject to the twin principles of distinction (discrimination) and proportionality. Willfully ignoring such constraints, as Rowe charges, constitutes a war crime.

INTERNATIONAL LAW AND STATE-SPONSORED HACKTIVISM

The problem of state-sponsored hacktivism is more complicated. Here, objections, such as those of Thomas Rid, that acts of hacktivism are merely criminal violations of the law or acts of conventional espionage and covert action, not war, seem more firmly grounded.

If we accept Rid's interpretation, then it would appear that our question about whether there is such a thing as cyber warfare is resolved. We would acknowledge, on the one hand, a very narrow class of effects-based activities in cyberspace that can be classified as acts of war and governed by the international law of armed conflict. We would consider all other cases of cyber conflict, the diverse cyber activities that pundits often loosely term cyber warfare, to be only criminal violations of the laws of an established legal regime or regimes. The problem would then have to do with properly attributing these actions to their state sponsors, and then figuring out how to locate, apprehend, and punish those specific individuals or responsible state organizations.

States, of course, deny that they sanction or engage in hacktivism. The "attribution problem," as this is usually called,[17] is simply more pronounced in state-sponsored hacktivism because no one who looks and acts suspiciously like an agent of the CIA, the KGB, or MI6 is actually caught in the act of committing the crime. And even if we set the attribution problem aside, if states were to be held to account for these cyber activities, it is unlikely that they will hand over their own agents to law enforcement officials representing the nations victimized by them.

By far the greatest challenge in state-sponsored cyber conflict, however, is very much like one posed by the use of drones in irregular warfare: the perpetrators are situated *a great distance* from the physical locations where the damage takes place, and thus their risk of harm or capture is largely obviated. The pilots sit in control pods thousands of miles from the drone bombing runs; intelligence operatives sit safely in Ft. Meade or Shanghai. This enables state agents to carry out a far greater number and range of operations than is possible with conventional manned missions.

While the individual covert activities themselves (for example, stealing plans for the F-35 strike fighter from Lockheed-Martin, or information from Department of Defense data banks) may still constitute prosecutable crimes, the covert actors are no longer (like the conventional spies in *Mission Impossible*) subject to being caught or killed while on a mission "in country." It is the increased access to state and corporate secrets via cyber intrusion, coupled with the reduction of personal risk to the agents of cyberespionage, that has led to the increase in the numbers, kinds, and range of covert operations that are possible. The peculiar cyber-ontological paradox where the espionage agents are located relative to the criminal acts in which they engage raises yet another legal wrinkle. Customary international law has never before attempted to hold states collectively responsible for criminal activities that originate inside their borders but victimize other states or individuals beyond those borders.

The actions of a corrupt financial manager, for example, who operates a large Ponzi scheme that is headquartered physically in one country but targets only individuals in other countries, never constitute grounds for those other countries *to declare war* on the first. Instead, international law enforcement relies on the cooperation among nations, in this case of the host government, to locate and apprehend the financial manager on their behalf or, at least, to put a halt to the Ponzi scheme itself, or finally, failing these efforts, to grant permission to law enforcement agents from the victimized countries to enter the host country and attempt to apprehend and extradite the criminal financial manager themselves.

This ad hoc system of cooperative international law enforcement as it pertains to crime was far from perfect, since many countries, in the name of sovereignty or political leanings, refused to comply with such requests. Some countries lacked formal extradition treaties with their neighbors; criminals actively sought them out for this reason, to claim sanctuary from the law enforcement officials of the victimized countries. (Many former Nazis, for example, escaped prosecution for their crimes against humanity during World War II by taking advantage of this fact and emigrating to countries in South America, where they would be safe from criminal extradition.)

This old system was less of a problem regarding acts of state-sponsored espionage, because to carry out their missions, espionage agents almost always had to be dispatched to the target or victim state. Once physically there, they risked being apprehended and jailed for their crimes, and perhaps sent home later (if they were not executed), as part of a political or diplomatic arrangement. Clearly, we must now recognize that the ever-increasing prospects of spies carrying out effective espionage entirely within their own national boundaries has largely erased this dimension of risk from espionage activities. As a result, clandestine intelligence and covert actions are now both *more feasible to carry out* and *less feasible to guard against*.

But surely, as with the crooked financial manager, the victimized state can appeal to the aggressor to stop the activity and turn over the agents, or risk the threat of armed retaliation, can it not? But again, customary law has never before regarded a state's refusal to put a stop to criminal acts or to turn over such "criminals" to authorities in the victimized countries as a casus belli—that is, as a justifiable cause for war.

Should this customary arrangement now be changed, perhaps by a treaty or legislation, in light of the proliferation of cyber trespassing and theft in the name of state-sponsored espionage? One scholar of international law, David Graham, has argued forcefully that no additional legislative activity is required. Instead, de jure customary international law has already been rewritten in this respect, in the light of the precedent set by two otherwise unrelated recent developments.

The first is the enactment of the International Convention on Cybercrime itself, which for the first time requires signatory and cooperating states either to apprehend criminals within their jurisdictions or to voluntarily tolerate the presence of law enforcement officials from the aggrieved state to assist in apprehending them. Under the Convention, failure to cooperate with international law enforcement may render the *state itself criminally liable* and subject to adverse action for the cyber crimes transpiring within its borders.

Meanwhile, Graham notes, following the attacks of September 11, 2001, the UN Security Council authorized an international military intervention to apprehend Al Qaeda's leaders and force the closure of the group's bases of operation and training in Afghanistan. The Security Council took this step only after the Taliban government had been asked for help. It had refused to cooperate, and the refusal was taken to be a justification for the international use of armed force against the government of a sovereign state. Hence, Graham argues, for the first time ever, the UN approved a military intervention that overrode national sovereignty.[18] Graham considers that these two historical developments together established a legal precedent and argues that, in principle, there is no legal reason why the UN Security Council could not do likewise in the case of cyberspace—that is, authorize a use of force, or even a full-fledged military intervention, against a state in which cybercriminals, terrorists, or even government agents are carrying out criminal acts of cyberespionage that victimize one or more UN member states. This is obviously a significant, but still quite plausible, precedent on which the international community might one day act.

THE *TALLINN MANUAL*

Rather than dismiss acts of state-sponsored hacktivism as nothing more than conventional acts of crime or espionage, we need a more robust account of how such behavior may be interpreted and encompassed within the jurisdiction of existing law. This is why the cyber DDoS attacks launched against Estonia during late April and May of 2007 continue to be of central importance. These attacks constitute the first known incidents of widespread suspected or alleged state-sponsored hacktivism of a serious nature. Richard Clarke, Joel Brenner, and many observers since have insisted that the Estonia attacks were, in fact, among *the earliest acts of cyber warfare*. Are they correct?

The questions of how properly to understand the Estonian attacks and what the appropriate level of response should have been were difficult to sort through in the drama of the moment. Soon after the cyberattacks, NATO sponsored the formation of the Cooperative Cyber Defence Centre of Excellence (CCD COE) in Estonia's capital city, Tallinn. An impressive array of internationally renowned scholars and practitioners in international law and other disciplines dealing with cyber conflict assisted an international group of experts to deliberate on the various dimensions of law and policy, in an attempt to determine the degree to which existing international laws and security agreements could encompass state-sponsored cyber conflict. Michael Schmitt was the logical choice to spearhead this effort, inasmuch as he had already been working on legal interpretations of cyber- and information-warfare issues for nearly a decade.[19] Like Randall Dipert in the area of cyber philosophy, Schmitt is easily the most accomplished and recognized authority in his field, international cybersecurity law, in the world today.[20]

The *Tallinn Manual* was the result of this effort. It comprises ninety-five "rules" and is divided into two parts. Part 1, "International Cyber Security Law," outlines the *jus ad bellum* for engaging in justified cyber conflict. Part 2, "The Law of Cyber Armed Conflict," describes how cyberattacks that are determined to have risen to a level equivalent to the use of conventional force must be conducted (what we might consider the *jus in bello* for cyber warfare).

Part 1 consists of two chapters; the first deals with state jurisdiction and responsibility in cyberspace, the second with the use of force, extrapolating customary legal provisions regarding justified use of force into nineteen rules, annotated with commentary indicating their basis in customary international law. Each chapter is divided into sections, and each rule is listed under the relevant conventional heading in current international law pertaining to *jus ad bellum*, such as state sovereignty and responsibility, prohibitions on the use of force, self-defense, and the responsibilities of international organizations for collective security.

Part 2 contains the remaining seventy-six rules, with similar commentary, stipulating how cyber conflict may and may not be conducted. Part 2 consists of five chapters, each covering one of the appropriate categories of the conventional and customary law of armed conflict. The topics range from the conduct of hostilities (who is and is not a participant or combatant) to the prohibitions against attacks on civilians and civilian objects to the proper means and methods of attack to the precautions that must be taken during attacks. Given a recent claim by Neil Rowe that cyber warfare consists almost entirely of illegal acts of perfidy,[21] there is an especially poignant section interpreting laws prohibiting conventional resorts to perfidy, ruses, and the improper use of various indicators, such as the UN or Red Cross/Red Crescent emblems, flags, uniforms, false surrender, and the like, as they apply to cyber conflict, including a specific rule (Rule 66) pertaining to cyberespionage.

The editor and contributors to the *Tallinn Manual* are at pains to point out that its contents do not constitute binding law but instead indicate how the *existing* law in each of the areas covered applies to the issues arising in cyber conflict.[22] This might prove confusing to some readers, since the titles of the parts and the descriptive titles of the rules seem to imply just the opposite: that each rule or ruling constitutes either new black-letter law or an interpretation meant to be taken as a settled matter of law—or even (more tendentiously) that there *already are extant* two regimes of law devoted to cyber conflict. Like the predecessor efforts Schmitt cites in the introduction,[23] however, the intended purpose of the manual is to guide deliberation and subsequent conduct in the face of questions or doubts about what a particular cyber event (or "object") is, and how one might respond to it while remaining in compliance with international law.

This is an inherently valuable but also tricky enterprise, since many of the conventional laws cited are subject to a variety of interpretations. In the case of perfidy, for example, pertaining to the prohibition of the improper use of enemy indicators (such as flags, military emblems, uniforms, and insignia) in an effort to mislead an enemy, Rule 64 cites article 23(f) of the Hague Regulations (1907) and article 39(2) of Additional Protocol I of the Geneva Conventions of 1949 to claim that this prohibition also applies in the case of cyberattacks. At the same time, the manual notes that, during the original drafting of Protocol I, Canada objected to the proposed extension of the conventional prohibition to apply also to efforts to "shield, favour, protect or impede" military operations. As a result, that original extension in Protocol I is not considered customary international law, even in the conventional case.

The commentary on Rule 64 likewise illustrates disagreements among the International Group of Experts on whether and how the rule distinguishes between the prohibited deceptions considered acts of perfidy and lawful lesser deceptions known as "ruses," such as, in the conventional case, making use of an enemy's signals, passwords, and code to encourage its own aircraft to drop supplies mistakenly or to land in hostile territory.

In the case of cyber conflict, deceptions of various sorts are routinely practiced, and determining which are lawful or prohibited is accordingly "somewhat problematic in the cyber context because of the possibility of remotely acquiring control of enemy systems without having physical possession of them."[24] In a conventional armed conflict, the "perfidy prohibition" would require that a military force that has captured an enemy's tanks must remove all of the enemy insignia before using the tanks again in combat against that enemy. How would this requirement apply to hacking into an enemy's air defense system in order to neutralize it prior to an air attack?[25] Is that a permissible ruse or an illegal act of perfidy? How, even more, does the law guide us if we launch a cyberattack that succeeds in commandeering (or hijacking) an enemy's lethally armed drones, and then use those drones in combat against that same enemy? It does not seem feasible to require that those remotely piloted aircraft first be landed and re-signed with the appropriate emblems or insignia. But does using drones against their former owners that still display the owner's insignia constitute a legal ruse or illegal perfidy?

To its credit, the manual attempts to address all such ambiguities in each of the areas involved in bringing cyber conflict under the umbrella of governance for conventional conflict. Its legal and technical experts appear to have thoroughly explored each problem, looked for useful analogues and legal precedents, and faithfully recorded both their consensus and disagreements on various issues. This is significant, inasmuch as a military legal adviser, known as a JAG (judge adjutant general), who is asked by his commander about the legal permissibility of launching an attack against an adversary using captured drones still bearing the adversary's insignia, obtained through an immediately prior cyberattack, will be greatly assisted by having the manual to consult, alongside his or her standard legal references and understanding of conventional international law and applicable rules of engagement.

However, the JAG and his or her commander will not find definitive answers in the manual. As with the dilemmas of both conventional and irregular warfare, he or she will find only more questions and equivocation or, at best, an authoritative interpretation that may or may not prove to be sound if tested in a court of law. The discussion and commentary in the manual may lead to more-informed command decisions, and having consulted it will surely demonstrate good faith by the command staff in attempting to abide by the rule of law.

The manual, that is to say, does not appear intended to resolve specific conundrums definitively, such as whether the cyberattacks in Estonia were equivalent to a use of conventional force or an armed attack. Rather, it attempts to advise and to better equip leaders, diplomats, lawmakers, and the appropriate bodies of the international community, such as the UN Security Council, to deliberate and adjudicate such matters when they are brought before them (and, by extension, to advise military tacticians and commanders in the field on how to understand and cope with cyber events that might reasonably be thought to be the equivalent of conventional armed conflict).

Many aspects of the manual's findings, however, are puzzling if not problematic. The rule governing cyberespionage, for example, might mistakenly be taken to imply that a relevant body of international law pertaining to conventional espionage has now been extrapolated to the cyber domain. That would be of enormous consequence for our discussion here, but, as the manual itself makes clear, there is no such regime covering conventional espionage. Instead, Rule 66 merely restates, in effect, that while espionage during wartime is not illegal, those engaging in espionage lack the protections afforded regular combatants, such as those accorded to prisoners of war. Likewise, Rule 66 says that espionage operations in the cyber domain, and cyber operations generally, when carried out in the midst of, and as a part of, conventional armed conflict between states, are subject to all the applicable laws of armed conflict. It also distinguishes cyberespionage per se from other kinds of cyber infiltrations, such as cyber reconnaissance or "computer network exploitation," which are neither illegal nor necessarily covered under the law of armed conflict. Otherwise,

> international law does not address espionage *per se*. Thus, a State's responsibility for an act of cyber espionage conducted by an organ of the State in cyberspace is not be engaged [*sic*] as a matter of international law unless particular aspects of the espionage violate specific international legal prohibitions (as in the case of cyber espionage involving diplomatic communications, Rule 84).[26]

The *Tallinn Manual* states repeatedly that acts of *cyber*espionage are not acts of war and do not rise to the equivalent of a use of force or an armed attack—presumably no matter what the severity of surveillance, compromised security, or information stolen. The sole exception seems to be, with specific reference to Stuxnet, the case in which an act of cyberespionage causes *physical damage* to hardware connected to or controlled through cyberspace.[27]

These findings invite us to return to our initial questions. Was Stuxnet an armed attack, a use of force? Was it an act of war? And what of the attack on Estonia that inaugurated the Tallinn process in the first place? Was *this* an act of war, a use of force, an act of espionage, or something else entirely?

INTERNATIONAL LAW AND THE ESTONIAN CYBER ATTACKS

In Rule 13 the *Tallinn Manual* affirms that a "state that is the target of a cyber operation that rises to the level of an armed attack may exercise its inherent right of self-defence." But it goes on to caution that "whether a cyber operation constitutes an armed attack depends on its scale and effects."[28]

The Estonian leadership's deliberations in the midst of the DDoS attacks launched against their cyber infrastructure revealed their confusion about how to respond. Might they have at first overestimated both their scale and their damaging effects? Or did they understand them at the time as no more or less than exactly what they were, and react accordingly? On some accounts, senior government leaders briefly considered asking NATO for help under the terms of article 5 of the so-called Washington Treaty (1949) pertaining to mutual security assistance.[29]

The *Tallinn Manual* stipulates what a victimized nation ought to do in such an instance—namely, bring the matter immediately to the attention of the UN Security Council, pursuant to its authority under chapter 7, article 39 of the UN Charter, to determine the existence of any threat to the peace, breach of the peace, or act of aggression and [to] make recommendations, or decide what measures shall be taken in accordance with Articles 41 and 42, to maintain or restore international peace and security.[30]

In commenting specifically on the Estonian incident, however, the manual observes that

> no international cyber incidents have, as of 2012, been unambiguously and publicly characterized by the international community as reaching the threshold of an armed attack. In particular, the 2007 cyber operations against Estonia, which were widely referred to as "cyber war," were not publicly characterized by either Estonia or the international community as an armed attack. The International Group of Experts agreed with this assessment on the basis that the scale and effects threshold was not reached.

Thus, having specified some criteria and a course of action for nations like Estonia to follow in assessing the severity of their situation, the manual says that the Estonian case itself is not a suitable candidate for availing itself of these remedies. That was apparently somewhat less clear at the time, however, than it seems to have become in hindsight.

In its commentary on Rule 20 (governance of armed conflict applied to the cyber domain), the manual goes on to acknowledge that the term *armed conflict* itself is not well-defined in international law:

> The term "armed conflict" was first used in a law of war codification in the 1949 Geneva Conventions, but has never been authoritatively defined as a matter of treaty law. It has today replaced the term "war" for law of armed conflict purposes.[31]

Nevertheless, regarding the Estonian attacks specifically, the consensus of the International Group of Experts was that the law of armed conflict did not apply because the situation did not rise to the level of an armed conflict.[32]

But the question remains, how is a nation to determine *at the time of an attack* whether it meets or exceeds the threshold of an armed attack as the manual defines it? Rule 22, characterizing (if not precisely defining the threshold for) armed conflict in the cyber case, states: "An international armed conflict exists whenever there are hostilities, *which may include or be limited to cyber operations*, occurring between two or more States" (my emphasis). Commenting again on the Estonian conflict in this context the Manual observes that

> there is no definitive evidence that the hacktivists involved in the cyber operations against Estonia in 2007 operated pursuant to instructions from any State, nor did any State endorse and adopt the conduct. For these reasons (besides the issue of whether the conflict was "armed"), the situation cannot be characterized as an international armed conflict.[33]

Rule 7, pertaining to "cyber operations launched from governmental cyber infrastructure," further cautions:

> The mere fact that a cyber operation has been launched or otherwise originates from governmental cyber infrastructure is not sufficient evidence for attributing the operation to that State, but *is an indication that the State in question is associated with* the operation [my emphases].[34]

Rule 9, meanwhile, pertaining to acceptable countermeasures in the face of an offensive cyberattack, states that "a State injured by an internationally wrongful act may resort to proportionate countermeasures, including cyber countermeasures, against the responsible State." Thus, in the case of Estonia:

> As to those acts which violated Estonian law, Estonia would at a minimum have been entitled to invoke jurisdiction over individuals, wherever located, who conducted the operations. In particular, its jurisdiction would have been justified because the operations had substantial effects on Estonian territory, such as interference with the banking system and governmental functions.[35]

According to the manual, Stuxnet appears on the one hand to be an act of espionage that resulted in physical harm. Ergo, it can be considered an act of war. State-sponsored hacktivism, on the other hand, at least in the case of Estonia, is less clear cut: these attacks were not espionage in any conventional understanding of this term. According to the manual, the closest kind of criminal activity to which they might be compared is vandalism—but vandalism that may have been ordered, aided, or carried out by agents of the state. So the legal interpretation fails to substantiate a case that the attacks were acts of conventional espionage, but they are also clearly something quite different from criminal activity, in that nothing was stolen or damaged, and no one was harmed. On the matter of whether state-sponsored vandalism is an act of war, it seems, the law is moot, if not entirely silent.

Indeed, what the law offers here by way of specific guidance to victims under attack thus seems almost viciously circular: international law cannot finally aid in determining what the cyber equivalent of an armed attack is. It can only offer a learned consensus that the Estonian situation did not constitute one. The *Tallinn Manual* stipulates what states might be entitled to do to protect themselves in response to such an attack, but does not allow that Estonia would have been entitled to do any of these things. These conclusions, furthermore, are based on the appraisal by the International Group of Experts of the scale and effects of the Estonian attacks, on one hand, and the lack of concrete evidence that another state was involved, on the other (notwithstanding that the attacks seemed to originate from the infrastructure of another state, a situation covered in Rule 7). But this is precisely what was unclear in the midst of the attacks.

If we wonder merely whether international law does or does not formally address the eventuality of cyber conflict, we have our answer in the affirmative. If we wonder instead, however, *how to comply with the law* in the middle of such an attack, or what guidance international law affords in a specific instance like Estonia, the answer is vague: *not much at all*. Not altogether surprisingly, even if we can successfully argue that international humanitarian law does apply in such situations, we discover that the content and quality of the manual's guidance is even poorer regarding these new and already quite puzzling cyber incidents than would normally be the case during a conventional armed attack. Or, to put it slightly differently: international law unquestionably "covers" or encompasses such an eventuality but offers little concrete guidance at the moment of decision-making regarding how to characterize the conflict or what kind of response would be legally permissible.

The waters are muddied even further in comment 13 to Rule 22:

> To be "armed," *a conflict need not involve the employment of the armed forces*. Nor is the involvement of the armed forces determinative. For example, should entities such as civilian intelligence agencies engage in cyber operations otherwise meeting the armed criterion, *an armed conflict may be triggered*. Similarly, using the armed forces to conduct tasks that are normally the responsibility of non-military agencies does not alone initiate an armed conflict. For example, the fact that the armed forces undertake cyber espionage directed at another State does not in itself result in an armed conflict, even if it is typically performed by civilian intelligence agencies [my emphases].

Once again, all these defining legal criteria were precisely matters of urgency and extreme uncertainty in the midst of the Estonian attack. How would these legal ruminations help resolve the matter? Suspicion fell upon pro-Russian hacktivist groups operating either independently or with state support. Likewise, the attacks could also conceivably have stemmed directly from sources controlled by the government, or else by either its military or intelligence apparatus.

As a consequence, in a future Estonia-like situation, characterized by the absence of clarity required to apply these legal interpretations to the situation at hand, what ought the legal advice of the JAG or inspector general to be? It appears that at best we might have to do what the Estonians, in some confusion, ended up doing—namely, wait until the attacks subside to assess the actual damage and harm done and determine who was responsible. Only then can the law be made to apply.

That does not seem as useful as are the corresponding legal criteria for identifying and responding to a conventional armed attack. If the manual's underlying claim is that international law not only applies in cyber situations but is as efficacious in outlining legally permissible actions and responses to cyberattacks as it is in conventional instances of armed conflict, then that underlying claim is extremely difficult to sustain. Certainly, there is much still to be decided, determined, or resolved in situ. Simply knowing that international humanitarian law or the law of armed conflict has (or will have) proper jurisdiction in cyber cases is of scant comfort, if we are unable at the time to determine what we can and cannot or should and should not do.

Two final questions clarify our remaining dilemma. First, would the Estonian government ministers have been better off in the spring of 2007 if they'd had the *Tallinn Manual* to turn to for guidance and advice? To that important question, my answer is that it is not clear it would have helped in the slightest degree.

Second, would the manual's application of international law in the cyber domain have guided the design and use of Stuxnet? It seems clear, instead, that *the designers of Stuxnet already thought themselves bound* by both international law and what we will next consider: the moral dictates of the just war tradition. Indeed, they had designed the weapon to conform to the fundamental principles of international humanitarian law and of just war theory explicitly. Furthermore, Stuxnet's designers had apparently *already* decided that their actions were justified as a form of anticipatory self-defense, without the benefit (or criticism) of the manual's new legal advice.

Does the *Tallinn Manual* refute the claims of the skeptics that international law is irrelevant in the cyber domain?

Unquestionably!

Does international law provide *adequate governance* of cyber conflict? Does it provide clear bases for resolving disputes, clarify the boundaries of ambiguity, and offer useful guidelines for carrying out activities (including conflict) in cyberspace? These are much harder questions to resolve. As noted earlier, the manual does not raise or answer these important questions. Indeed, in their rush to assert unilateral jurisdiction over these new forms of activity and conflict, it is as though the authors of the *Tallinn Manual* were providing answers to other questions entirely—questions that very few, in the end, were really asking.

Law governs best when its dictates are clear, equitable, and even-handed, and when its provisions embody goals that are widely shared by the individuals, organizations, and nations who will be governed by that law. Limitations on wanton, senseless killing, prohibition of the unjust exploitation of the weak by the powerful, restrictions on child labor, and the protection of women's rights in patriarchal societies are all candidates for the goals of governance that are readily amenable to the rule of law. Thomas Hobbes argued that individuals are only grudgingly willing to cede their freedoms and to accept restraints on their behavior when they believe they will get a better bargain in the process. Put quite simply, the members of a society will submit themselves to the rule of law only when the majority of them are made so miserable or become so outraged at the abuse of freedom by others that they collectively exclaim, "There oughta be a law!" against this or prohibiting or punishing that, whatever the offensive behavior may be.

Cybersecurity experts of all stripes lament that an awakening of a desire for more law and order in the cyber domain has not yet come. The cyber domain's citizens—whether biological individuals, organizations, or nation-states—seem largely satisfied with the status quo.[36] Until people are sufficiently frightened, victimized, or simply unsettled by their vulnerability to cyberattack (like the Estonians), it is unlikely that this complacency will change. Indeed, as we have already noted, some Internet groups, such as Anonymous, actively resist attempts to regulate the cyber domain as infringements of our individual and collective rights.

So far, the sole exception to this apparent desire to dwell in anarchy in cyberspace has been in the field of criminal law. Cyber techniques have greatly expanded the possibilities of and reduced the risks of engaging in, well, crime! Bank robbing, for example, is a very familiar crime, and clever cyber thieves can steal much greater amounts of money at less risk to themselves than their 1930s counterparts could do with pistols, tommy guns, and automobiles. And the victims are harmed whether the thief is a thug brandishing a revolver in a local bank branch or operating on a laptop or tablet out of the local coffee shop. So it is not surprising that by far the greatest strides in governance in the cyber domain have been in the area of combating, controlling, and preventing crime. As has already been noted, national law enforcement agencies around the world have been scrambling to keep up with the ingenuity of cyber criminals—and with the outrage of victims, who want the crimes stopped and the perpetrators held to account.

What is the corresponding case for international law governing armed conflict? The body of that law pertaining to warfare, as we saw, consists of two parts.[37] The portions known as *jus in bello*, governing how armed conflict is conducted, actually long preceded the portions known as *jus ad bellum*, governing when it is acceptable for nations to resort to force to resolve conflicts. The international public impetus for establishing rules of conduct was a desire to to limit war's violence and to protect its most vulnerable victims (civilian noncombatants, refugees, the wounded, and prisoners of war). While segments of the public were skeptical about the force and effectiveness of such laws, no one wished to argue in favor of allowing indiscriminate violence and causing unnecessary suffering. Banning certain weapons of war, such as poison gas, and restricting or prohibiting the use of weapons that have no real military value was in everyone's interest.

Likewise, following two world wars of previously unimaginable scale and misery, that same international public (what we now sometimes loosely term "the international community") was willing to consider and support measures to limit states' rights to use military force to resolve conflicts. By April 1945, when representatives of fifty-one countries of the soon-to-be United Nations gathered in San Francisco to begin drafting what became the UN Charter, one could safely conclude that the world had had its fill of war and violence, and that those nations were ready to come to the bargaining table (just as Hobbes had predicted) to hammer out a better way to resolve their differences.

I rehearse that well-known history so that we can now ask whether, in the case of cyber conflict, there is anything even remotely resembling this kind of desire or resolve to make such a grand bargain, even among the most farsighted leaders of the international community? If anything in this complex and convoluted domain is abundantly clear at the moment, it is that the answer to this question is an unequivocal "no!" Some developing nations, and even whole continents—for example, Africa—regard the debate over the rule of law in cyberspace as merely a first-world, northern-hemisphere problem shared only by wealthy elites. The citizens in developing countries don't have Internet connectivity, and their governments are not dependent on cyber infrastructure, and in any case, they face far more daunting problems on which they would rather focus.

Other nations do not resist the rule of law per se, but do actively resist the Western extension of it into the cyber domain. China, for example, enjoys parity in its ability to wage cyber conflict in pursuit of its national interests. Indeed, cyber experts in other countries, such as the Russian Federation, recognize that China's mastery in the cyber domain is the equivalent of military capability and that its dominance in the cyber domain is second to none. Why, then, should the Chinese now agree to enable what they perceive to be the West's interest in ensuring its hegemony in cyberspace by establishing the rule of international law there?[38]

Finally, as we have seen, there are cyber experts as well as shadowy denizens of the cyber domain, wearing "black hats" or "white hats," who value their privacy, anonymity, and freedom to act without accountability in the cyber domain. Why should they submit to governance when, apart from criminal activity, *nothing whatsoever is actually happening there*? All cyber activity is virtual, proponents of liberty and anarchy might argue. *No one gets hurt*, they might claim, although conceptual interests like property, commercial advantage, and national security are being compromised. Since that kind of competition and virtual, conceptual harm has transpired, one way or another, since the beginning of human history, there is no urgent need to bring it under the rule of law, especially if that move involves a loss of advantage with no comparable or offsetting gain.

A philosopher might complain that the debate about the rule of law in the cyber domain focuses only on superficial, competing national interests, and that there appears to be no deeper or more profound shared conception of "the Good" that can be achieved by imposing law and order in this lawless new frontier. This is in marked contrast to the situations early in the histories of countries like the United States and Australia, which had actual lawless frontiers, where average citizens who were victimized and terrorized by bandits and bullies were all too eager to see law and order established.

Again, despite the admirable progress being made in criminal law enforcement of cybercrimes, the constituents of the cyber domain have no desire to strengthen the rule of international law. Indeed, the United States, which has been among the leaders in complaining of its victimization by political and economic adversaries in the cyber domain, quietly decided, in July 2015, not to continue making a public issue of the Chinese government's alleged theft of those twenty-two million secure personnel files of federal employees in the OPM described earlier.[39] This is despite the government's earlier decision to indict five PLA intelligence officers by name for stealing commercial and industrial secrets from American companies, including Westinghouse, United Steel, and Alcoa.[40] The decision not to pursue the OPM theft in part reflected the United States' desire to not reveal too much about its cyber forensic abilities, as well as its tacit recognition that "we do this, too!" America's leaders acknowledged, if grudgingly, that China's alleged behavior, unlike burglary and industrial espionage, fell within what one senior cyber strategist and former intelligence official described as the "unwritten norms" governing interstate espionage.[41]

We will return to these so-called emergent, often unwritten norms and their importance for ethics and the law in the remaining chapters. With respect to the *Tallinn Manual*, unfortunately, we are obliged to conclude that it did not "emerge" from any such authentic process or set of practices, but instead appears to have been little more than an act of disciplinary hegemony, carried out either in ignorance of or in total disregard for the moral and philosophical grounding of both the content and the authority of that law. Good governance never arises merely from a preemptive attempt to force the collective views of a few experts (no matter how distinguished) down the throats of an unwilling and rebellious international community. As a gifted young colleague and UN staff expert in international law and governance summarized what is now universally referred to as "the Tallinn debacle":

> I am very frustrated with so-called "legal" approaches [to cyber conflict], as I think there is a very limited value of merely claiming that something would or would not be covered by the law. The interesting and important questions are *whether* the law does its job—namely protecting a community's values, and asking what these values are.[42]

WHY THE *TALLINN MANUAL* FAILED

Many conceptual deficiencies led to what, by early 2013, was already being described as the "spectacular failure" of the *Tallinn Manual* to garner widespread international support or to galvanize the opinion of the international community around its findings. Chief among these problems was the underlying legal positivism of those engaged in interpreting the law. Legal positivism is, in essence, the philosophical view that "the law is the law," that unlike natural law, the law itself is utterly distinct from moral concerns, and that what the law thus stipulates (in the form of written rules or statutes, issued by those entitled to govern) is therefore authoritative without question.[43]

This conception of the law as little more than a somewhat arbitrary social construction may function adequately within domestic jurisdictions—assuming they possess, and can effectively exercise, what the social philosopher Max Weber termed a "monopoly over the use of force" sufficient to ground their authority both to issue and to enforce specific "positive" legal statutes. In that sense, law may be little more than the brute exercise of power.

This conception is utterly inadequate as a governing legal philosophy in the case of international law. Indeed, assuming legal positivism's validity (as is routinely done in English-language legal education today) betrays a fundamental ignorance about what international law is and whence it derives whatever minimal degree of normative force or authority it enjoys. In particular, this conception is useless in addressing the question at hand—namely, to what extent should international law now assume the mantle of authority in a new domain where its black-letter provisions were never designed specifically to apply and in which the citizens, practitioners, or "inhabitants" have no apparent desire to see the reach of the law extended?

One cannot simply *stipulate* answers to these hotly contested questions. Such normative claims must be grounded in sound jurisprudence and conceptually coherent legal philosophy. This the *Tallinn Manual* utterly failed to do, thereby leaving the authority of international law itself in a kind of precarious limbo.

This simply will not suffice in the cyber domain. Fixing what is profoundly mistaken here is no simple matter. It will require nothing less than addressing the underlying intellectual poverty into which legal education, both domestic and international, has hopelessly fallen, willingly sacrificing any genuine efforts at jurisprudence in favor of the technical mastery of superficial legal casuistry and what can only be described as extraordinary hermeneutical gymnastics.

Lest I appear to be privileging my own discipline, moral philosophy, let me say that the situation is hardly any better there. Moral philosophy and its practitioners address perceived lacunae in international law (and engage in largely fruitless disputes with international lawyers) largely by appealing to the just war tradition or just war theory. It is a matter of historical fact that each and every positive statute of treaty law in international humanitarian law has its origins or conceptual grounding in the findings of that particular tradition of moral discourse. But adherents of that discourse have scarcely more understanding of its alternative claim to authority than international lawyers possess respecting the law. Both are therefore equally prone, in Michael Schmitt's apt phrase, to "badly mangl[e] the law"—as well as, I would add, to distort its conceptual foundations in moral philosophy.

It is not as if this larger problem cannot be adequately addressed. And the pressure exerted by new developments in the cyber domain, regarding cyber conflict in particular, demand that this underlying philosophical problem no longer be simply ignored, dismissed, or swept under the rug as a conceptual diversion or inconvenience. Law may effect a separation, if not a divorce, from its philosophical ground and historical origins in domestic jurisprudence, where we might view these as, at best, loosely coupled. But this separation, let alone divorce, will never survive in the international arena, where all three are inextricably intertwined.

Lawyers and moral philosophers, working more closely together, will simply have to think harder about what they propose to promulgate and why their proposals ought to meet with widespread approval and acceptance. This is especially true whether we are talking about vigilante groups like Anonymous or competing, adversarial nation-states, such as China and the Russian Federation, let alone when we are trying to decide whether state-sponsored hacktivism is or is not a new form of unarmed conflict or "soft war" that should be brought under the jurisdiction of international humanitarian law. Such a rapprochement and subsequent good-faith collaborative effort is what any reasonable attempt at good governance will ultimately require.

NOTES

1. Thomas C. Rid, *Cyber War Will Not Take Place* (Oxford: Oxford University Press, 2013).
2. Council of Europe, "International Convention on Cybercrime," Budapest, November 23, 2001, http://conventions.coe.int/Treaty/EN/Treaties/html/185.htm (accessed July 21, 2015).
3. See "Major Computing Hacking Forum Dismantled," Justice News (Washington, DC: U.S. Department of Justice, July 15, 2015), http://www.justice.gov/opa/pr/major-computer-hacking-forum-dismantled.
4. For one of the first treatments of this topic from the standpoint of law, see David R. Koepsell, *The Ontology of Cyber Space* (Peru, IL: Open Court Publishing, 2003). This work explored the unique ontology of cyber objects, primarily from the standpoint of intellectual property law. Dipert was the first to call attention to both objects and events from the perspective of law and the morality of war and conflict.

5. Ryan Jenkins observes that this kind of argument is often adduced against software weapons: because they are not physical objects, existing international conventions regarding the use or threat of force do not apply (e.g., UN Charter 2 (4)), since these provisions prohibit the use of *physical* force. Jenkins finds that reasoning to be implausible. See Ryan Jenkins, "Is Stuxnet Physical? Does It Matter?," *Journal of Military Ethics* 12, no. 1 (2013): 68–79.

6. Ohlin, Govern, and Finkelstein, *Cyberwar* (2015), v–vi.

7. Singer and Friedman, *Cybersecurity and Cyberwar*, 118–120. Singer subsequently suggested that he was merely paraphrasing my characterization of Stuxnet as an "ethical weapon," made in a presentation at a UNESCO conference in July 2011, shortly after the worm's discovery. See George R. Lucas, Jr., "Permissible Preventive Cyber Warfare," in *The Ethics of Information Warfare*, ed. Luciano Floridi and Mariarosaria Taddeo (Amsterdam: Springer, 2014): 81–82. I repeated that characterization later that year in an exchange with Singer at a meeting of the Society for Philosophy and Technology at North Texas State University (at which I had arranged for him to be the keynote speaker). In my 2012 "Stutt Lecture on Ethics" at the US Naval Academy, in addition, I noted that the features exhibited by Stuxnet mysteriously seemed to track very closely the principles for the ethical conflict of cyber warfare that John Arquilla had outlined a decade earlier, in 1999, in "Ethics and Information Warfare." See "Just War and Cyber Conflict," Annual Stutt Lecture on Ethics, US Naval Academy, April 9, 2012, http://www.youtube.com/watch?v=hCj2ra6yzl0. Text at http://www.usna.edu/Ethics/_files/documents/Just%20War%20and%20Cyber%20War%20GR%20Lucas.pdf.

8. Significantly, and in support of my position against Langner on this point, the *Tallinn Manual* does not concern itself with his assessment, and finds specifically that Stuxnet did not violate its Rule 43 prohibiting use of cyber weapons that might prove to be indiscriminate. See *The Tallinn Manual on International Law Applicable to Cyber Warfare: Prepared by the International Groups of Experts at the Invitation of the NATO Cooperative Cyber Defense Center of Excellence*, ed. Michael N. Schmitt (Cambridge: Cambridge University Press, 2013), comment 5, p. 146 (hereafter cited as *Tallinn Manual*. All citations are to this edition).

9. For a brief period, a virus known as "Duqu," which operates in a manner similar to Stuxnet but is spread through infected thumb drives rather than through self-replication and peer-to-peer tunneling through networked hardware, was thought to have been a sinister knockoff. But Symantec's cyber forensic experts eventually determined that Duqu had been designed and released by the same organization that had manufactured Stuxnet, and was most likely also part of the Olympic Games offensive.

   In general, the claim that something can't be done because it hasn't been observed amounts logically to what philosophers term a "counterfactual," and so is impossible to verify absolutely. That difficulty is all the more apparent when one reads the post mortems on these events. David Kushner, writing in the *IEEE Spectrum* offers a well-grounded account of Stuxnet, the subsequent discovery of the surveillance software Flame, and other components of Olympic Games. He, too, engages in the hypothetical discussion of reverse engineering and malevolent reuse of these weapons, but succeeds only in documenting one case in which a few components of the Flame surveillance program appear to have been successfully incorporated into a new weapon targeting civilian industrial systems. See David Kushner, "The Real Story of Stuxnet," *IEEE Spectrum*, February 26, 2013, http://spectrum.ieee.org/telecom/security/the-real-story-of-stuxnet (accessed 5/21/2016).

Another oddity in this discussion: the wild variance in allegedly factual accounts, such as who discovered the malware first, who was first to identify its properties, to successfully reverse engineer it, and so forth. Owing to rivalries between some of the principals (e.g., Langner, Kaspersky Labs, Symantec) and the outsized egos of some of these otherwise very intelligent individuals, the "factual accounts" one reads differ markedly.

10. Neil C. Rowe, "The Ethics of Cyberweapons in Warfare," *Ethical Impact of Technological Advancements and Applications in Society*, ed. Rocci Luppicini (Hershey, PA: IGI Global, 2012), 195–208. Interestingly, Rowe subsequently reversed his judgment on nonreplicability and limited prospects for multiple use, stating that "the ideas behind Stuxnet are now being used by the criminal cyber-attacker community at a net negative cost to world society." See Neil C. Rowe, "Perfidy in Cyberwarfare," *The Routledge Handbook of War and Ethics*, ed. Fritz Allhoff, Nicholas G. Evans, and Adam Henschke (London: Routledge, 2013), 394. But as evidence, he cites only an undocumented and misleading claim by David Kaplan, similar to that of David Kushner, to the effect that some elements of the Stuxnet strategy may have influenced the design of subsequent "rootkit" attacks launched for explicitly criminal purposes. See David Kaplan, "New Malware Appears Carrying Stuxnet Code," *SC Magazine*, October 18, 2011, http://www.scmagazine.com/new-malware-appears-carrying-stuxnet-code/article/214707. This "new" malware turned out to be Duqu. This serves to illustrate the whirl of misinformation that is quickly generated, even among experts, about cyber conflict.

11. Langner recently issued a lengthier and more detailed post mortem that offers a considerably more nuanced account of the risks inherent in the fallout from Stuxnet, Duqu, and Flame, as well as of the nature (and future prospects for exploitation of) the remaining long-term vulnerabilities in widely used industrial control software that might still be targeted. But again, those vulnerabilities do not involve "reusing Stuxnet," so much as teaching by example how less-skilled or less well-resourced hacktivists (whether or not they are agents of a nation-state) might go after more modest targets in the future. See Ralph Langer, "To Kill a Centrifuge," *State of Security* blog, TripWire.com, http://www.tripwire.com/state-of-security/latest-security-news/stuxnet-expert-ralph-langner-offers-latest-analysis-cyber/.

12. Major General Charles Dunlap, quoted in Singer and Friedman, *Cybersecurity and Cyberwar*, 124.

13. Cf. "International Cyber Security Law," comment (2), *Tallinn Manual*, 13.

14. This concurs with the findings of the International Group of Experts regarding this matter, as reported in the *Tallinn Manual*, although this conclusion requires a juxtaposition of some of the scattered comments on this event, for example, Rule 10 (*Tallinn Manual*, 42): "A cyber operation that constitutes a threat or use of force against the territorial integrity or political independence of any State, or that is in any other manner inconsistent with the purposes of the United Nations, is unlawful," coupled with comment 13 on Rule 13 (pertaining to the inherent right of self-defense): "A closer case is the 2010 Stuxnet operations. In light of the damage they caused to Iranian centrifuges, some members of the International Group of Experts were of the view that the operations had reached the armed attack threshold (unless justifiable on the basis of anticipatory self-defence)" (*Tallinn Manual*, 58). Thus, the manual may be taken as ruling that while likely impermissible, Stuxnet would constitute an armed attack subject to

applicable law, but defensible in principle as an act of anticipatory self-defense rather than one of unwarranted aggression.

15. See Lucas, "Permissible Preventive Cyberwar," 73–83. See also Rule 22 (*Tallinn Manual*, 79) pertaining to the initiation of a state of armed conflict subject to the law of armed conflict, and comments 14 and 15 on the degree to which Stuxnet had or had not exceeded this threshold (*Tallinn Manual*, 83–84).

16. Neil C. Rowe, "War Crimes from Cyber Weapons," *Journal of Information Warfare* 6, no. 3 (2007): 15–25.

17. Cf. Singer and Friedman, *Cybersecurity and Cyberwar*, 72–76. Actually, the so-called attribution problem in cyber conflict refers more broadly to the initial difficulty in accurately or unmistakably linking specific actions in cyberspace to their perpetrators (whether these be states, organizations, or individuals). This obviously constitutes, at first glance, an enormous obstacle to legal and moral accountability for malevolent actions. Huge strides in cyber forensics, however, enable skilled information experts, such as the Langner Group, Symantec, or Kaspersky Laboratories (not to mention government organizations engaged in cybersecurity) to offer ever more reliable accounts of who has done what, with what, and to whom in the cyber domain, and thus render deniability ever less plausible.

18. David E. Graham, "Cyber Threats and the Law of War," *Journal of National Security Law* 4, no. 1 (2010): 87–102.

19. See, for example, two articles by Michael N. Schmitt: "Computer Network Attack and the Use of Force in International Law: Thoughts on a Normative Framework," *Columbia Journal of Transnational Law* 37 (1999): 885–937; and "Wired Warfare: Computer Network Attack and *Jus in Bello*," *International Review of the Red Cross* 84, no. 846 (2002): 365–399. The latter can also be found in Michael N. Schmitt and Brian T. O'Donnell, eds., *Computer Network Attack and International Law*, International Law Studies 76 (Newport, RI: U.S. Naval War College, 2002), which grew out of an international law symposium on this topic convened by Professor Schmitt very early in the history of this discussion. Schmitt brought his impressive experience and credentials to these efforts as well, having served for over twenty years as a lawyer and intelligence officer in the US Air Force, and subsequently as the dean of the George C. Marshall European Center for Security Studies, in Garmisch, Germany.

20. Others would include Erik Jens, who assisted Schmitt in the Tallinn process, and affiliate scholars like Duncan Hollister and Scott Shakleford, together with General Charles Dunlap.

21. Neil C. Rowe, "Perfidy in Cyberwarfare," 395. Rowe argues that perfidy in cyberspace occurs "whenever malicious software or hardware pretends to be ordinary software or hardware, where its goal is to harm software or hardware *as part of a military operation*" (my emphasis). As the highlighted phrase indicates, however, the discussion reveals a fundamental and serious "category mistake" on Rowe's part, in which he conflates what he correctly identifies as forms of individual behavior that are "illegal in nearly every country of the world" (i.e., criminal behavior), with *military behavior* during a state of armed conflict that is both widely practiced and universally tolerated in international law. As explained earlier, all individual acts of espionage are illegal under domestic criminal regimes, but certainly not because the actions involve perfidy! Rather, they involve trespass, theft, and destruction of property, carried out in part through deception. That the author has, to borrow Schmitt's phrase, "seriously mangled" domestic

criminal law and international law pertaining to armed conflict seems evident in his claim that Stuxnet constitutes an example of perfidy, when its deceptive elements constitute at most a permissible ruse of the sort otherwise widely practiced and tolerated during both conventional and irregular warfare. In addition, the remaining acts of cyberespionage that Rowe considers are likely not covered under international law to begin with, and so their use of deception (whether ruse or perfidy) is irrelevant.

22. E.g., *Tallinn Manual*, 11.
23. P. 1 of the introduction to the *Tallinn Manual* cites earlier efforts to produce legal guidelines governing cyberwarfare, such as those that resulted in the International Institute of Humanitarian Law's *San Remo Manual on International Law Applicable to Armed Conflicts at Sea* and the Harvard Program on Humanitarian Policy and Conflict Research's *Manual on International Law Applicable to Air and Missile Warfare*, as examples of nonbinding legal interpretation in specific contexts needing greater clarification.
24. *Tallinn Manual*, Rule 66, comment 6, p. 192.
25. This was the essential feature of a massive cyberattack against Syria in 2007 discussed in chapter 5.
26. *Talinn Manual*, Rule 6, "State Responsibility," comment 4, p. 30.
27. *Tallinn Manual*, Rule 66, "Cyber Espionage," comment 9, states: "Certain acts of cyber espionage involve more than mere information-gathering activities and can cause damage to computer systems. Therefore, acts whose primary purpose is cyberespionage may sometimes amount to a cyberattack, in which case the Rules as to cyberattack apply" (195).
28. *Tallinn Manual*, 54
29. Singer and Friedman, *Cybersecurity and Cyberwar*, for example, follow the earlier standard accounts I cited in the introduction, describing the 2007 cyberattacks on Estonia as "allegedly assisted by the Russian government" (98), and subsequently offer a description of a private, pro-Putin "patriotic group" of more than twelve thousand members, whose leader they report actually admitted to participating in these attacks (110–112). Citing BBC news reports at the time, they also describe how the Estonian foreign minister "called for help, believing that the massive cyberattack threatened its security, and hence the [NATO] alliance's as a whole. [Estonia] argued that under the Washington Treaty NATO was obliged to defend against this start of a new 'cyberwar'" (100).

    However, a comprehensive report from the CCD COE on the full range of cyber "incidents" (including Estonia), cites a subsequent interview with Estonian defense minister Jaak Aaviksoo, claiming that notification of NATO or invoking article 5 was never considered. The actual quotation from Minister Aaviksoo, however, does not include such an assertion, nor can it plausibly be construed in this way, especially when the same minister (as reported in the *Tallinn Manual*) declared at the time that the 2007 DDoS attacks against his nation "can effectively be compared to when your ports are shut to the sea," drawing (the manual's authors infer) an implied parallel between the closure of ports [a blockade] and DDoS attacks that blocked Estonia's important websites. See *Tallinn Manual*, comment 4, p. 196, n. 265. The manual cites as its source Johnny Ryan, "'iWar': A New Threat, Its Convenience, and Our Increasing Vulnerability," *NATO Review* (Winter 2007), www.nato.int/docu/review/2007/issue4/english/analysis2.html (accessed July 31, 2015).

    This and other claims in the CCD COE report of 2010 (such as that the attacks originated solely from Estonian dissenters inside Estonia) cannot be

substantiated, and seem sharply at odds with the numerous other authoritative accounts of this incident cited earlier, including, once again, in the *Tallinn
Manual*, p. 20, which describes the attacks, contrary to this report, as having
issued at least partially from abroad. Indeed, the narrative in this report of the
Estonian incident appears to be an act of historical revisionism rather than objective historical accuracy, designed to portray the leaders of that government
as more calmly in control of the situation than press interviews portrayed them
at the time. See Eneken Tiki, Kadri Kaska, and Liis Vihul, *International Cyber
Incidents: Legal Considerations* (Tallinn, ES: Cooperative Cyber Defence Centre of
Excellence, 2010): 25–26.

30. *Tallinn Manual*, Rule 18, comment 1, p. 69.
31. Cf. *Tallinn Manual*, comment 11 on Rule 82, p. 82, which further states: "The law
of armed conflict [likewise] does not [itself] directly address the meaning of the
term 'armed conflict,' but the notion clearly requires the existence of hostilities."
32. *Tallinn Manual*, comment 3 on Rule 20, pp. 75–76.
33. *Tallinn Manual*, comment 8 on Rule 22, p. 80.
34. *Tallinn Manual*, comment 4, pp. 34–35, suggests, without further elaboration,
that this provision proved relevant "to Estonia (2007) and Georgia (2008)."
35. *Tallinn Manual*, Rule 2, "Jurisdiction," comment 9, p. 34.
36. Singer and Friedman (2014) dispute that the cyber domain is "ungoverned,"
rather stating (with reference to Anonymous and a variety of "patriotic" individual counterterrorist hackers) that it is "self-governed in strange and fascinating
ways" (*Cybersecurity and Cyberwar*, 103–106).
37. For a fuller account, see my historical and conceptual survey of the rise of international law, and its relationship to the ethical codes of the military profession,
in *Military Ethics: What Everyone Needs to Know* (New York: Oxford University
Press, 2015), chap. 2.
38. And here one might ask why representatives of these nations and organizations,
especially some of their most thoughtful and accomplished cyber experts, were
not included in the Tallinn process? This inexplicable exclusion of key stakeholders from the deliberation about future governance seems to constitute an additional, purely political flaw in the process that would likely have guaranteed its
failure in any case.
39. See Ellen Nakashima, "U.S. Avoids Blaming China for Data Theft," *Washington
Post*, July 21, 2015, http://tablet.washingtonpost.com/rweb/world/us-avoids-
blaming-china-in-data-theft-seen-as-fair-game-in-espionage/2015/07/21/
03779096-2eee-11e5-8353-1215475949f4_story.html (accessed August 1,
2015). Evidently, the policy is now to distinguish acts of espionage, such as
the OPM hack, from acts of industrial or corporate theft (also espionage?),
based on the notion of the importance of intellectual property versus the
toleration, otherwise, of customary state behavior in this respect. See Ellen
Nakashima, "U.S. Is Crafting Sanctions on China," *Washington Post*, August 31,
2015, A1, A7.
40. See the indictment filed and posted by the Department of Justice: attachment
to "U.S. Charges Five Chinese Military Hackers for Cyber Espionage against U.S.
Corporations and a Labor Organization for Commercial Advantage" (press release, Office of Public Affairs, US Department of Justice, Washington DC, May
19, 2014), http://www.justice.gov/opa/pr/us-charges-five-chinese-military-
hackers-cyber-espionage-against-us-corporations-and-labor.
41. Ms. Nakashima reports: "Former U.S. intelligence officials said the OPM hack is
in some ways regarded as fair game because of unwritten spying norms that took

shape during the Cold War. "This is espionage," said Michael Hayden, a retired Air Force general and former head of the CIA and the National Security Agency, of the OPM hacks. "I don't blame the Chinese for this at all. If I [as head of the NSA] could have done it, I would have done it in a heartbeat. And I would have not been required to call downtown, either to seek White House permission." It is in part the nature of this (implied) form of *self-governance* (as opposed to externally imposed legal governance) to which we will turn in the remaining chapters. See Nakashima, "U.S. Avoids Blaming China."

42. Ms. Elena Finckh, a staff member specializing in international law at the United Nations Institute for Disarmament Research (UNIDIR) in Geneva, offered this and other thoughtful characterizations in personal correspondence to the author. It was another UNIDIR senior staff official who characterized the *Tallinn Manual* as a "spectacular failure," at a meeting of the International Committee of the Red Cross in its Geneva headquarters' "Humanitarium" in the spring of 2013, shortly after the initial release of the manual, and following a contentious public meeting in Rome in November 2012, convened by the CCD COE to disseminate and discuss the results and future work of the so-called Tallinn process. This assessment of failure was universally shared without dissent by the UN, ICRC, and UNIDIR experts in international law in attendance, with the same dismay, surprise, and regret that I have expressed here. All of us concurred that this was an easily avoidable result of a fatally flawed process and personnel dynamic.

43. Those interested in delving further into "legal positivism" may begin by consulting the Lexis-Nexis legal dictionary, http://legal-dictionary.thefreedictionary. com/Legal+Positivism.

 Legal positivism actually had its origins in what was originally a profound philosophical examination of the foundations of jurisprudence, undertaken early in the nineteenth century by Jeremy Bentham and John Stuart Mill as part of a quest by the former to reform some of the worst excesses found in the routine practice of English common law. While Bentham, in particular, was dismissed by the legal establishment at the time for being "merely a philosopher," and not a "real" lawyer or legal scholar, his and Mill's profound philosophical influence on jurisprudence transformed the underlying foundations of legal reasoning in subsequent decades, and it is their thinking that forms the unconscious background presuppositions of most practitioners and teachers of law in the Anglo-American tradition today. Ironically, the philosophical ingenuity of both men is lost in this history, leaving only the relic, what is now an equally inadequate and impoverished conception, of the ground of legal authority and practice. Astute readers will discern that I am attempting to reintroduce some of the conceptions that Bentham and Mill originally attacked, such as my new conception of "emergent norms" as a kind of natural law. This is a wholly secular conception of such law and the historical emergence of norms through reflection on practice, and owes more to the work of Harvard scholar Lon Fuller and philosopher Alasdair MacIntyre (and Aristotle), than to the religious and theological conceptions of classical natural law, which both Bentham and Mill rejected. And to that is added a further dimension of "moral law" as, like international law itself, a universal form of a rhetoric of persuasion rather than coercion, as reflected in the work of the philosopher Jürgen Habermas, in particular. I explore these notions in detail in subsequent chapters.

CHAPTER 4
Genuine Ethics versus "Folk Morality" in Cyberspace

It is the threat of harm to the interests and welfare of virtually all of the diverse entities, agents, and events in the cyber domain that forces the question of ethics upon us, particularly with respect to cyber conflict. One might plausibly claim, in fact, that inhabitants or agents operating in this new domain now face a corresponding set of interests, conflicts, and legitimate fears of injury to those that motivated inhabitants of lawless geographical frontiers, on land and sea, finally to embrace a robust form of law and order. As noted in chapter 3, on those historical frontiers, the evolution away from anarchy began as an unwritten consensus regarding what was morally unacceptable conduct and gradually grew to include laws governing conflict, both between rival interests in conventional settings (for example, with respect to trade and commerce among nations on the high seas beginning in the seventeenth century), all the way to the conduct of armed hostilities among rival national armies and navies by the early twentieth century. Should we anticipate a similar kind of evolution with respect to conflict and competition in the cyber domain as well?

I would not hold my breath. Why expect ethics (on whatever definition) to succeed where the law has thus far failed? Is it not the case that the law at least has the benefit of clarity and precision, while ethics suffers from ambiguity and endlessly unresolved disputation in comparison?

Cyber conflict, as we have seen, confronts nations and industries with a new form of unrestricted, relentless, and indiscriminate conflict, with attacks on military, industrial, and civilian infrastructure and objects that violate conventional norms of war. One might then wonder whether it even makes sense to turn toward ethics or morality in such a context! Why, for example, should we worry about whether to impose moral or legal limits on our abilities to develop and use cyber weapons and engage in cyber conflict when adversary nations, criminals, and terrorists are relentlessly engaged in attacking us, harming us, and robbing us blind without regard for either? The vulnerabilities, the threats posed, and the genuine harm already done (as we have observed) are all very real. Would not imposing one-sided ethical constraints on ourselves merely disadvantage us and advantage our adversaries who (on our account of them, at least) give such matters absolutely no credence whatsoever?

THE ADVANTAGES OF TAKING THE "MORAL POINT OF VIEW"

There are two possible strategies for addressing this skepticism about the constructive role of moral considerations in cyber conflict.[1] The first involves exploring the relative advantages of morality as a form of self-governance in contrast to the constraints externally and somewhat arbitrarily imposed by the law. The second follows from the first and requires us to inquire more deeply into just what "ethics" represents as a kind of social institution, and how it can plausibly claim to provide *universal* guidance for human conduct and the exercise of human (moral) agency. Both are important considerations in justifying claims for the efficacy of morality in cyber conflict.

The first of these two strategies is largely subjective and psychological, regarding the attitude of the governed toward self-imposed constraints that arise from considerations of common notions of their individual interests or from a widely shared conception of the Good (that is, of the goal or purpose which their actions are aimed to achieve). Such self-imposed principles governing actions seem practically to stand a greater chance of winning widespread respect, approval, and compliance, especially when contrasted with what seem to be arbitrary and externally imposed constraints arising in the law.

In terms of the canons of good governance discussed in chapter 3, for example, we noted that the rule of law is most effective when it arises from the felt need of the governed to impose order on a state of anarchy for their collective benefit. And we recognized that, to date, no such desire can be discerned within the cyber domain. Indeed, it is just the opposite: the denizens of the cyber realm often resist any possible curtailment of their privacy, anonymity, and freedom from accountability. All the more so when the push to establish legal jurisdiction in cyberspace comes from a narrow group of stakeholders whose main interest seems to be asserting their authority and extending their hegemony into the uncharted territory of cyberspace. As noted earlier, it was that widespread public perception of the Tallinn process that led to the failure of the *Tallinn Manual* to gain widespread support.

The moral point of view is *structural* rather than psychological. We have discerned that international law generally, and the law of armed conflict in particular, is *state centric*. While there is a robust body of international humanitarian law pertaining to biological individuals, the bulk of international law reflects the prerogatives of states and is designed primarily to ensure and protect their sovereignty, territorial integrity, and monopoly on the use of force. While this arrangement had its historical justification in attempts to limit competition, conflict, and war in the early modern era, it poses a decided disadvantage in the cyber domain, where geographical boundaries, territory, and national sovereignty are largely meaningless concepts.

To frame this dilemma formally: international law is *paradigm dependent*—contingent, that is, on the paradigm of the nation-state. That paradigm is what is in jeopardy in the cyber domain.[2] Moral principles, by contrast, are largely *paradigm independent* and can function to discern order and resolve conflict in a variety of different cultural and political arrangements. Indeed, the specific forms of moral discourse pertaining to war, conflict, and the use of force arose well before the paradigm of the nation-state came into existence, during a period when sovereignty was distributed (as it seems to be now in the cyber domain) over a variety of organizations and institutions, none of which enjoyed any sort of monopoly on the use of force.[3]

Thus, while moral principles and the demands of ethics have the disadvantage of seeming ambiguous and open to a variety of interpretations, they function to discern order and protect basic rights across a far broader range of political and cultural situations than does the law, international law in particular. Indeed, we are frequently driven back to moral considerations as the foundational principles from which specific legal arrangements arise, whenever those foundations themselves shift or alter dramatically. This is an especially crucial feature of the historical dependence of the international law of armed conflict—as well as of human rights law— to bear in mind, as we find ourselves immersed in the cyber domain, which lacks many of the essential defining ontological structures upon which customary international law has come over the centuries to depend.

THE CHALLENGE OF FOLK MORALITY FOR AUTHENTIC ETHICS

The second strategy for dealing with the skepticism about the role of morality in cyber conflict involves delving into just what ethics is, and how it purports to govern or hold sway with us. To do this, we have to dispense with some of the common public misperceptions of which a widespread "folklore" regarding ethics is composed. As discussed in chapter 2, I use the term "folk morality" in this context to reference widely held popular beliefs about ethics that are often either false or superficial, inconsistent, and seriously misleading. An example of that popular folklore is the notion that choosing to honor and uphold moral principles in one's own behavior puts one at a competitive disadvantage.

This familiar piece of proverbial wisdom—basically, "nice guys finish last"—is an example of an ancient kind of folk morality, often called *moral realism*, which, while easy to refute, is extremely difficult to dispel. It is advocated at present by political scientists and the occasional, presumably tough-minded, business leader as constituting the most "realistic" lesson concerning what life itself is like in the "real world" of rough-and-tumble competition. But we encounter identical formulations, and decisive refutations, of this incoherent and empirically falsifiable belief as early as 2500 years ago.

The ancient Greek philosopher Thucydides has his Athenian delegation utter a verison of the "nice guys finish last" doctrine in his famous "Melian Dialogue," where (in contrast to its treatment in political science) the view of the Athenians is portrayed as a summary of the diminished moral values of a once-great civilization skidding headlong down a slippery slope of cultural decline that will lead finally to its decisive military defeat during the Peloponnesian Wars. Plato similarly has one of his characters, the eminent sophist Thrasymachus, voice this doctrine in the opening dinner scene of *The Republic*, whereupon Socrates proceeds to make short work of him and of this patently absurd and self-contradictory view, to the amusement of the other dinner guests (who describe their teacher as having thus "cut off the head of a snake"). And yet, somehow, the belief that moral considerations have no place in ruthless competitions such as war or commerce has persevered.

"Realism" is thus sharply at odds with the considerations of the so-called state of nature: in classical social contract theory, an initially (hypothetical) condition of society prior to the establishment of law and government that provides a strikingly accurate description of the status quo in the cyber domain. According to the state of nature, individuals who find themselves dwelling in the legal or moral anarchy that the moral realists describe always eventually see it to their advantage, not their disadvantage, to surrender a portion of their liberty, privacy, and individual freedom of action to purchase the security and stability afforded by morality. "Nice guys," we might crudely summarize, avoid finishing last by banding together to identify, punish, and expel the "bad guys" from their community. This, at least, is the political function of morality as a social arrangement in any culture. Even the figure of Glaucon in Plato's *Republic*, who also purported to feign skepticism regarding the institution of morality in any deep or profound sense, was obliged to grant this much, that even a resulting "outward semblance" of law and ethics is preferable to ruthless, unregulated, cutthroat competition.

That process of defining and weeding out "the bad" cannot take place, however, unless there is a nearly universal consensus among all stakeholders about what moral principles are operable in their situation. Here we encounter the second misperception about what morality is—namely, that it is a host of competing, mutually exclusive, and culturally relative claims about what constitutes right and wrong. Moral values and ethical standards are often said to be grounded in individual beliefs or in variant cultural practices. Inasmuch as these beliefs and practices differ greatly among individuals and across cultures and historical epochs, "morality" is thus a largely empty notion, involving endless unresolvable disputes. Unlike the law, which stipulates what conduct is permissible and impermissible, morality merely embroils us in ambiguity and uncertainty.

This particular variation of folk morality arises in large part from the public's views on vexing social dilemmas—abortion, euthanasia, and capital punishment, for example—which are thought to involve irreconcilable moral positions. This misperception is reinforced in social sciences such as anthropology, which often identifies "morality" with the mores and behaviors of distinct societies, and then goes on to observe how these vary across societies as they pertain to significant social institutions, such as marriage, property, punishment of wrongdoing, treatment of women and minorities, and the like.

It often seems that moral philosophers and ethicists engage in a running skirmish against these folk views and delight in pointing out how confused, foolish, and inconsistent they are regarding the supposed relativism of morality. Discussions (and debunkings) of so-called moral relativism, pertaining to both individual beliefs and social practices—as well as to empirical accounts of these undeniable differences and to normative approaches, where the problems and confusions arise—abound in the philosophical literature about ethics. It would take us too far afield to consider all of them in detail here. Suffice it instead to attempt to move beyond this impasse by making a few straightforward observations.

First, disagreements over sensitive cultural dilemmas like abortion and capital punishment stem less from differences over ethical principles (such as respect for persons, the importance of privacy, or the right to life), than from ontology—that is, questions about the nature and status of the entities (e.g., criminals, the unborn) that are put forward for consideration under the principles. In that sense, the question of whether the biological human fetus is an unborn child with the same rights of respect and consideration that extend to human beings generally is of a piece with the kinds of disagreements that moral philosophers like Randall Dipert pointed to in the cyber domain regarding the nature and status of the entities and events encountered there.

Our relative unfamiliarity with the objects, agents, and events in the cyber domain gives rise to a similar kind of uncertainty about how they should be considered from the perspectives of morality and law. We might expect to see the same differences of opinion on ethical issues in the cyber domain that we see in the cultural and social realms of everyday life—but that is less a defect of moral argument than a feature of their puzzling ontological constitution. Neither constitutes grounds for giving up on ethics! Quite the contrary, it is a call for us to tackle these important conundrums, and try to sort them out in a manner that seems fair and equitable to all parties!

As to the irreconcilability of individual and cultural differences in moral values and ethical principles, this, too, is frequently overstated. Virtually every known culture, past and present, evinces some version of what is usually termed the "principle of reciprocity" (sometimes called the Golden Rule or the Silver Rule). That is, one finds widespread consensus that a fundamental principle regarding the treatment of others can be expressed in the aphorism, "Do not do to other persons what you would not wish done to yourself." Formulations of this dictum vary, but they all amount to a recognition of equivalence of moral status among human beings, demanding equity and probity in moral consideration and treatment. Exceptions to or disagreements with this principle, moreover, are judged almost universally *not* to reflect legitimate differences of opinion. Instead, they are usually taken to reflect the opinions of persons who range from being merely morally untrustworthy and unreliable to downright psychopaths, whose behavior is to be feared or punished rather than emulated. Thus the familiar version of folk morality known as moral relativism relies on vastly overstating cultural differences while ignoring areas of widespread agreement and consensus.

What tends to differ across cultures, ironically, is not the fundamental moral principles themselves (such as the principle of reciprocity) but ontological beliefs about the status of entities in a given society and the social mores and customs in that society regarding how those entities are to be treated. But, ironically, it is *laws and legal regimes* that codify this perceived status and enshrine these customs and mores in different cultures.[4] Legal regimes in different cultures specify what sorts of considerations each entity is due—for example, women, children, prisoners, fetuses, minorities, and outsiders (those from other societies)—and these legal systems, unlike fundamental moral principles, are variable and culturally contingent, so much so that many moral philosophers mainly agree that the term *ethics* (from the Greek *ethos*) ought to be reserved to describe the specific fundamental customs and values of a culture—or else the study of these—while the term *morality* ought to be reserved to describe only the basic fundamental principles regarding respect, rights, and equivalence that, like the principle of reciprocity, are universally held.[5]

THE ORIGINS OF UNIVERSAL MORAL NORMS

Based on this distinction between the meanings of ethics and morality, we may proceed to observe that the moral principles that claim universality carry normative force from one or more of several kinds of considerations. According to Thomas Hobbes, as we saw earlier, morality and political institutions arise primarily as the result of a kind of hypothetical risk analysis and risk management. Individuals seeking to maximize or protect their individual interests from ruthless competition with other individuals achieve this goal by ceding some of their individual authority and autonomy to a central government or power that, in return, wields the authority of the sword to provide security. John Locke amended Hobbes's basic claim of security toward a broader guarantee of the protection of the state for certain basic and universal rights of the individuals, such as the rights to life, liberty, and property. Whether it is basic security or fundamental human rights that are ultimately guaranteed, however, on this conception, the authority of morality stems from the concatenation of individual self-interests in having these guarantees in force. This would be the proper understanding of what Locke described somewhat vaguely as the "tacit consent" of the governed to these political arrangements.

The authority of morality, and its ability as a social institution to govern effectively, however, can arise from other sources than an equilibrium of individual self-interests. Religious belief is most frequently invoked in this regard. But accounts of morality that rely on religious authority alone suffer from a number of practical disadvantages. Chief among them is the plurality of plausible, or implausible, accounts of the origin and ground of moral authority found in competing and culturally idiosyncratic notions of nature or "the gods." Many of these competing accounts yield what might prove to be plausible and viable conceptions of governing moral principles whose authority and "claim" on others—that is, whose normative force— is, nonetheless, contested. The resulting systems of religion-dependent morality, like systems of domestic legislation, vary from culture to culture or nation to nation, relegating us once more to the relativist stance and undermining the ultimate authority of the moral point of view.

An equally old and venerable conception of the origins and authority of morality, however, more indebted to Aristotle than to Hobbes, Locke, or theology, portrays it as a property or virtue of human social institutions generally. Given a plurality of individuals dwelling together in a community or engaged in common practices and enterprises, it behooves those individuals to reflect on the better or worse ways to realize the shared goals of those practices. Ancient communities, such as the Greek city-states for example, constituted reasonably well-defined and limited polities in which a broadly shared conception of the goods (the aims or goals) to be realized through their cooperative practices served as a guide to discern the better and worse ways of carrying out those practices. That is to say, through immersion in common practice (*praxis*), together with reflection on the adequacy or comparative efficacy of alternative forms of practice (*phronesis*) aimed at some common end, members of the community of practice could be led to discern for themselves both the forms of "best practice" (ideals, aspirations, or forms of excellence) and, perhaps more basically, those forms of practice that should be clearly labeled as prohibited and unacceptable, as fundamentally inimical to any conceivable realization of the Good. The ensuing moral principles that come to govern the community (to wield normative force) are those that either guide individual action toward aspirations, moral ideals, and forms of excellence (the so-called virtues), or else condemn and prohibit destructive and inimical forms of practice (vices) that are incommensurable with the Good.[6]

Aristotle himself thought there was a natural limit or "upper bound" on the size of the polity that might entertain the requisite common conceptions of the Good, let alone engage in reflection upon the better or worse means of attaining it.[7] Alasdair MacIntyre, on whose account of this procedure I am relying, seems to hold, as a matter of historical consideration, that any prospects for such commonality of social purpose in the modern era, whether on account of size or scale or of commitment to something beyond the self-interests of individuals, is impossible to achieve. Instead, the most we might hope for is, once again, the kind of ethics, such as the Hobbesian variety, that is merely a form of risk management—of the sort parodied by the aforementioned skeptic, Glaucon (in book 2 of Plato's *Republic*), as merely an outward semblance of authentic morality. Even more discouragingly, the variety of particular practices engaged in by human communities are so diverse as to render implausible any sense of commonality or universality in the moral principles thus adduced. Moral relativism, and the absence of any meaningful conceptions of morality that might claim to be universal, is thus an irreducible feature of the modern human condition, nowhere more evident than in the divided and dissolute anarchy of the cyber domain.

We will return to these considerations in the chapters that follow. For the present, suffice it to say that what I want to characterize as "emergent moral norms," sufficient to guide and govern the choices and actions of moral agents, offers a hopeful prospect for obtaining some greater cooperation and constraint of activities as these choices and actions unfold in the cyber domain. One must be cautioned, however, that if the desired end is the governance of the cyber domain by means of an authentic moral point of view that is internalized, self-imposed, and widely shared (rather than the mere outward semblance of such morality), then we are still confronted with a profound obstacle. The pessimistic assessment by Alasdair MacIntyre, in particular, on the prospects for attaining anything like a shared conception of the Good that is necessary to an authentic morality or common ethos (as opposed to its semblance as an outward equilibrium of competing self-interests) may prove all but unattainable in the modern era, especially in so diffuse, diverse, and divided an environment as the cyber domain represents.

One possible response is a prospect, first outlined by Immanuel Kant, for persuading or leading persons who are preoccupied by self-interest toward a commitment, even if unconsciously, to a wider and more substantive notion of the goods to be gained through lawful governance, as well as to the order and security that the moral point of view offers as an alternative to unrestrained or unrestricted conflict. Kant called this moral evolution from outward semblance to authentic moral reality the "cunning of nature."[8] This conception arises from a once widespread debate about the nature of individuals and the influence of society.

The Swiss political philosopher Jean Jacques Rousseau first posed the question of human nature in his novel *Émile* (1762). The question was essentially whether individual human beings are basically little more than nasty "stinkers" (as Socrates's rival, Thrasymachus, had taught), or whether instead we are all born into the world basically good-natured but are quickly "corrupted" by an immoral society. Though Rousseau seemed to believe the latter, things turned out rather badly either way because, Rousseau concluded, it appeared to be impossible for a morally worthy individual, if there even were such a person, to survive and flourish in the modern world.

Kant took up Rousseau's dilemma in his own later essays on politics and ethics, and posed a way of resolving the dilemma that he termed the "cunning of nature." Kant allowed that individual human beings are indeed largely selfish and corrupt (whatever the cause), but he also believed they have the capacity for rational thought, by which they can learn about nature through the development of science and mathematics (as indeed, over centuries, we have managed to do). This rationality also teaches each of us what is proper practical, social behavior in accordance with what he termed "the Moral Law." Unfortunately, few of us pay any attention to these lessons.

But all our varied capacities have generated additional outcomes. Each of us, for example, seems to desire to live together with our fellow human beings in society. At the same time, each of us desires to, or is unwilling to give up the hope that we can, dominate our fellow human beings. This "unsocial sociability" and ongoing "strife" between each person's competing capacities—desiring to live socially with but also dominate others and to pursue our desires while knowing rationally that some are inimical to a good life—generates a widespread dissatisfaction and restlessness within human beings and leads us in all sorts of directions. Higher civilization, in the form of science, technology, art, and culture, had emerged, Kant argued, from this perpetual strife, along with the kind of impetus that led to the external equilibrium of desires that Thomas Hobbes had postulated as the foundation of law and political order. We have, in effect, been driven by our perverse and conflicted natures to create or generate all these good things.

In particular, as I have emphasized, to manage conflict we are all forced into a compromise which results in the *outward semblance*, or appearance, of law and order and of civilization itself: everyone doing more or less what they should, resulting in a well-ordered and flourishing society. Nature, it seems, has given human beings just the right mix of opposing instincts and capacities, forcing all of us, in effect, to "behave ourselves."

But this outward semblance of authentic morality is not the final chapter. Once this fortuitous external result has been attained, it becomes possible for a genuinely good individual to survive, function, and flourish—thus realizing the moral goal that Rousseau believed we could never attain. This last twist is the cunning of nature, according to Kant. Authentic, or "inward," morality arises "naturally," that is, solely from the interplay of our natural instincts and endowments. As a result of this interplay, something that starts out as a pursuit of self-interest, can, if intelligently constrained and guided, eventually morph into something far more worthy: what we earlier described (with Aristotle and MacIntyre) as a *widely shared conception of the Good*, not the mere external equilibrium of selfish desire.

Despite their interesting differences, these philosophical accounts offer reasonable, plausible explanations of how moral norms can be said to possess a claim to universal adherence. For the moment, and in contrast to MacIntyre's negative assessment of the modern era, I would also observe that professions (such as medicine, law, education, the clergy, and the military) represent communities of shared practice that are on a sufficiently small and close-knit scale that they do embrace—or are at least capable of embracing—commonly held, widely shared conceptions of the Good. The precise kind of substantive emergent norms that MacIntyre believed governed ancient communities of practice could likewise be said to arise and govern internal practice in these contemporary settings.[9] I will hold that it is to communities of shared practice, such as physicians and healthcare professionals reflecting in the aftermath of their own peculiar crises of malpractice or malfeasance at venues like Nuremburg, Belmont, or Helsinki, that one must look in order to find examples of the kind of Aristotelian process of moral self-governance at work in the present.[10] Reflections by medical personnel at the those gatherings, for example, generated ethical codes composed of widely held normative moral principles that rest on something more morally substantive than mere risk management or the concatenation of their self-interests. The question is whether something like that same dynamic, if engaged in by denizens of the cyber domain, might hold out broader promise of generating principles of common governance that might come to enjoy widespread respect and common authority.

In regard to cyber conflict, it surely seems from what we have studied about conflict, competition, and malevolent behavior thus far that both we and our potential adversaries would derive considerable advantage by giving some consideration to the benefits of moral governance. Like the medical personnel at Belmont and Helsinki in particular, we might find that reflection on past practice encourages all concerned to think more carefully and cogently about the larger strategic goals they hope to realize through cyber conflict, and to take the initiative to impose some principles and constraints upon themselves that permit the attainment of these goals while discouraging behaviors that all might soon come to regret.

At a minimum, an ethical analysis of cyber conflict simply invites all parties to think clearly about what they are doing, what they are willing or unwilling to do, and why. We should talk about whether there are ethical limits on what we are willing to do in response to espionage and cyberattacks directed against our and our allies' military, commercial, and vital infrastructure targets and about whether, just as in conventional or counterinsurgency conflicts, it is really true in the cyber domain that acknowledging and abiding by such limits automatically puts us at a disadvantage.

THINKING ETHICALLY ABOUT CONFLICT
IN THE CYBER DOMAIN

If we succeed in rescuing morality from the grasp of folk morality and the skeptics who contend that it is irrelevant in the cyber realm, then we are free to move to a more practical question: Toward *which* universal moral principles ought we to look in in attempting to bring ethical considerations to bear on the problem of cyber conflict? Certainly, the principle of reciprocity applies—but what, if anything, does it actually tell us about how to act? And how does respect for fundamental human rights guide us in a virtual-reality domain composed not of persons but of electrons and photons?

Faced with these questions, the International Group of Experts at Tallinn rightly wondered whether the answers could be found in existing international legislation. Thus, for example, we all came to agree that "a weapon of war is a weapon of war," no matter its physical form or composition, so that the use of cyber weapons came under the sway of laws governing the development and use of conventional weapons of war. By analogy, we might argue that the moral reflections in the centuries-long tradition of just war theory, from which specific legal statutes originally devolved, might be the best place to begin in our quest for insights to guide our actions and limit conflict in cyberspace. To successfully mine this tradition, we will eventually require a better understanding than we enjoy at present of what just war theory is, and whence it derives its authority and jurisdiction.

For the present, however, let us set that problem aside and simply inquire what guidance the just war tradition offers us regarding conflict among and between nations, apart from crime or espionage, that rises to the level of a use of armed force. Those who are already familiar with this historical "conversation" about the moral justification of war typically think of it as a culturally limited phenomenon based on centuries of reflection about the problem of warfare by a succession of respected figures in Western philosophy and Christian theology, from Augustine and Thomas Aquinas to numerous scholars in the present. The question with which such figures are preoccupied is when, if ever, is it morally permissible to resort to war and armed conflict to settle political disputes in the international arena. The discussion of this question also ranges over the permissible and impermissible methods of waging war.

Historically, the first question concerned, as St. Thomas put it, "whether it is always sinful to wage war."[11] This has come to be designated in the idiomatic Latin terminology of medieval law as *jus ad bellum*, roughly, "the justification(s) for entering into a state of war," as noted in chapter 2. With reference to our earlier brief discussions of "professional ethics" as a form of internal self-governance, by contrast, the second set of questions might be framed collectively as "professional" questions of how a war is best waged by those actually involved in fighting it, with special attention paid to constraints and prohibitions on the proper and morally justified use of force against adversaries and innocent third parties (noncombatants). This second discussion regarding the conduct of war and of the preparation, training, character, and conduct of combatants in war is designated by the Latin legal idiom *jus in bello*.

Historically, there is considerable reflection, especially, as I have noted, in the philosophical literature of Western culture, on both sets of questions, which are thought to be conceptually distinct though obviously related. *Jus ad bellum*, is thought to be the purview primarily of statesmen and political leaders, who are charged with the welfare and defense of the state. *Jus in bello* pertains primarily to the military forces deployed under the command of the state, and seems to entail or encompass reflections on the "ethics of the profession of arms" itself.[12]

Discussions of war and ethics, and, separately, of military ethics, are, to be sure, often disparaged as irrelevant, or worse, as disadvantaging the side that takes such issues to heart by constraining their physical power and *materiel*, using it more sparingly and, hence, less effectively than their adversary. The latter is an empirical observation, however, and once again, there is little evidence, historically or otherwise, that militaries that honor professional norms and customs, such as refraining from attacking noncombatants and mistreating prisoners of war, fare any less well in war than forces who ignore them.

This kind of reasoning about war has a long history in Western culture, but it is as far from being merely a Western cultural artifact as the practice of war itself. In the literature of other cultures, we find, for example, Arjuna and Krisna, the principal characters in the great Hindu classic the Bhagavad Gita, debating these questions, and laws in ancient India clearly defined those who were to be exempt from attack during a war. The Confucian military strategist Sun Tzu famously offered delicately nuanced and often understated prudential views on precisely these questions in *The Art of War*. In twentieth-century China, Chairman Mao denounced his culture's earlier forms of discourse and limitations on the practice of combat as "asinine," but then proceeded to proclaim his own "Eight Points for Attention" governing the conduct of his insurgency forces in their guerilla war in 1938.[13] The Qur'an and its accompanying Hadiths declaim frequently and at length upon when, how, and to what extent to make war on unbelievers and when, if ever, Muslims should raise the sword against fellow Muslims.

The renowned political philosopher Michael Walzer, the leading just war theorist of the twentieth century, writes, "For as long as men and women have talked about war, they have talked about it in terms of right and wrong." "Reiterated over time," he observes, "[these] arguments and judgments shape what I want to call *the moral reality of war*—that is, all those experiences of which moral language is descriptive or within which it is necessarily employed."[14] For our present purposes, moreover, this important moral discourse seems to stem from and to reflect individual and collective human agency—that is, just war discourse is a direct expression of human freedom and the human ability, individually and collectively, to deliberate rationally and choose among alternative courses of action and thus to act (or refrain from acting) as appropriate, and to offer reasoned explanations of their decisions. In short, just as with MacIntyre's account of the origins of professional norms in deliberative discourse about shared practices, just war theory appears to represent the norms collectively elicited through reflective discourse by its practitioners.[15]

JUST WAR THEORY AS PART OF A "MORALITY OF EXCEPTIONS"

An interesting fact is that the moral discourse about war is akin to the moral discourse about a variety of other exceptional practices with which all humans are all too familiar—killing, lying, breaking promises or contracts, betraying loyalty, civil disobedience, and law-breaking, for example—all of which are, with virtually no divergence, the kinds of practices from which persons in every known culture and every known historical epoch are exhorted by one another to refrain.

And yet humans engage in these prohibited activities all the time. Usually, they are thought to be wrong, and those engaging in them are held accountable under prevailing principles of law, morality, and customary behavior for their wrongdoing. In culturally and historically dependent fashions, the wrongdoers are punished, excoriated, imprisoned, exiled, or executed—unless, that is, they can be found by their peers to have had justificatory reasons, motives, or intentions. We hold lawbreakers, such as Mahatma Gandhi and Martin Luther King Jr., accountable for violating established legal norms; we hold whistleblowers, such as Daniel Ellsberg and Edward Snowden, accountable for violating obligations of loyalty and betraying their trust; we hold killers accountable under both law and morality for taking the lives of others. But in every case, we ask if the civil disobedient, the whistleblower, the killer, or the liar had good cause to do what he or she did. Was the killing done in self-defense, for example?

Warfare, because of the devastation, death, and destruction it causes, is thought to be chief among the list of things that we ordinarily *are not supposed to do*, even if we sometimes do it anyway. In fact, the theological, political, or intellectual leaders or members of the society who are witness to or wronged by such actions have a right to ask the wrongdoer two basic questions:

(1) Did you have good and sufficient reasons—*justified cause*—for your actions?
(2) Did you go about deciding and carrying out these normally prohibited actions *in the right fashion*?

In the case of *jus ad bellum*, or the decision to go to war, the justifying reasons, while not identical, are roughly similar to those governing decisions to override prevailing norms in these other cases:

- One should have a compelling reason (*just cause*) to override the prohibition against fighting and killing.
- One should have undertaken every possible measure short of war to resolve the conflict. War should be the *last resort*.
- One's intentions in resorting to warfare must be beneficial rather than malevolent—the restoration of peace and satisfaction of the demands of justice, or prevention of harm to others, for example, as opposed to revenge, terror, or self-aggrandizement (*right intention*).
- There must be *proportionality*—that is, commensurability between the justifying cause and the ends being sought through war as compared to the damage and destruction it will surely inflict.
- Such reasoning on the part of the responsible decision makers, the "moral agents," must be capable of withstanding peer review or judicial review—that is, it must meet the test of *publicity*, in which impartial, reasonable observers confronted with the same situation could be expected to reach the same or similar judgment.

The final or *legitimate authority* to authorize such exceptional actions, that is to say, ultimately rests not with one individual alone but with the community on whose behalf these activities are allegedly being undertaken. This list of necessary conditions, or prompts, for practical deliberation in advance of war, in particular—just cause, last resort, right intention, proportionality, and publicity or legitimate authority—are among the historically familiar criteria, what moral philosophers term "necessary conditions," generally adduced in the just war tradition. But as we can now see, they are applicable beyond justifying war alone.

Exclusive focus on the problem of warfare in some more philosophically inclined cultural traditions has produced other nuanced conditions or criteria that should be considered, such as, in the case of going to war, requiring not only an advance public declaration of intent to go to war but also a reasonable expectation that doing so will result in a satisfactory or successful resolution of the conflict. Such demands seem compatible in principle with the other instances of what I term a morality of "exceptions," including civil disobedience, whistleblowing, or decisions to engage in strategies of promise-breaking, disloyalty, secrecy, deceit, or deception in pursuit of some "greater good." The moral justification of these otherwise distinct actions or policies require good justificatory reasons embodying right intentions and may be undertaken only after less-extreme options have been exhausted and proportionality has been considered. Finally, such exceptional strategies may be pursued only if they are publicly acknowledged, likely to succeed, and likely to be endorsed by disinterested others in a post facto review.

Warfare, unlike the other activities from which moral agents should normally refrain, however, embodies unique elements that arise from a fundamental equivocation over agency—that is, over the "one" or the "we" who makes these determinations. Decisions to deceive, blow the whistle, or break the law most often reside with individual human beings (or, at most, a small group of persons) capable both of making them and of being held accountable for the results.

The question of collective agency—that is, "sovereignty," or possessing the legitimate authority to commit a society to a course of action threatening the entire body politic with harm, and acceptance of accountability for the infliction of that harm—is considerably more vexed. This is especially true with respect to irregular warfare, terrorism, and insurgency, in which decisions reached by individuals and small groups may unknowingly or unwillingly subject a much wider society to the risk of harm.

In conventional thinking, sovereignty (and hence, legitimate authority) resides in a leader—monarch, prime minister, the leader of a parliament, or elected president—who symbolizes and is at least tacitly deputized to speak for the body politic collectively. Increasingly in the past century, such authority is even thought to exceed that of the heads of individual nation-states and requires a collective judgment on the part of a representative congress of nations, such as the United Nations, in which the principle of publicity is inherently vested and guaranteed. This makes unilateral decisions by individual nations to declare war (other than in exigent circumstances of armed self-defense in response to an unprovoked attack) deeply suspect, let alone decisions by nonstate actors or organizations, such as the radical Sunni Islam organization, Al Qaeda, or its apparent successor, the self-proclaimed Islamic State, to declare war upon others. Indeed, we might observe that the question of sovereignty and legitimate authority in just war doctrine now constitutes the single most vexed and contentious issue in international relations in the twenty-first century.[16]

Otherwise, and quite unlike an individual's personal decision to blow the whistle, break a promise, or violate the law, the decision to go to war commits a subset of the society, nation, or coalition—normally its military and security forces—to carry out the general will on behalf of the declaring authority. Thus, if we customarily hold individuals accountable for making themselves exceptions to the normal constraints that define justifiable behavior, how does that translate into a canon of expectations and constraints imposed on that designated subset of agents? And, even more problematically, to what extent will past answers to this important question automatically carry over into the realm of unrestricted or irregular warfare in the present? The question is especially urgent when irregular warfare is waged by agents of the state against terrorists or insurgents, who lack any legitimate authority to wage war themselves, and who are therefore often contemptuous of any constraints on their behavior. Certainly, all of these considerations must figure into the evaluation of adversarial behavior in a cyber conflict as well.

JUS IN BELLO AND PROFESSIONAL MILITARY ETHICS

As noted earlier, reflections on *jus in bello* and *jus ad bellum* have taken place in many historical eras and cultural traditions. Sun-Tzu provides some of the earliest examples in *The Art of War*, as does Socrates in Plato's *Republic*, discussing such issues as when to fight and when to refrain from fighting, the proper targeting of enemy combatants, noncombatant immunity, and the distinction between true military necessity in campaigns and indiscriminate, gratuitous destruction: a fundamental principle often labeled "the economy of force."

As often as not, the impetus behind such considerations is as much a matter of prudence and common sense as of morality. Why, Sun-Tzu wonders, would a commander risk harm to his army if the military objective could be achieved without a battle? Why, Socrates asks students as they reflect upon the Peloponnesian War, would we slaughter the innocent bystanders and helpless family members of the enemy or raze the enemy's cities and destroy its land, when we hope to restore political and economic relations with them following their defeat?

Such principles, dimly discerned, survive in modern-day reflections as well, such as those that Franz Lieber sought to embody in "General Orders #100." And in so codifying these intuitions, the Lieber Code incorporated what the Dominican priest Francisco de Vitoria, decrying the harsh treatment of indigenous populations during the Spanish Conquest, had described as the "customs and habits of civilized peoples and nations" (ius gentium).[17]

Such fundamental norms and long-prevailing intuitions, as we noted earlier, are enshrined in the present-day law of armed conflict, specifically in the moral norms that (as noted in chapter 2) are sometimes characterized among the basic principles of international humanitarian law, including

- prevention of superfluous injury and unnecessary suffering (humanity)
- military necessity
- proportionality (the economy of force)
- distinction (discrimination or noncombatant immunity)
- command responsibility (accountability)

JUS IN SILICO: ETHICS AND JUST WAR THEORY IN THE CYBER DOMAIN

Can such considerations play a role in guiding and governing conduct in the cyber domain? Inasmuch as they are not state-centric or paradigm-dependent principles, then, quite in contrast to the state-centered concerns embodied in international law, there is no reason to think that just war reasoning could *not* work as well in analyzing cyber conflict.

With regard to what we might then term *jus in silico* or the "justification of cyber conflict," we would expect that nations or other agents would refrain from engaging in such conflict (presuming they are not engaged in criminal activities) unless there was *a compelling and justifiable cause* for doing so. They would likewise refrain from engaging in cyber conflict, save as *a last resort* (or else, as a next-to-last resort before engaging in conventional armed conflict). They would do so only with the proper authorization and under the supervision of recognized and responsible state authorities. Finally, nations would only engage in cyber conflict that was, or was likely to prove, *proportionate to the harm* they had suffered or to the grievance which they sought thereby to address.

And when nations turned to actually carrying out such conflict, they would target only legitimate enemy military or state targets and would *refrain from deliberately targeting civilian persons or objects*, in keeping with existing laws of armed conflict. They would exert only as much cyber force as was necessary to achieve their aims and would seek to prevent or limit the collateral harm or damage that might be otherwise inflicted on public infrastructure or innocent third parties not engaged or implicated in the conflict.

In sum, nearly all of the principles of just war moral discourse that guide decisions and actions in conventional and irregular conflict would find their counterpart or analogue in the cyber domain: just cause, legitimate authority, last resort, and proportionality, for example. And likewise, in the development and use of cyber weapons against enemy targets, the principles of strict military necessity, civilian immunity, and proportionality of means would continue to apply to constrain excessive and unwarranted damage or use of force. Whether or not one could gain acceptance of these restrictions as constituting matters of law, they would remain in force as matters of morality and professional ethics governing the combat personnel charged with carrying out the cyber conflict. Far from simply disadvantaging the side that complied in good faith with such measures, compliance would ensure that limits were placed on the damage done, and even more importantly, serve to distinguish legitimate or "justified" combatants and tactics from the efforts of mere criminals, vandals, or vigilantes, who seldom concern themselves with such moral restraints on their activities (which is precisely why we believe ourselves to be justified in fighting them).

Ethics and recognized, familiar traditions of moral discourse about armed conflict thus do provide resources from which we can at least derive preliminary insights into how to guide and govern conflict and competition in the cyber domain as well. Although the results prove more straightforward and more generally accepted than disputed extensions of international law, however, our task is far from finished. Even in attempting by analogy to extend the parameters of just war discourse into the cyber realm, we encounter problems of interpretation, as well as of the limitations on acceptable or permissible action. Some of these have analogues in recent debates about irregular warfare, from which we can learn a great deal: for example, the status of civilian dual-use targets, the notions of noncombatant immunity in practice, and the precise meaning of "last resort" in instances where cyberattacks might offer a less-destructive alternative to conventional attacks. And, of course, we have yet to resolve the problems caused by the blurring of boundaries between kinetic and low-intensity conflict—uses of armed force, for example, rather than espionage and covert action. And we will need to consider whether this new form of conflict confronts us with the need for an equally new kind of moral education and professional military preparation: the duty to develop and disseminate a "code of the cyber warrior."

NOTES

1. I have borrowed the term "moral point of view," describing what will be seen as a stance in favor of a particular conception of morality, from a once widely read and influential book by Kurt Baier, which attempted to address the question that occupies us here: How, if at all, can morality as a distinctive human social institution be justified beyond, or apart from, appeals to a kind of risk management driven by competing self-interests? See Kurt Baier, *The Moral Point of View* (Ithaca, NY: Cornell University Press, 1958).

2. This constitutes another point in favor of the analogy of problems in the governance of cyberspace and those already addressed in other contexts regarding the rise of irregular warfare, in which the widespread involvement of nonstate actors and demands for overriding national sovereignty through international military interventions intended to defend the human rights of victims of genocide put tremendous pressure on the so-called Westphalian paradigm of state sovereignty.

3. In the late medieval and early modern period, for example, power in global affairs was not only exercised by nations (Japan, China, Portugal, and Spain, for example), but by a variety of nonstate federations and international organizations, ranging from the papacy and worldwide religious orders, such as the Dominicans and Jesuits (who were nominally under the jurisdiction of the Pope), to trade organizations like the Hanseatic League, the East India Company, and others that operated largely outside the control of any formal government. This system of "distributed sovereignty" provides a good analogue for the cyber domain at present, given the relative powerlessness of state governments in the face of international commercial organizations, such as Google, Yahoo, and Microsoft, as well as of nonstate actors ranging from Anonymous to the Russian Business Federation.

4. Supreme Court Justice Stephen Breyer's book *The Court and the World: American Law and the New Global Realities* (New York: Alfred K. Knopf, 2015) makes just this point, arguing that domestic jurisprudence itself has become exceedingly more complicated as a result of the entanglement of foreign practices with domestic law. He does not comment on how or why this revelation has come so late to American jurisprudence or on how the legal education system might be reformed to provide future lawyers with an adequate grounding in "comparative law" as well as international law.

5. Such formal distinctions are not hard and fast inasmuch as, originally, the two terms are derived from Greek and Latin words denoting the same set of questions, namely, "How best should I live my life, toward what should I aspire, and what duties or obligations do I owe to others?" The late English moral philosopher Sir Bernard Williams and the eminent German ethicist Jürgen Habermas are among those who use the terms in the formal fashion outlined above.

6. This is sometimes labeled "virtue ethics" to distinguish it from other kinds of moral reasoning grounded principally in consideration of fundamental moral principles defining one's duties (deontological ethics) or from efforts to realize the Good (utilitarianism). These distinctions, largely reified in the twentieth century for purposes of moral instruction, strike me as unhelpful and misleading, inasmuch as Immanuel Kant, famously labeled a deontological ethicist, lectured widely on the virtues, as well as on moral education and development, which were thought to be the purview of virtue ethics alone, while J. S. Mill read Aristotle assiduously, derived the principle of utility itself from analysis of Aristotelian considerations, and offered conceptions of moral rights and duties as especially vigorous and efficacious summations of behaviors that maximized utility—while Aristotle, for his part, devoted copious attention to justice (*dike*) and the duties of justice, as well as to the duties of virtue, distinctions we find enshrined in Kant's reading of Aristotle in *The Metaphysics of Ethics* (1795). I would prefer to bypass what I regard as this specious and destructive pedagogical dialectic of moral philosophers in these chapters.

7. The first book of Aristotle's *Politics* postulates an upper limit to the *koinonia* (the community of free citizens) to some ten thousand adult males.

8. Some philosophers devoted to the work of G. W. F. Hegel will complain that it is in Hegel's sophisticated and well-developed philosophy of history that we find the concept to which I allude, under the heading of the "cunning of *history*." I wrote my doctoral dissertation on Hegel; this concept regarding what Hegel described as the "unfolding of Absolute Spirit" is indeed to be found there, but it fleshes out an outline first sketched by Kant in scattered essays on social and political issues written in the mid-1780s, before the young Hegel had even begun to study at university. This, however, is among those dry philosophical disputes with which I promised not to burden the general reader.

9. MacIntyre does not acquiesce in my understanding and use of his work in this context. For example, on the matter of (modern) professions and (ancient) practices, he writes:

> On my view, practices are one thing, professions quite another. Professions are institutions and like other such [institutions] distribute power, prestige, and money, goods external to practices the pursuit of which is always in tension with devotion to the goods internal to practices. ... My use of the notion of a practice is such that there is no question of comparing better and worse practices. ... I do not believe that norms "worthy of universal jurisdiction" arise from practice. ... It is only within disciplined practices (the plural is crucial) that we first identify goods and standards and then rules required to achieve those goods and conform with those standards. Those rules are very different from the rules that reflection on practice in general without knowledge of goods arrive at. What you do arrive at is Rawls or Habermas, both of whose conclusions are deeply incompatible with mine. (pers. corrs., November 10, 2015)

While attempting carefully to distinguish MacIntyre's conceptual framework from my appropriation and use of it, I do not yield to these interpretations, and it is this presumed incompatibility between the Kantian and Aristotelian frameworks against which I am arguing. To these specific objections, I replied:

Of course your account explains why, for the modern world, it is not "society" or societies as such, but only specific situations of smaller, well-defined communities of agents engaged in well-defined practices that are informed by shared conceptions of the good thereby achieved—such as "professions" (where these can be said to exist)—each of which can collectively cultivate and practice virtues.

My extended case relies, not so much on Hobbes and compromises consciously born of self-interest per se, but on Kant, and the "cunning of nature." It is engagement in activities lacking any sense of shared purpose or of the good to be realized, coupled with reflection on better or worse ways of carrying out those activities, which transform the latter into (rule-governed) practices embodying a shared conception of the good, which must lie inherently beneath each, awaiting discovery or elicitation through the kind of education that reflection on practice eventually provides.

It is that "Kantian turn" on your own conception which I have insufficiently explained, but also to which I expected you (once it was apparent) to object, or to find implausible, not the least b/c I recall you telling me once, years ago, that you viewed Kant as a "madman." I took this merely as a rejection by you of any attempt to view morality in some abstract, featureless sense, unconstrained by embodiment or cultural horizons, whether describing a supreme principle of morality, or (as with Rawls) some abstract stance from which justice or the good might nonetheless be articulated.

This is why I rhetorically substitute Aristotle's practical reasoning (ordinary, human deliberation on better and worse tactics in pursuit of some goal) in place of Rawls's "reflective equilibrium" in the "original position." Even Kant envisioned nothing quite so abstracted from any context whatever. Naturally one's interests, as well as attendance to outcomes (for that is largely what is reflected upon as being "better or worse"), would play a role. But participants (such as even adversaries in a war) have more content to their deliberations in this situation than would be provided by the astonishingly narrow conception of "self-interest" put forward by Hobbes. In any case, it is the education of desires through experience that tempers such reflection, sometimes sobering experience in the case of war, and forces a more enlightened approach toward discerning the good that all participants in the practice seek. This is how moral norms can be said to "emerge" through practice and reflection.

10. Here I refer to three significant congresses (at these respective geographical locations) of medical and healthcare personnel, convened to evaluate and redress perceived errors and excesses in the behavior of individual members and organizations of their practitioners with respect to medical research carried out on human subjects. The Nuremburg Code, reflecting on torturous experiments carried out on helpless and unwilling human subjects, concluded principally that useful or even valuable scientific results alone did not warrant or justify such experimentation, unless undertaken with the informed consent of the subjects. The Belmont convention yielded protocols for human-subjects research in response to the US Public Health Service's conduct of experiments on unknowing

subjects in Tuskegee, Alabama, while the Helsinki Congress reflected on, and issued a code of prohibitions and ideals of best medical practice in response to, questionable research conducted by the World Health Organization.

11. Thomas Aquinas, *Summa Theologica* II, part II, Q: 40 (art. 1). In *The Summa Theologica of Thomas Aquinas, Fathers of the Dominican Providence* (London: Burns & Oates, 1911).

12. Here colleagues in international law might object to the characterization of its treaties and statutes as a reflection of the professional code of military personnel, but this would betray yet again a fundamental misunderstanding of the history of that body of law. As one example: early in the American Civil War, a German-born American legal scholar and former Prussian Army soldier, Franz Lieber, was asked by President Lincoln to convene a committee of senior military officers to draft a series of regulations and guidelines for troops in the Union Army. The result, "General Orders #100" (known the "Lieber Code"), enshrined a great many principles of professional decorum and constraint regarding the use of force, noncombatant immunity, treatment of prisoners, and other matters pertaining to the proper professional conduct of armed hostilities. Interestingly, the result was so admired that the document was subsequently adopted as doctrine by the Prussian Army, considered at the time the premier professional military force in the world, whence it spread to the military services of other European militaries and policymaking communities. Key elements of the Lieber Code eventually served as the basis for the first Geneva Conventions in the late nineteenth century, prescribing the appropriate conduct of armed hostilities. This founding document of professional military ethics thus became simultaneously a key founding document in the historical evolution of the international law of armed conflict (international humanitarian law). For a more detailed discussion of other examples of this ethical reflection on military professionalism and its place in international law, see George Lucas, *Military Ethics: What Everyone Needs to Know* (New York: Oxford University Press, 2015), esp. chap. 2.

13. Indian law and Chairman Mao are quoted in Michael Walzer, *Just and Unjust Wars* (New York: Basic Books, 1977), 43, 225–227.

14. Ibid., 1, 15.

15. Here again, MacIntyre dissents from my reading of his work. He writes:
    The just war case illustrates my point adequately. What the kind of Aristotelianism that I advance can account for is first how individuals through initiation into practices—in the AV [*After Virtue*] sense—may become just and secondly why those who are just find themselves constrained by the norms of justice in going to war and in waging war. What such Aristotelianism has nothing to say about is the condition of those who out of fear of the consequences of lack of constraints enter into agreements to abide by or enforce just war norms, agreements sustained by calculations of reciprocal advantage. Of course practical experience may play a part in bringing them to enter into such agreements, but nothing analogous to a practice in the AV sense is involved. . . . Thomas Hobbes is relevant to their concerns, Aristotle is not. The theses and concepts of Aristotle's politics and ethics find application where there is at least rough and ready agreement on goods and how they are to be rank ordered. Where such agreement is lacking, as in the cultures of modernity, it is Hobbes's theses and concepts that find application. (pers. corres. July 21, 2015)

16. See James Turner Johnson, *Sovereignty* (Washington, DC: Georgetown University Press, 2014).
17. Francisco de Vitoria, *de juri Belli* (1539), in *Vitoria: Political Writings*, ed. Anthony Pagden and Jeremy Lawrance (Cambridge: Cambridge University Press, 1991): 233–292.

CHAPTER 5

If Aristotle Waged Cyberwar

How Norms Emerge from Practice

One view of the normative status of international law that we considered in chapter 3 was that this law consisted in large part of a codification merely of "what states do, or tolerate being done." That leads us to ask in the case of cyber conflict, what exactly are states currently doing and tolerating being done to them? And to what degree are these practices amenable to, or even worthy of, codification in either law or morality? The answer to the first question seems to be that they are both doing, and apparently tolerating, just about anything.

North Koreans allegedly hack into private corporate files and leak embarrassing emails from Sony Pictures executives, in an attempt to blackmail the executives into suppressing the release of a movie comedy that portrays their country's leader in a bad light. Iranian cyber operatives allegedly launch DDoS attacks against selected American financial institutions and hack into Saudi Arabia's (ARAMCO's) oil-drilling infrastructure and steal, deface, or damage computers and data, possibly in retaliation for the Stuxnet cyberattack on their nuclear development site in Natanz. The PLA's Shanghai Cyber Unit steals blueprints for an advanced jet fighter from Defense Department data files, while allegedly looting valuable patents and industrial trade secrets from American and Canadian commercial manufacturers, and PLA Unit 78020 in Kunming subsequently steals the private personnel files of some twenty-two million Americans who work for or have recently retired from the OPM. And, at the time of this writing, there are likely a few well-placed government and corporate executives, fearing prospects of blackmail or extortion, who are also wondering, "Who has control of the data stolen from dating website Ashley Madison?"

As we have seen, the victims of these cyberattacks often refuse to retaliate or even to formally protest the actions because they, too, engage in cyber conflict. Any attempts to interject "lawfulness" into this wild scenario are met with howls of protest, claims of "cultural hegemony," or even random attacks on those who dare advocate in favor of cyber law and order by vigilante groups determined to preserve this status quo. All of this transpires against a backdrop of criminal activity that is quite serious and costly, and may at times involve either state agents or active complicity by tacitly approved, state-sponsored institutions. Ironically, the only pushback so far has come from citizens in the United States and Europe, who often feel more threatened by the efforts of their own intelligence and national security agencies to countermand these attacks through big-data collection and analysis than they do by the attacks themselves.

The classical social-contract portrait of international anarchy in interstate relations, then, seems in full force in the cyber domain. Is there any reasonable hope that we will be able to establish greater safety and security? Or are we condemned to dwell in the invaluable free and open resource that is cyberspace without restrictions of any kind? Chinese officials, as we have seen, object to what they characterize as Western attempts to "control the cyber domain," characterizing cyberspace instead as a "commons," like the public meadows and pastures in cities and towns in the eighteenth century, freely available for use by any and all without regulation.[1] Demographer Garrett Hardin observed that those eighteenth-century public spaces were subject to destruction, calling this "the tragedy of the commons." Might the same fate be in store for their mid-twentieth-century counterparts?[2]

We have considered the view of the cyber doomsdayers, such as Richard Clarke, that nothing short of a cyber Pearl Harbor or Armageddon will force participants to the bargaining table. An alternative view is that an evolutionary process in international relations, sometimes characterized as *the emergence of new norms of responsible state behavior*, will accomplish the same end. In this chapter, we will examine several well-studied instances of recent state behavior, in order to determine

(1) whether there are norms governing cyber conflict practices (apart from criminal activities) that are currently emerging from the engagement in these practices by adversaries; and if so,

(2) whether these emergent norms sufficiently resemble the moral underpinnings of conventional armed conflict, so as to provide reasonable

assurances of the possibility of responsible and accountable future behavior in the cyber domain; and

(3) perhaps most importantly, whether this evolution of "international
norms," grounded in consensus, agreement, and the advocacy of best
practices by the nations involved thus far affords a greater probability
of acceptance and compliance than would formal legislation.

As we also saw in chapter 4, morality, properly understood, addresses u-
niversal concerns like justice, fairness, and human rights that are widely
acknowledged, and more or less respected or observed by the citizens and
governments of many nations. Ethics, in contrast, describes the manner in
which specific communities of common national citizenship, or of professional practice, inculcate, imbue, institutionalize, and finally operationalize
these universal concerns in culturally specific laws, customs, and practices.
We likewise discovered that the latter, more immediate experiential feature
of morality as a culturally distinct and diverse ethos often downplayed, ignored, or obscured the recognition of common concerns and values, giving
rise to the popular and intractable folk mythology of moral relativism and
incommensurable moral *différance* in the field of ethics.

Interstate conflict is an area in which there is a clear need for compromise and restraint. In this chapter, accordingly, I return to Aristotle,
particularly as his ideas are portrayed in the work of Alasdair MacIntyre,
in which the origins of what we otherwise call "emergent norms" in international relations can be further analyzed. I draw particular inspi-
ration from MacIntyre's examination of the origins of ethics in shared
professional practices, such as military and medical ethics.[3] I broaden
MacIntyre's example of communities of shared professional practice to
examine how widespread conflict involves the interaction of the ends,
purposes, or "strategies" with which individuals and states seek to realize, more broadly through experimentation, better and worse means of
realizing their desired ends. The better (or best) practices can be said to
constitute the "emergent norms," while the worst and most undesirable
practices help eventually define recognized boundaries or limitations on
permissible practice.

To be sure, this might seem to constitute unnecessarily hazy and abstract theorizing. But, as we shall see, these fundamental philosophical
ideas concerning the basis of moral behavior turn out to be operational-
ized in very interesting ways in the current behavior of agents and their
actions within the cyber realm—leading to the expectation that the quest
for adequate and reasonable governance is in the interests, and serves the
otherwise diverse purposes, of all concerned.[4]

Laws and regulations are stipulative: they are defined, codified, and externally imposed by institutions of authority upon unwilling subjects or agents. Best practices, by contrast, *emerge* from the common experience of shared practices among the interested parties, and reflect their collective experience and shared objectives. Aspirations and ideals are *hammered out cooperatively by the relevant stakeholders* in specific instances, making it relatively easy for all stakeholders to recommend and consent to them as authentic expressions of shared intentions and common general interests. Who, after all (as Kant might remind us), can object to conforming to standards that they themselves have formulated and subsequently imposed upon themselves in order to guide and regulate their shared pursuits?

In international relations, as mentioned, this process is commonly referred to as the "emerging norms of responsible state behavior." These "norms" are thought to differ from both formal legislation and prior established moral principles. Norms (from *normative*, pertaining to agreed standards like weights and measures, as well as from *nomos*, or law) instead are widely recognized and generally acknowledged standards of conduct by which individuals and nations evaluate their own and others' behavior. Sometimes in international law these norms are termed *ius gentium*, "customary law," or "the standards and customs of civilized nations and peoples." Admittedly, this is neither very clear nor very precise, nor does it seem very powerful, especially when there are no treaties or bright-line statutes in international or domestic law to clarify them, and little in the way of effective sanctions to enforce them. But it is remarkable how, over the centuries—and long before these concepts ever found their way into written, statutory form—nations and peoples developed and respected a family of norms in international relations pertaining to things like ambassadorial immunity, treatment of prisoners of war, and respect for other basic principles (even when such respect is sometimes accorded more in the breach than in the observance).[5]

With respect to the cyber domain, my own understanding and treatment of this topic is deeply indebted to recommendations by Panayotis Yannakogeorgos and Adam Lowther regarding the prospect of US sponsorship of global norms for cyberspace.[6] This also happens to be the approach to the governance of cyber conflict I have advocated ever since the discovery of Stuxnet in 2010.[7]

But this approach to governance entails its own difficulties, especially from the standpoint of both ethics and law. First: *How can norms be said legitimately to emerge from practice?* This seems worth explaining, inasmuch as norms are thought to be wholly distinct from—"orthogonal" to—practice, precisely in order to be able to offer a stance or perspective independent of practice from which to constrain it. Doesn't the concept of "emergent norms" in international relations thus involve endorsing some version of "the naturalistic fallacy" by attempting to derive "ought" from "is?"[8]

In domestic and international law and public policy, of course, we do not trouble ourselves with this intriguing philosophical puzzle. Instead, as noted earlier, norms are constructed from the precedents set by state practice or from the legal judgments reached in disputes over specific practices. In public policy and in international relations, that is to say, the status of norms is similar to that of causality in the natural sciences: both have remained, in the amusing summary of Alfred North Whitehead, "blandly indifferent to their refutation by Hume."[9] And even if this problem can be addressed, lawyers and ethicists might, in any case, question the degree of authority or normative force that such emergent norms might actually possess. Each of these two fundamental concerns deserves its own response.

THE METHODOLOGY OF UNCERTAINTY: HOW DO NORMS "EMERGE"?

How do we handle uncertainty, especially uncertainty stemming from novel developments, new technologies, or contrasting or competing ways of living? How do we grow comfortable with novelty and accustomed to the need for a new kind of order in our lives? How do we discern the new rules of the game, when we don't know precisely what the game is? In the interpretation of his work I offer here, Alasdair MacIntyre can be shown to have shed considerable light on these problems several decades ago. He noted that we can find clues to the answers to such questions in works by Aristotle and St. Thomas on ethics and political theory. Indeed, the formal procedure is described in detail in one of Aristotle's logical treatises, the *Posterior Analytics*.[10]

Basically, the method is this: when we are unfamiliar with and uncertain about what is taking place, let alone about what rules or principles properly apply to our actions, we start by gathering all the relevant data we can about the practice in question—for example, moral customs in different cultures, various kinds of constitutions and political arrangements—or, in our case, the various activities and practices taking shape in the cyber domain. We begin intuitively to discern *better* from *worse* practices, based in large part upon their relative degree of what we might term "operational effectiveness" in realizing ends or goals, which we may only imperfectly grasp or understand. We also draw comparisons between what we know and what we are newly confronting. We engage in reflection, dialectic, and sustained philosophical argument in order to analyze both the practices in question and our comparative experiences with their results. We extrapolate from the known to the unknown, and gradually begin to discern inductively what Aristotle termed the *archai*, the "first principles" governing these practices.

Certainly, this Aristotelian process was at work with regard to the advent of nuclear weapons. The United States developed and then used these weapons against Japan. And while the justification for using them in the context of a war against an enemy deemed guilty of its own war crimes is still hotly debated, few have doubted that our using these indiscriminate and destructive weapons against civilian targets was an undesirable practice and one not to be encouraged. The fear that the United States might one day fall victim to the bad precedent it had set helped to generate a dangerous and costly arms race—but that very precedent and arms race *also* led responsible states to advocate for nuclear nonproliferation and to discourage threats involving the "first use of nuclear force" by nuclear powers. The resulting "emergent" norm of nuclear nonproliferation, while not inviolable, has proven to be an especially strong international norm over the past half century.[11]

Despite the concerns raised about the *Tallinn Manual*, the evolution of law itself in response to novel developments in most respects is a good case in point. The complex relationship between law and morality is always of great interest, but it need not detain us now. In both fields, we frequently tease as well as complain that both morality and the law are constantly playing catch-up with technology. But if Aristotle is right, this is not a flaw; it is exactly what is to be expected, and it is precisely what we are now engaged in rectifying. Legal scholars work by analogy and with past experience in the form of precedent. In order to cite precedent and draw analogies, however, they need a body of new experiences to work with. Confronted with emerging examples of the new and the unknown, they turn to precedent to help classify and categorize the new behaviors, and reason by analogy and extrapolation from past practices to present governing principles. Sometimes, solving the stubbornest and most recalcitrant legal problems, in turn, requires elaborate and tortured and contorted interpretations, what I characterized earlier, in the Tallinn case, as "hermeneutical gymnastics."[12]

Apart from Stuxnet, we don't yet have a great deal of experience with full-fledged cyber conflict on the scale of conventional warfare, although we might say that our familiarity is increasing daily, in accordance with what is known as Moore's Law.[13] But, arguably, we have now experienced at least four instances of cyber conflict that *could not properly be classified merely as criminal acts, or even simply as acts of espionage and covert action.*

While most cyber experts concur in calling the four instances of conflict I will enumerate below cyber warfare, recall that Thomas Rid of King's College had objected that none were acts of war but instead were merely acts of either espionage or sabotage. But acts of sabotage *are* currently classified as acts of war under international law. *Sabotage* constitutes an act that, in effect, crosses the boundary between ongoing low-level conflict between states, such as espionage, and a genuine resort to force, or to the equivalent of an armed attack by one nation against another. Otherwise, however, Professor Rid is basically correct that virtually all cyber conflict boils down to straightforward crimes or criminal acts of espionage. There is a spirited discussion currently underway about whether infusing a nation's civil infrastructure with backdoor booby traps likewise crosses the line between espionage and sabotage and might constitute something equivalent to a use of armed force.[14]

So far, it appears that crime is what has seemed most familiar (for all the novel new ways of carrying it out in the cyber realm). Cybercrime is the arena in which we have seemed generally most confident and effective in classifying and responding to threats and challenges. Notwithstanding the novelty and ingenuity of cybercriminals, the basic nature, intentional structure, and effects of their criminal activity seem familiar, common, and generic: we've seen it all before, especially when the crime is the theft of money or property. The Internet, to revise bank robber Willie Sutton's famous phrase, is now simply "where the money is"! Hence, we discover that we can reasonably well classify the crimes, take steps to combat and prevent them, and apprehend the perpetrators, within the bounds of the law—in short, make the same efforts made by constabulary forces everywhere.

So we ask again, how do we stand currently with respect to cyberwar? To answer that question, it is useful to examine illustrative cases of what various nations have recently undertaken, how other nations have reacted, and what, on balance, most experts seem to conclude about all this.

Richard Clarke in 2010 offered detailed and dramatic accounts of four now-classic cases of cyber conflict that, in his opinion, qualified as acts of war. There have, of course, been numerous other examples since,[15] but these four are still cited in virtually all accounts of cyber warfare written to date, and I focus on them as occasions for observing norms that are actually emerging in an ongoing process of engagement:[16]

(1) The first is the DDoS attacks in Estonia in 2007 that we have already discussed from a legal perspective in chapter 3. To recap: After the

Estonian government moved an unpopular Russian war memorial from the center of Tallinn to a military graveyard outside the city, Russian citizens and their government were outraged, as were Estonian citizens of Russian descent. Soon thereafter, the government of Estonia reported that the country was "under relentless attack." Estonian websites were flooded with enormous volumes of traffic, effectively shutting down newspapers, banks, government websites, and financial and civic transactions. In this highly wired, tech-savvy nation, commercial and government affairs ground to a halt. The government allegedly contemplated appealing to NATO to come to its aid under the collective security provisions of the NATO treaty, claiming that the attacks originated in Russia. The government of the Russian Federation, however, denied responsibility, claiming in effect, "We can't be blamed if individual patriots take matters into their own hands." NATO declined to become involved, stating that the massive cyberattacks did not rise to the level of armed conflict.

(2) In September 2007, the Israeli Air Force apparently carried out a successful nighttime bombing raid in Diaya-al-Sahir in Syria on what was believed to be a nuclear power and weapons facility being built there with technical assistance from North Korea. The success of the raid was attributed to a prior cyberattack that had disabled and spoofed Syria's Soviet-era air missile defense system, making it impossible for the Syrian military air traffic controllers to detect the malfunction or track the flight of the Israeli bombers into Syria's airspace. The nuclear facility was destroyed, and six North Korean workers were killed in the attack.

(3) Russia preceded its conventional armed intervention in the breakaway province of Ossetia in Georgia, in 2008, with DDoS attacks designed to frustrate Georgian command and control systems and interfere with government communication and the coordination of a response. These attacks appeared to be aimed solely at government and military sites.[17]

(4) Last is the Stuxnet attack aimed at the nuclear weapons development program in Iran. To recap: the Stuxnet worm gained control of the centrifuge array in Iran's Natanz nuclear power facility, causing the individual machines to malfunction and self-destruct, while transmitting false data to the operators indicating that they were functioning properly. It was thus several months before the problem was discovered, and more than two years before external security expert analysis, coupled with security leaks, revealed that the Stuxnet worm was a cyber weapon allegedly created by Israel or the United States or both in a collaboration and was part of a larger surveillance and sabotage operation known as Olympic Games.

What can we now glean from these case studies of cyber conflict?

A great deal. The disabling of Syria's missile defense system, the DDoS attacks in Georgia, and Stuxnet, for example, appeared to be part of serious, grave conflicts transpiring between sovereign states: the sort of things that constitute acts of war or can lead to the declaration of war. I strongly disagree with Thomas Rid's assessment that none of them constitutes "war": the last three are certainly acts of war. As I argued at the UNESCO symposium in July 2011, however, the Stuxnet example is unique in that it resulted in physical damage to a military target solely through use of software designed to serve as a weapon, and may have been the first purely ethical weapon ever deployed.[18] By contrast, I noted, the Estonia example seemed somehow out of proportion to the remaining three. The justification for armed conflict or the threat of force was nearly nonexistent in this case. This incident was, at most, a diplomatic matter. The attacks, moreover, were directed indiscriminately at civilians and civilian infrastructure. It does not seem morally justifiable, quite apart from the issue of legality, to seem to pose ominous threats to vital civilian infrastructure (e.g., to deny ordinary citizens access to their financial resources) because of a dispute over the placement of a single bronze war memorial. As we know, the Russian Federation's denial of any knowledge, involvement, or responsibility for the attacks invoked the so-called attribution problem. But even taken individually, the Estonia attacks were certainly criminal activities, and though the Russian Federation is not a signatory, the CCC commits nations to policing cybercrimes that are carried out within their borders.

Meanwhile, the rulings of the UN Security Council authorizing the US-led intervention in the matter of the Taliban and Al Qaeda in Afghanistan in late 2001 established that the government of a sovereign nation could be held liable for failing to put a stop to or expel nonstate actors involved in international criminal conspiracies arising within its borders. Some of the leading international lawyers engaged in the Tallinn process, such as Michael Schmitt and David Graham, concluded at the time that NATO would have been justified in holding Russia to account for the attacks.[19]

NATO officials apparently judged at the time that the harm inflicted did not rise to the level of an armed attack. But what would have happened and what reponse would we have *wanted* to see if the attacks had persisted, so that the harm done became more than a massive inconvenience and resulted instead in widespread death, personal injuries, immiseration, and loss of property? Would NATO *then* have been justified in undertaking some kind of retaliation? If so, what sort of attack would have been called for? For example, should the response have been limited to an "in-kind" cyberattack, or would a conventional, kinetic response have been justified?

At the opposite extreme, the Stuxnet/Olympic Games attacks allegedly undertaken by Israel and the United States on nuclear facilities in Iran were apparently aimed at stopping activities by Iran that clearly violated the UN nuclear nonproliferation treaty as well as defying express orders from the International Atomic Energy Commission to cease and desist their illegal nuclear program. Hence, the Stuxnet attack seemed to constitute a justified military response to a legitimate military threat. The attacks themselves appeared to have been undertaken in response to Iran's refusal to follow a direct order from the international community to abandon its illegal and unauthorized program and were aimed at purely military facilities or installations, not civilians. The damage done seemed proportional to the threat of of harm.

Similar conclusions can be drawn regarding the Russian conventional attacks and cyberattacks on Georgia. Despite Georgia's membership in NATO, the opposition to its government seemed legitimate; the aspiration of the Ossetians for independence was worthy of expression, and the Russian intervention, directed solely against military targets, seemed far more justified and proportional than the attack against Estonia (although, at the time of this writing, substantial harm and damage to civilians in Ossetia from the Russian–Georgian conflict remain unaddressed and uncompensated). These are the kind of political disputes, Carl von Clausewitz might remind us, that wars are designed to resolve.

Is there any legitimate basis for inferring that the Russian Federation, the United States, and other participatory nations are stumbling, blindly and inadvertently, toward a consensus about what behavior is permissible during a cyber conflict? I think that these four instances, along with some others, demonstrate that we *are* converging on a kind of normative policy of best practices and limitations on practices during a cyber conflict. The norms that nations appear to be recognizing and increasingly practicing [20] can be summarized as follows:

(1) Cyberattacks ought never to be directed against civilians, civilian objects, or civilian infrastructure.
(2) Cyberattacks should only be directed at legitimate military targets, with the twin aims of minimizing collateral damage or loss of life, and inflicting only as much damage as is commensurate with the degree of threat the target represents.
(3) A cyberattack can be deemed equivalent to a use of armed force whenever it inflicts harm or damage equivalent to what would be generated by a conventional attack. For instance, it does not matter whether the Iranian centrifuges were destroyed by bombs dropped from aircraft or

by a cyber weapon. We might call this "the principle of equivalence" or of "equivalent harm," which entails that whenever presented with a choice of means and methods of force to be directed against a justified military target, *the weapon that is capable of neutralizing the target with the least threat of collateral damage is to be selected whenever feasible*, consistent with the principles of "economy of force" and military necessity.

That leaves a lot unsettled, for example, the threshold of cyber harm that would justify use of force in retaliation and whether, when, and how to retaliate against a serious cyberattack with a conventional attack rather than a proportionate cyberattack. Note also in the Stuxnet case, the use of force was anticipatory or preemptive—indeed, it was really *preventive*, directed against a possible future threat, rather than a clear and present (imminent) danger. Does the advent of discriminate and relatively nondestructive cyber weapons *lower the threshold* against preventive war? Or do the same prohibitions on the use of conventional force apply? That remains to be seen. However, many observers, myself included, have argued that the types of preventive war involving cyber weapons are now more likely, and also likely to be tolerated, if not indeed fully justified.[21]

However we may subsequently choose to answer those additional questions, much has already apparently been accomplished. The process or method of discerning responsible norms of state behavior based on common experience and concerns proves to be far less presumptuous and far more inclusive than the practice of international law, at least as it was exhibited in the composition of the *Tallinn Manual*. Even more importantly, it is subject to far greater political success in governing state behavior. There is much that nations could agree on, mutually uphold, and enforce without any of the stakeholders feeling they had been ignored, bullied, or painted into an unacceptable corner. Moreover, some of the thorny questions still remaining to be addressed have been clarified, and a more acceptable methodology for future work demonstrated that is likely to succeed in other disputed areas as well, such as in governing the use of military robotics, or reigning in the use of large-data surveillance in cybersecurity, areas in which efforts at formal legal governance have likewise thus far failed.[22]

DO EMERGENT MORAL NORMS PROVIDE EFFECTIVE GOVERNANCE?

But, both lawyers and philosophers might object, how much normative force do these emergent and (allegedly) commonly agreed-on moral principles possess? And in any case, what guarantees do we have that countries like Russia and China (not to mention North Korea) will abide by these international norms of responsible state behavior? The answer, apparently, is that they possess about as much authority and sanction as does present-day international law—which is to say, not very much at all.

Most of international law, in contrast to domestic legislation, in fact consists of little more than a somewhat inflated attempt to write down, in treaties or statutes, principles that have been long been implicitly agreed to and practiced as norms. Were it not so, there would be little reason to write them down. And if they were being "dreamed up" and arbitrarily imposed, rather than emerging from a widespread and growing consensus regarding limits on acceptable practice, nations would tend to ignore or belittle such statutes as constituting "bad governance." Beyond the codification and sometimes helpful clarification of norms emerging from practice, international law accomplishes little on its own (if "accomplishment" is taken to mean the ability to coerce behavior unilaterally).

So-called killer robots (i.e., autonomous unmanned platforms that are lethally armed), for example, will only be regulated or outlawed when and if the nations that build and deploy them and the nations that are victimized by them agree to abide by a set of common principles governing their use. The same is true in the cyber domain. This is precisely how the "methodology of uncertainty" works, and how norms themselves emerge from practice and reflection on practice.

We may now have a basis for agreement on how to limit ourselves in carrying out cyber campaigns aimed at the effects-based attacks that are the equivalent of conventional war. But what about state-sponsored hacktivism and other large-scale acts of espionage and corporate theft? How does this retrospective analysis of more-or-less conventional warfare help us with the new forms of unarmed conflict that are now often termed "soft" war?

NOTES

1. Thus, following the Snowden revelations, the *China Daily* carried an editorial protesting, "For many Chinese, it is bizarre how Washington can continue to pose as the biggest cyberespionage victim and demand that others behave well." The editorial concluded that "by dividing cyberespionage into 'bad' and 'good' activities, Washington is trying to dictate the rules for global cyber domain, which is a public space." To be certain, it appears from this comment that the Chinese (or, more accurately, whoever composed and approved of this editorial) consider the cyber domain not merely a public space but a "commons," that is,

an arena or resource available to all without constraint or restriction. And they are objecting, not consenting, to the imposition of rules, norms, or values on that space. At face value, this seems to portray a very different conception of the cyber domain than that advanced by the United States and NATO countries. See David E. Sanger, "Differences on Cybertheft Complicate China Talks," *New York Times*, July 10, 2013, www.nytimes.com/2013/07/11/world/asia/differences-on-cybertheft-complicate-china-talks.html.

2. Based upon the history of "grazing commons" (a pasture for grazing cattle available to the public without charge) during the seventeenth and eighteenth centuries in England and the American colonies, this famous ecological metaphor is generalized to formulate the following principle: "Any natural resource available for general public use without restriction will inevitably be overused, consumed, and eventually destroyed." See Garrett Hardin, "The Tragedy of the Commons," *Science* 162, no. 3859 (1968): 1243–1248.

3. Interested readers will find this account thoroughly developed in my recent book, *Military Ethics: What Everyone Needs to Know* (New York: Oxford University Press, 2015), esp. chaps. 2 and 5.

4. While it does not unilaterally prove my point, the Honorable Michelle Markoff, deputy coordinator of the US State Department's Office of the Coordinator for Cyber Issues, reported in July 2015 that twenty nations, including Russia and China, had reached a strong consensus on norms regarding responsible state behavior in cyberspace, including three that had long been proposed by the United States: "protection of critical infrastructure, the protection of computer incident response teams, and cooperation between States in responding to appropriate requests in mitigating malicious cyber activity emanating from their territory." Markoff also noted, however, that "more robust statements on how international law applies were contested by a few key States, and we did not achieve all of the progress we would have liked in this area." This was a very diplomatic way of describing the fate of the *Tallinn Manual* (see chapter 2). See Michelle Markoff, "Advancing Norms of Responsible State Behavior in Cyberspace," *Dipnote: US State Department Official Blog*, July 9, 2015, https://blogs.state.gov/stories/2015/07/09/advancing-norms-responsible-state-behavior-cyberspace#sthash.6OZmB9K1.dpuf.

5. Diplomatic or ambassadorial immunity is by far the oldest of these norms, cited and honored (more or less) since ancient times but only codified and written into international law in 1963, as article 43 of the Vienna Convention on Consular Relations.

6. P. A. Yannakogeorgos and A. B. Lowther, "The Prospects for Cyber Deterrence: American Sponsorship of Global Norms," in *Conflict and Cooperation in Cyberspace: The Challenge to National Security*, ed. P. A. Yannakogeorgos and A. B. Lowther (Boca Raton, FL: Taylor & Francis, 2014), 49–77.

7. See the following works by George R. Lucas Jr., "Just War and Cyber Conflict." Annual Stutt Lecture on Ethics, U.S. Naval Academy, April 9, 2012, http://www.youtube.com/watch?v=hCj2ra6yzl0. Text at http://www.usna.edu/Ethics/_files/documents/Just%20War%20and%20Cyber%20War%20GR%20Lucas.pdf; "Can There Be an Ethical Cyberwar?," in Yannakogeorgos and Lowther, *Conflict and Cooperation in Cyberspace*, 195–210; "*Jus in silico*: Moral Restrictions on the Use of Cyber Warfare," in *The Routledge Handbook of War and Ethics*, ed. Fritz Allhoff, Nicholas G. Evans, and Adam Henschke (London: Routledge, 2013), 367–380; "Emerging Norms for Cyber Warfare" (keynote address,

"Conference on Ethics and Cyber Security," Center for Applied Philosophy and Practical Ethics, Australian National and Charles Sturtt Universities, Canberra, AU, August 5–6, 2013), http://philevents.org/event/show/11114; "Navigation, Aviation, 'Cyberation': Developing New Rules of the Road for the Cyber Domain," Inaugural Public Security Lecture, National Security College, Australian National University, Canberra, AU, August 7, 2013, http://www.youtube.com/watch?v=cs7RXAPzG84; "Permissible Preventive Cyber Warfare," *The Ethics of Information Warfare*, ed. Luciano Floridi and Mariarosaria Taddeo (Frankfurt: Springer, 2014), 73–82.

8. There are two distinct versions of this fallacy, one put forward by the Scottish Enlightenment philosopher David Hume, and one later described by the English moral philosopher G. E. Moore. It is Hume's version of the naturalistic fallacy, found in his *Treatise on Human Nature* (1739) rather than Moore's to which I refer, to wit: the presumably fallacious derivation of "ought" from "is." Moore, who coined the term "naturalistic fallacy," actually had a very different concern in mind—namely, that moral goodness was not a "natural kind," and so could not be defined in terms of something occurring in the natural world (such as pleasure or happiness), as utilitarian moral philosophers had attempted to do. Hume, by contrast, did not take his to be an absolute prohibition. Rather, he argued, one was always obliged to *demonstrate* how one might derive an "ought" from an "is" (something that R. M. Hare proceeded to do via deontic logic in the 1950s). I take Hume's turn to the histories of England to be a different kind of that required derivation, one that demonstrates precisely what I assert in this chapter: that agents' reflective analyses of their customary behaviors and best practices are the origins of norms and principles.

9. Whitehead's famous phrase is found in *Science and the Modern World* (New York: Macmillan, 1925), 16.

10. Interestingly, MacIntyre's clearest explicit accounts of what I term "the methodology of uncertainty" as well as of his derivation of norms from concrete practices, comes toward the end of his discovery and elucidation of that method, for example, in *Whose Justice? Which Rationality?* (South Bend, IN: University of Notre Dame Press, 1988), and even more in his Aquinas Lecture of 1990 at Marquette University. See Alasdair C. MacIntyre, *First Principles, Final Ends, and Contemporary Philosophical Issues* (Milwaukee, WI: Marquette University Press, 1990). MacIntyre offers a complete description of the method of "imperfect" sciences, in which the grounds or "first principles" of the science are not fully disclosed and are subject to provisional elucidation, as in ethics or politics as well as physics and biology, in sharp contrast to geometry, where the first principles are evident from the start. With these later works in hand, one reads with much greater insight MacIntyre's earlier works, such as the magisterial *After Virtue* (South Bend, IN: University of Notre Dame Press, 1981), in which the method of inquiry, and the commentary on the nature of emergent moral norms, in particular, is implicit in his critique of modern conceptions of morality. And, while MacIntyre clearly had no patience with Kant, it is interesting that the account by MacIntyre of Aristotle's development of this "methodology of uncertainty" (as I am calling it) is not unlike the emergence of Kant's methodology of "reflective teleological judgments." The latter is first discerned implicitly, while remaining formally undisclosed in a number of Kant's essays on history, political life, and the quest for peace in the mid-1780s, prior to being more systematically and explicitly elucidated in the second part of *The Critique of Judgment* (1790).

11. An excellent account of the nuclear nonproliferation case, alongside other examples of "emergent norms" of responsible state behavior in development and use of weapons of war that perfectly illustrate the process I am describing here, is found in Peter B. Postma, "Regulating Lethal Autonomous Robots in Unconventional Warfare," *University of St. Thomas Law Journal* 11, no. 2 (2015): 300–330.

12. For example, see Albert R. Jonson and Stephen Toulmin, *The Abuse of Casuisty* (Berkeley: University of California Press, 1990), for an account of case-based legal and moral reasoning that offers accounts of unusual and sometimes invalid application of principles based on precedent to new cases.

13. The "Moore" is Gordon Moore, founder and CEO of Intel Corp. In keeping with the pace of miniaturization of transistors and the increase of the number that can be included upon a single silicon chip of a given size, Moore's Law now holds that the pace of technological change doubles every eighteen to twenty-four months, helping to explain why we persistently feel so overwhelmed by rapid transformations in the cyber domain.

14. This debate occurs in the *Journal of Military Ethics* primarily between Chris Eberle, Edward Barrett, and myself. See Edward Barrett, "Warfare in a New Domain: The Ethics of Military Cyber Operations," *Journal of Military Ethics* 12, no. 1 (2013): 4–17; Christopher Eberle, "Just War and Cyber War," *Journal of Military Ethics* 12, no. 1 (2013): 54–67; and my response to both in "Ethics and Cyber Conflict: A Review of Recent Work," *Journal of Military Ethics* 13, no. 1 (2014): 20–31. Eberle, in particular, thinks cyber activities like infrastructure backdoors and logic bombs are comparable to the building and positioning of strategic nuclear weapons, which is not subject to retaliation unless the weapons are actually used. I challenge that analogy on the basis of the Cuban missile crisis, and also find grounds to compare this more to the actions of foreign agents in planting actual explosives for future detonation on the United States' civil infrastructure in the event of the outbreak of hostilities. The latter strikes me both as closer to what cyber trapdoors and Trojan horses really represent in way of a threat that is more immediate, serious, and thus more amenable to retaliation, than the development and placement of nuclear weapons. But this is all obviously far from settled.

15. Jeffrey Carr offers additional counts of these four and a number of others that are clearly espionage, not war. See Jeffrey Carr, *Inside Cyber Warfare: Mapping the Cyber Underworld*, 2nd ed. (Sebastapol, CA: O'Reilly Media, 2011). Ryan Jenkins offers a decisive rebuttal to the absurd claim that Stuxnet, constructed of computer software, cannot constitute a use of physical force that would fall under legal regimes governing the use of force in armed conflict. See Ryan Jenkins, "Is Stuxnet Physical? Does It Matter?," *Journal of Military Ethics* 12, no. 1 (2013): 68–79. The more interesting feature, given that it constitutes the equivalent of the use of force in terms of physical effects, is that it is a preemptive (actually, a preventive) use of force, which is certainly outside existing legal regimes but can be morally justified. See the continuing discussion of preventive war generally in Deen K. Chatterjee, ed., *The Ethics of Preventive War* (New York: Cambridge University Press, 2013).

16. My earlier analysis of the significance of these four cyber events can be found in "*Jus in Silico*: Moral Restrictions on the Use of Cyber Warfare," in Allhoff, Evans, and Henschke, *Routledge Handbook of War and Ethics*, 367–380.

17. Cyber weapons appear, by contrast, to have played a less prominent role in the separatist armed conflicts in eastern Ukraine, also carried out with Russian support. The hacking collective CyberBerkut, which is allegedly affiliated with the Russian Federation, carried out a series of attacks apparently intended to disrupt the voting in Ukraine's presidential election in 2014. That attack failed to derail the election. Similar attacks on Ukrainian government websites have continued intermittently, but without the impact of the Georgian attacks. Notwithstanding, note the choice of wording in the news headline reporting the Ukranian attacks: Margaret Coker and Paul Sonne, "Cyberwar's Hottest Front," *Wall Street Journal*, November 10, 2015, A1, 12.

18. See George R. Lucas, Jr., "Permissible Preventive Cyber Warfare," in *The Ethics of Information Warfare*, ed. Luciano Floridi and Mariarosaria Taddeo (Amsterdam: Springer, 2014), 73–82. See the subsequent account by Singer and Friedman, *Cybersecurity and Cyberwar*.

19. See David E. Graham, "Cyber Threats and the Law of War," *Journal of National Security Law* 4, no. 1 (2010): 87–102; and Michael N. Schmitt, "Cyber Operations and the *Jus in Bello*: Key Issues," *U.S. Naval War College International Law Studies*, 87 (2011): 89–110. Both advance forms of this argument.

20. Once again, I cannot help but note that these basic principles that I first laid out in the immediate aftermath of these four incidents seem to have been largely (re)affirmed by the twenty nations, including Russia and China, that participated with the United States in discussions on responsible state behavior in the cyber domain, as reported in Markoff, "Advancing Norms." *This really is* how this emergent norm process unfolds.

21. See Lucas, "Permissible Preventive Cyber Warfare," in Floridi and Taddeo, *The Ethics of Information Warfare*, 73–82.

22. My proposed precepts for the governance of lethal autonomous systems, which attempt to summarize areas of consensus following nearly a decade of contentious public debate on this topic, can be found at the end of George R. Lucas, Jr., "Automated Warfare," *Stanford Law and Policy Review* 25, no. 2 (2014): 1–23. The precepts are somewhat lengthy; they involve knowledge of and consent to certain principles governing research, development, manufacture, and use, and specify the nature of criminal liability for willful violations.

Emerging norms for cyber surveillance on the basis of the recent Snowden/NSA controversy can be found at the end of George R. Lucas, Jr., "NSA Management Directive #424: Secrecy and Privacy in the Aftermath of Snowden," *Journal of Ethics and International Affairs* 28, no. 1 (2014): 29–38. These are similar to those constraining cyber conflict generally, but contain procedures for obtaining informed consent on the part the general public surveilled.

CHAPTER 6

Privacy, Anonymity, and the Rise of State-Sponsored Hacktivism

One weakness in Aristotle's methodology, unfortunately, is that it is retrodictive: inherently backward looking and wholly reliant on what has historically transpired in the past. The nineteenth-century German Romantic philosopher Georg Wilhelm Friedrich Hegel (who was deeply indebted to Aristotle) stated the problem succinctly at the conclusion of his lectures on the history of philosophy: "nur bis hierher hat daβ Bewusstsein gekommen"—whatever truth or wisdom we can glean from the past only extends as far as our present moment in time and history. Such comprehension is enlightening, to be sure, but with no authoritative predictive power.

In chapter 5, I tried to construct what Alasdair MacIntyre terms a "master narrative" of cyber conflict, that is, an all-encompassing story of the experience of cyber conflict up to this point that tries to encompass all known facts and disputes in as coherent, inclusive, and plausible a sequence as possible. A master narrative endeavors to take full account of all rival conceptions (like those of Rid, Clarke, Dipert, Singer, Harris, Schmitt, and other writers, journalists, scholars, and cyber experts), addressing and encompassing the concerns they raise, while analyzing additional data that they either ignore or else cannot adequately incorporate within their own interpretive frameworks.

The goal of assembling a master narrative is *verisimilitude*. This is demonstrated in the present instance by our narrative's ability to help us distinguish between cyberwar and more general cyber conflict, and to say with some confidence which is which and what laws or norms apply to each. This is among the problems that frustrate or undermine the claims to plausibility of alternative competing narratives, tending to render them less reliable as comprehensive and accurate accounts. In contrast to the purely legal formulations of cyber conflict, for example, the account of e-mergent norms can offer guidance for effective governance in situations in the cyber domain that are not strongly coupled to the paradigm of the nation-state, and so are likely to be acceptable to nations and stakeholders who reject the exclusively legal accounts. Finally, a master narrative of cyber conflict can explain the developments in technology and practice to this stage, and why they have not (yet) turned out to be as dire as first predicted.

What neither these rival narratives nor Aristotle's master narrative can handle well, however, is the foreword-looking element of novelty and surprise. All such retrodictive accounts are thus liable to be overtaken by events.

EMERGENT NORMS AND THE RISE OF STATE-SPONSORED HACKTIVISM

The cyber events that followed the Stuxnet attack have taken a surprising turn, wholly unanticipated by the experts and largely inexplicable in terms of the just war narrative. That unexpected turn takes us back to the recent development with which we began—namely, away from cataclysmic apocalyptic effects-based physical destruction and toward hacktivism, vandalism, and crime—even (as in the North Korean case) petty, petulant crime—carried out by state agents.

We can now say, to our great relief, that the United States is not currently threatening to attack the Three Gorges Dam, while the Chinese and North Koreans for their part have not yet attempted to destroy the Hoover and Grand Canyon dams. Likewise, the massive cyber-driven blackouts of power grids in Brazil, North America, and portions of Western Europe, so prevalent only a few years ago, have largely ceased.[1] No airplanes have yet fallen from the sky and no trains have been derailed because of cyber-attacks (although several air traffic control outages have been caused by aging equipment, and several tragic and destructive freight train derailments have occurred, including loss of life, through the normal, random incompetence of operators attempting to manage an overtaxed and decaying rail transportation infrastructure).[2]

Instead of the threat of wholesale interstate cyber warfare receding, it has taken an entirely new form and direction in which reasonable constraints seem to play no role. State-sponsored hacktivism is the new face of warfare in the twenty-first century—carried out with "weapons of mass disruption" rather than weapons of mass destruction.

One reason for this transformation is practical. Early on, I dismissed out of hand the prospect that terrorists or alienated teenagers could produce weapons like Stuxnet or single-handedly take down the Hoover Dam. They have instead found ways to carry out lesser forms of mischief that end up having nearly as much political impact as effects-based cyberattacks. Less technologically sophisticated nations, such as Iran and North Korea, which do not yet have the capacity to develop a Stuxnet, have found it far easier to expand and improve upon the methodologies of individual and nonstate cyber hackers.

Another reason for the transformation stems from the attribution problem. Cyber forensic capabilities have improved dramatically over the past several years. It is really not possible for large-scale operations like Olympic Games to remain anonymous for very long. Clever cybersecurity experts will sooner or later track them down. Shane Harris, in his book *@War*, for example, offers compelling case studies of efforts by the FBI, allied nations, the NSA, and other information intelligence bodies over the last decade to get to the bottom of even the cleverest and most well-disguised attacks.[3] But such efforts are difficult, time-consuming, and costly. The advantage, as the cybersecurity experts themselves admit, always lies with "the offense."

State-sponsored hacktivism could be described as an offensive tactic that lies just under the threshold of full attribution and response. It is worth it to understand what damage was suffered in such an attack, where it came from, and what enemy capabilities the attack demonstrated. But it is not always clear whether an attack is worth "going to the mat for," when its perpetrators publicly deny any responsibility or accountability for it. While the Department of Defense document on cybersecurity strategy, released in 2012, threatened in effect to "put a missile down someone's smoke-stack"[4] for carrying out such attacks, it is not at all clear that the hack of Sony Pictures or the theft of twenty-two million OPM personnel files warranted such a response. As we saw earlier, the United States decided not to retaliate against China for the OPM hack, even though it was virtually certain it had been carried out by the People's Liberation Army. The best we can do in most cases is to

(1) try our best (both individuals and organizations) to avoid being victimized through the continuing installation and improvement of robust defensive security measures;

(2) have our own defense forces retaliate in kind to such attacks, when possible, to try to deter future attacks; or

(3) *adopt an offensive cyber posture ourselves*, as a national defense strategy designed to preempt future attacks before they occur.

It is the third strategy of national self-defense that has generated the most public consternation and alarm.

THE CUNNING OF HISTORY

The slightly ominous phrase "the cunning of history," found in Hegel, captures perfectly the dilemma we face now. Human beings may propose, experiment, hypothesize, and reflect on their activities to try to make some sense out of them. But history, like some sort of mysterious, independent, self-conscious entity (one that Hegel termed "Absolute Spirit"), seems to have its own intentionality, purpose, and goals, which are realized unwittingly instead through human actions.

While we proposed at first to disadvantage rivals with our technological superiority in cyberspace, and then gradually came, through the experience of conflict, to enunciate and put forth reasonable standards of good behavior and restraint, history itself has other plans. We find ourselves, instead, confronted with a new form—"soft," "unarmed" warfare—that we unwittingly developed and let loose into the world precisely through these technological innovations.

It is a dishearteningly familiar old story, dressed up in the latest technological garb: we have made ourselves more vulnerable through our development and increasing reliance on the IOT. Adversarial and rogue states can exploit these vulnerabilities just below the level of armed conflict by exploiting the inevitable security weaknesses in smart phones, drones, automated industrial processes, traffic signals, and computerized cars, among many other things. Our most private beliefs, opinions, and activities can be unearthed and exposed, sometimes after decades, to ruin careers and destroy lives.[5] If conventional war means "killing people and breaking things," as Clausewitz maintained—to destroy the enemy's army, occupy his cities, and break his will to fight—state-sponsored hacktivism, the main weapon in this new "soft" war, does all this nearly as well simply by immobilizing and confusing the enemy's army, ruining the lives and careers of its citizens (leading some of them to kill themselves), and thereby breaking the enemy's will to fight just as effectively as conventional war. In contrast to the hopeful moral historical narrative of emergent norms in chapter 5, it seems as if the kind of unbridled and unscrupulous competition unwittingly licensed by our stubborn adherence to folk morality has turned on us with a vengeance. Rather than these self-centered or culturally relative conceptions of ethics serving to increase tolerance and understanding of our behaviors, they have helped instead to foster social conformity, political oppression, and widespread personal fear.[6] To borrow the grim imagery of *The Circle*, Dave Egger's apocalyptic novel about the ultimate fate of the "Google culture," it is as if a great, transparent, ravenous shark has run amok in our midst, devouring everything that is personal, unique, or significant about human social life, and ultimately excreting it uniformly as "a thin grey ash."[7] If this is history's ultimate purpose and destiny for us in the cyber age, it results in a dystopian nightmare, rather than in either the Aristotelian vision of cultural flourishing or the gradual evolution of political democracy and individual human freedom that Hegel had portrayed as "the End of History" in his lectures on the *Philosophy of History*.

PERMISSIBLE PREVENTIVE CYBER SELF-DEFENSE

Recall that it is a shared conception of the Good, a common desire for something more substantial than anarchy, that is missing in citizens of the cyber domain. So is there any reason to hope that state-sponsored hacktivism and soft war present an occasion for this positive and favorable moral evolution?

There is nothing "inevitable" about this. We are discussing real people and the real history their actions and choices generate, not some metaphysical Hegelian force that pushes events into a preconceived pattern. There is no divine providence in our account, only the hope that, in the end, Reason (and what Abraham Lincoln appealed to as "better Angels of our Nature") can still prevail.

I contend that the latest form of that very "unsocial sociability" and conflict of desires that Immanuel Kant originally described as the drivers of history and cultural evolution can be discerned in the current tension between our collective (social) desire for security and well-being, and our individual desires for privacy and anonymity. Both are rational, reasonable desires, and each constitutes a legitimate goal. But these twin goals stand in marked tension with one another.

I believe we need to confront the possibility that some dimensions of these desires—for anonymity, in addition to personal privacy, in the cyber domain—are misplaced, misconceived, and fundamentally mistaken. While we can defend a right to privacy in the cyber domain, for example, I do not believe that we can or should continue to defend the cyber citizen's demand for a "right to anonymity" as well. Anonymity, in marked contrast to privacy, is unhealthy and unworthy and needs to be exposed for what it really is in this new context of crisis, so that (along with the last vestiges of folk morality) it can be expunged and repudiated.

To consider how and why this is so, let us return to a vignette with which we began: the massive, unprecedented attack on major US financial institutions carried out by the so-called Cyber Fighters of Izz al-Din al-Qassam. Recall the portrayal of this attack through reliance on the NSA's hitherto top-secret software program, Treasure Map. How did the NSA know this attack was spoofed? How were they trying to defend against it?

The answer, of course, is their controversial big-data collection and surveillance effort: the Enterprise Knowledge System, with its PRiSM database in Utah and its XKeyscore threat-analysis algorithm—in short, all the things we learned about through the revelations of the NSA contractor-turned-whistleblower Edward Snowden. To complete our examination of the role of ethics and emergent moral norms in the quest for greater individual and national security in the face of relentless state-sponsored hacktivism, we will need to turn to these topics and episodes. We need, that is, to explore the real significance of Snowden's revelations and ponder carefully the threats posed to personal privacy and anonymity by our simultaneous quest for cybersecurity.

PRIVACY, ANONYMITY, AND THE SECTORS OF VULNERABILITY

We have before us at present a very controversial and unresolved question: To what degree are rank-and-file citizens of democratic nations willing to surrender some of their privacy to protect themselves collectively against cyber snooping, Internet criminals, corporate espionage, and cyberattacks on their nation's power grid or air traffic control systems? Would not it behoove any nation and its citizens to be willing to enact reasonable precautions for the sake of greater security now, so that they can avoid having to make far more difficult decisions later, regarding, for example, the conventional kinetic military-force retaliation that cyberattacks, cyber harm, and self-defense might require?

In his State of the Union address on February 12, 2013, President Barack Obama pleaded for legislation that would address the security threats to vital national infrastructure posed by cyberattacks while simultaneously protecting the privacy of individual US citizens. His was only one prominent voice in a rising chorus of concern being expressed by political and military leaders in Europe, including the United Kingdom and elsewhere, lamenting the explosion of military and industrial cyberespionage; the theft of state secrets and technological innovations; and the increasing vulnerability of the world's energy, financial, and transportation sectors to potentially devastating cyberattacks.

Our society's answer to this question depends, of course, on what measures the proponents of greater Internet security might actually require. There are three main sectors of vulnerability in any nation's cyber domain: (1) government and military; (2) industrial (including energy, finance, communications and transportation); and (3) individual users in the civilian or private sector, who may interact in myriad ways with either of the two foregoing sectors, as well as with each other.

As we now know, by far the greatest ongoing and persistent vulnerabilities come from individual users in the last sector. For example, it was an individual lab technician who inadvertently spread the Stuxnet worm worldwide.[1] As in epidemiology, the vector of infection of a computer virus—and for that matter, the ability of an enemy agent to infect and control individual computers as zombies in a massive botnet—is almost entirely a matter of one infected, unprotected individual user inadvertently spreading the virus to other unsuspecting and unprotected users.

Most national militaries, military agencies, and national government agencies have moved over the past several years to adopt more-secure systems and policies, either because they have experienced attacks themselves or have observed serious national security breaches in allied nations. Private and quasi-national industries, such as utilities, transportation, communication, and finance, have made preliminary strides to improve their information security but are reluctant to take more-decisive measures that would prove costly and inconvenient to clients and customers. This is an area that will almost certainly require government intervention, legislation, and perhaps funding.

Apart from the costs and inconvenience to private industry, the obstacle constantly cited by political leaders in democratic and rights-respecting states is the need to protect individual privacy. Ironically, it is the individual, private sector of the cyber domain that is most insistent on privacy, even though that sector constitutes the source of the greatest remaining vulnerability of any nation to a cyberattack.

CYBER SECURITY MEASURES FOR INDIVIDUALS

Two factors thus stand in the way of enhanced security: (1) the increased costs of such measures and (2) the intrusions on individual privacy that might result. Figuring out how to bear the costs and how to distribute the resulting financial and administrative burdens of enhanced security in the industrial sector are strictly matters of public policy that, on their face, appear amenable to rational solution. Governments might provide legislative impetus accompanied with basic financial incentives (through the tax system, for example), while the remaining costs could be apportioned to the industries and their paying customers, who would both benefit from enhanced security measures.

The dilemma of individual privacy, however, will not be so easily solved. As noted earlier, this concern is confined almost exclusively to the "third sector" of the cyber domain. Individuals can have no reasonable expectation of privacy in either of the first two sectors—for example, when as employees, they are using military, government, or even industrial resources to conduct official business. It is only when individuals are communicating privately with one another, handling their personal financial affairs, perhaps paying their annual taxes, or engaging in e-commerce on the Internet that the concern for privacy becomes an issue. We do not want our purchases, preferences, finances, or private communications with friends, family, and loved ones revealed or made public or to become subject to scrutiny by agents of the nation's security sector. This is, I believe, the most difficult obstacle to cybersecurity that thoughtful individuals and policymakers must seek to address.

One promising avenue of discussion might be to clarify more precisely *just what dimensions of privacy are at risk* in the quest for greater cybersecurity and to further determine just how great that risk actually is. It actually proves to be a far less difficult and abstract exercise than we might have feared when we stop to consider the actual privacy implications of some of the concrete and feasible security measures that have been proposed.

So, for example: in addition to the numerous measures instituted or proposed in the government and private industrial sectors (none of which pose immediate threats to individual privacy), two security proposals have been advanced for individual Internet users. Both are relatively straightforward to operationalize and, if implemented, promise to be extremely effective. Yet both are vehemently opposed by critics.

The first proposal would require that Internet service providers (ISPs), such as Verizon, Comcast, Sympatico, or Orange, verify, upon an individual's initial logon connection, or "handshake," with the provider, that the user has installed the latest security software (currently available from most ISPs at no charge, for recommended but voluntary installation). Under this regime, an unsafe or unsecured individual user would not be permitted public access to the "information superhighway," just as it is prohibited to drive an unsafe vehicle on public thoroughfares.

Secondly, and even more controversially, a nation's intelligence and surveillance architecture, such as that of the NSA in the United States, could be harnessed to institute routine, random "packet sniffing," using mathematical algorithms to scan the so-called metadata accompanying the enormous volume of a nation's email and other Internet traffic, especially at key trunk points of entry into the national system, for abnormal or suspicious patterns of communication. This does not involve a human user reading or scanning the contents of those communications. Instead, a complex mathematical algorithm essentially "data-mines" the traffic for patterns of contact: for example, an IP address in a country that is receiving an unusually large volume of communications from three international sites suspected of being used by terrorists. In this instance, the pattern would be flagged for human scrutiny. If it appeared that international terrorists might be communicating with the site of a financier in the host country, a warrant would be sought to examine the contents of the communications further, to see if money was flowing from an agent or organization in the host country to finance international terrorist operations.

As stated, however, both measures were strenuously resisted by Internet privacy advocates (even before Snowden's revelations) as constituting or threatening serious violations of individual privacy. If, critics argue, even in an allegedly democratic, rights-respecting country like the United States, the FBI is already able to intercept and examine the private correspondence of even powerful individuals such as the director of the Central Intelligence Agency and the Commanding Officer of NATO's ISAF forces in Afghanistan (as was widely publicized in November of 2012),[8] how is any ordinary citizen safe against intrusions by government agencies into their private lives if these cybersecurity measures are enacted?

PRIVACY VERSUS ANONYMITY

Prior to the Snowden fiasco, the battle lines had shaped up largely as a conflict between those in the national security and intelligence communities who favor greater security and control of the Internet and those who believe that cyber vulnerability is exaggerated and that such measures are little more than the ongoing attempt by the institutions and agencies of government to infringe on individual privacy and liberty.

We will never be able to resolve this issue until we first learn to distinguish legitimate privacy from anonymity—something entirely different. Much of the seemingly intractable controversy rests upon the confusion or conflation of these concepts. If we can sort out that confusion, I believe we might, together, more calmly agree on a reasonable roadmap toward greater cybersecurity—one that leaves our privacy and essential personal liberties fully intact.

Privacy itself seldom involves attempts to cloak one's actions from public scrutiny, let alone seek to avoid responsibility or accountability for the legality, moral propriety, or harmful consequences of one's actions. Privacy is merely a demand that the requirements for public security and individual accountability *not spill over into otherwise unreasonable intrusions into one's personal beliefs or activities that have little or no relevance or consequences for the public.* The concern over the FBI's investigation a few years ago of the private email correspondence of two prominent US government officials was, in the end, over whether it had been warranted by any threat to national security or potential breach of their public duties that this correspondence might reveal. Privacy, therefore, as the right (or claim) of noninterference in personal thoughts and actions is not, and ought not to be, viewed with suspicion.

The same is decidedly *not* the case with anonymity. In general, claims of anonymity for individuals mirror the claims of governments and organizations to secrecy and lack of transparency that arouse public suspicion and hostility because they are generally thought to be a license to hide possible mistakes, mischief, violations of law, or even outright corruption. Demands for anonymity serve principally to cloak our activities in order to evade detection and, by extension, avoid being held accountable for them. As such, demands for anonymity should always be viewed, prima facie, with the deepest skepticism and suspicion.

The infamous shepherd, Gyges, in book 2 of Plato's *Republic*, did not acquire and use his "magic ring" in order to protect his privacy but to gain the capacity for complete anonymity and thereby escape all accountability for the consequences of his subsequent unscrupulous actions. In that spirit, NATO's much-heralded anticorruption "Building Integrity"[9] campaign among its partner nations and allies followed the anticorruption organization "Transparency International" in stressing "integrity, transparency, and accountability" as the watchwords for the conduct for individuals in government and industry. Anonymity, however, is the political opposite of transparency. And the emphasis on anonymity among Internet users is little more than an invitation to escape accountability and to act with impunity. It tends to undermine, rather than to promote, integrity.

To state the contrast with the utmost clarity: anonymity involves the desire to *hide the identity* of the perpetrator of actions that may have *grave and harmful public consequences*, while privacy is merely the demand that the public not interfere in an individual's thoughts or actions *that have no practical public consequences* or significance whatsoever.[10] That is an enormous conceptual difference. And it is important to clarify this difference, inasmuch as most demands for Internet privacy turn out to be demands for anonymity instead—even to the point of asserting, with a straight face, that anonymity itself is a right.

The assertion that everyone has a fundamental right to anonymity over and above their right to privacy is an astonishing claim—unprecedented and, with one important exception, almost entirely without justification. The attempts of a self-proclaimed hacktivist to steal data or reveal private or confidential information of another person or entity, or to deface or destroy an organization's website—let alone the Internet activities of a pedophile—are not at all equivalent to the reasonable desire of an individual consumer not to have his or her product preferences captured by commercial surveillance software or cellphone apps and divulged without permission to commercial and business organizations for purposes of targeted marketing.

Privacy is a broad demand that society, commerce, and the government stay out of personal matters that are *none of their business*. Anonymity, by contrast, is a very focused demand that society and governments be prevented from discerning, even under tightly controlled legal conditions, the identity of individuals who appear to be engaged in sinister and malevolent activities—*whose deterrence is everyone's business*.

Proponents of anonymity do not seek to protect their own or others' privacy. Instead, *they seek to hide their very identities* in order to escape accountability for their actions, believing, falsely, that, in cyberspace, unlike physical space, they are entitled to do whatever they please, to whomever they please, without fear of consequences.

A LIMITED JUSTIFICATION FOR ANONYMITY

The general benign attitude toward anonymity (and its prospects for abuse) must be vigorously contested, especially in light of the grave consequences of the obstacles it otherwise presents for effective cybersecurity. As a general rule, we must come to recognize that, with one important political exception, *there is no legally justified or morally legitimate activity pursued anonymously that could not just as well be pursued with full transparency and disclosure in public.*

That sole exception to this general rule pertains to a relatively few but very well-defined contexts characterized by radically unequal distributions of political power.[11] Individual citizens in ruthless, repressive totalitarian societies that don't tolerate political dissent constitute the clearest example of such asymmetries of power. Citizens in these countries might reasonably lay claim to anonymity or desire to preserve their anonymity on the Internet in order to be able to express their political opinions without fear of reprisal.

In such cases (which unfortunately are widespread), it is never anonymity for its own sake that such individuals claim is their right but *protection against persecution and unjustified infringement of their other authentic rights*, including both their legitimate rights to privacy and to freedom of expression. Contrast this with the case of members of the vigilante group Anonymous, whose members do not fear persecution: rather, they are the self-appointed persecutors. They wish to avoid being held accountable by those whom they decide to persecute or by agents of the governments of the jurisdictions in which their illegal activity occurs.

A second, familiar example of this sole exception pertains to employees in government or large industries who are engaged in morally justifiable whistleblowing in an attempt to expose corrupt or dangerous practices within their organization, or even to express reasonable dissent from established policies. Note, however, that even in this generally justifiable exception of unequal power relationships, anonymity still can be abused by unscrupulous employees in morally unjustifiable attempts to leak confidential information or slander the reputations of supervisors or fellow employees when there is no evidence of actual wrongdoing. Thus, even in these cases, claims for the protection of anonymity ought to be viewed with cautious suspicion.

It is a measure of the extreme irony of this otherwise cynical and pernicious equivocation that anarchist and hacktivist Internet groups like Anonymous and WikiLeaks demand, and attempt on their own recognizance to enforce, a degree of transparency on the part of governments and the public that they refuse to acknowledge or practice themselves. The activities of both groups might be usefully contrasted with those of former US Defense Department consultant and military analyst Daniel Ellsberg when he released the "Pentagon Papers" in 1971.[12]

Mr. Ellsberg made no claims to a right of anonymity. His anonymity, in any case, could have easily been ensured had he simply concealed his identity when he passed along classified government documents to the major newspapers. Neither he nor his severest critics claimed that his actions had anything to do with personal privacy. Instead, his was an act of civil disobedience; Ellsburg defied US law regarding the custody of classified documents in order to blow the whistle on covert and questionable military activities about which he firmly believed the general public had every right to know.

His public act (even for many who disagreed with his judgment) was an act of courage and principle.

The actions of Anonymous and WikiLeaks, by contrast, often strike the public merely as acts of random vandalism, more akin to teenagers spray-painting graffiti on public buildings—little more than a public nuisance, save when the lives and welfare of innocent persons are inadvertently and thoughtlessly placed at risk—or, even worse, vigilantism, with all the wrongful harm and injustice that routinely accompanies such one-sided and self-appointed "law enforcement."

RESTRICTING ANONYMITY WHILE PRESERVING PRIVACY

The distinction between privacy and anonymity is important, primarily because it is not the violation of individual privacy but a somewhat greater restriction on individual *anonymity* that greater Internet security requires. The login handshake and email packet sniffing merely disclose the identity of the communicators, not the content of their communications, and so override user anonymity without necessarily compromising privacy. We should ask whether this in itself constitutes an unprecedented or harmful thing.

For example, the content of the letter I write and send through conventional mail is considered private, and therefore the letter is not to be opened or inspected without my consent—or without a warrant from law enforcement authorities, obtained based on substantive evidence and submitted to an independent judiciary. However, my name is on the envelope, identifying me as the letter writer to anyone who handles it. I have a right to privacy regarding the content of that piece of mail, but I am not anonymous as the correspondent. A government's postal workers are perfectly within their rights and, in fact, have a public obligation to report any suspicious behavior on my part (such as addressing the letter to known terrorists, or receiving mail from known or suspected purveyors of pedophilic materials) to the appropriate authorities, who must then seek additional evidence in order to justify any further attempts to examine my mail more closely.

I cite this familiar and relatively uncontroversial example because, by analogy, the email and automated data packet sniffing long sought by government works exactly the same way: the contents of my emails are not revealed. Rather, picket-sniffing software detects only suspicious patterns of contact.

As we learned during the Snowden affair, when these patterns are detected or suspected, the investigating authorities are then required to go through an additional, presumably rigorous and adversarial, screening or vetting procedure in order to obtain any further evidence. Assuming the requisite degree of rigorous adversarial review, these procedures help to ensure that due process and responsible diligence have been followed when allowing authorities to undertake a closer and more thorough investigation of the significance of these patterns, precisely in order to protect my right of privacy from such investigation or intrusion.

Such controls are more than sufficient to deter or frustrate criminals or spies, or to detect terrorist networks, without any appreciable limitation on, or invasion of, any individual's privacy. In fact, such security measures on the Internet would do little more than put in place in that domain the kind of security and safeguards we already have in place with respect to conventional mail delivery, as well as with the transportation of goods and services nationwide.

What could be wrong with that?

NEW "RULES OF THE ROAD" FOR CYBER NAVIGATION

Likewise, the handshake between my private computer and a public ISP does not violate my privacy, though it surely does compromise my anonymity. Yet to permit the ISP to scan my PC in order to detect the presence (or absence) of appropriate security software before it grants me access to the Internet is hardly different from requiring that people who want to drive a car obtain a driver's license and equip their cars with safety equipment, like brake lights and seat belts, before driving on public roadways. In both cases, this very modest abrogation of their privacy and personal liberty serves both their own safety and security interests and those of others.

Indeed, the confused and often exaggerated concerns about the loss of individual privacy at the expense of public safety closely resemble the concerns regarding the proper use of highways and public thoroughfares at the dawn of the automobile age in the late nineteenth and early twentieth centuries. Attempts to regulate the presumed privacy and freedom of individuals to travel in whatever conveyance they pleased, obeying whatever rules of the road they chose to acknowledge, were likewise strenuously resisted at first. As a result, public thoroughfares in Europe and America at the dawn of the twentieth century resembled the information superhighway at the dawn of the twenty-first: lawless frontiers in which each individual asserted his rights to freedom and privacy regardless of the harm posed to others.

Traffic regulations, however, proved not to be a violation of privacy or an unwarranted limitation of individual freedom. Simply demanding that all conveyances on public highways be equipped with safety equipment, and operated by trained and licensed drivers, obeying traffic rules designed largely for their own and public safety served the best interests of all concerned, without sacrificing the most salient features of privacy and freedom of action. Indeed, one might plausibly claim that both individual liberty and personal privacy are enhanced by these innovations. I suspect the same would prove true with Internet privacy and freedom of action were more-responsible security measures enacted for the security of its users.

Notwithstanding the present climate of hysteria, fear, and confusion, especially following Snowden's revelations, one might still hope that reasonable security constraints proposed or currently in place for cyberspace solely for purposes of safety and security will meet with similar acceptance. There is otherwise very little way to defend effectively against further state-sponsored hacktivism, unless we are willing either to enact or, despite our outrage over the NSA's deception, continue such policies and procedures.

In the realm of individual behavior in cyberspace, we have yet to gain widespread public support for enhanced security measures. In the wake of the Snowden revelations, we are faced instead with a widespread demand to dismantle such security as we now have in place. And this, in turn, is because, despite public pronouncements to the contrary, the United States and its four long-standing intelligence allies—Canada, the United Kingdom, Australia, and New Zealand[13]—had apparently put even more stringent measures of surveillance and data collection in place than they had dared admit to the public, attempting to establish a widespread covert program of anticipatory self-defense.

What we need to do now is examine what we have learned about these programs, and about whether the secrecy with which they were instituted serves, after all, to justify the public concern that the State can never be sufficiently trusted for us to give up our anonymity in cyberspace, even at the cost of having to endure cyberbullies, trolls, and state-sponsored hacktivism.[14]

NOTES

1. To be sure, an unknown person or persons shot up seventeen transformers in a regional power substation in San Jose, California, in April 2013. But the attack has never been solved, or repeated. See Rebecca Smith, "Assault on California Power Station Raises Alarm on Potential for Terrorism," *Wall Street Journal*, February 5, 2014, http://www.wsj.com/articles/SB1000142405270230485110457 9359141941621778. A massive power outage in Ukraine in early 2016 has been attributed to Russian cyberattackers. Despite earlier attributions of such attacks

elsewhere in the world, this one is now being touted as the "first documented case" of a power outage caused by a cyberattack. See Andrea Peterson, "Hackers Caused a Blackout for the First Time, Researchers Say," *Washington Post*, January 5, 2016, https://www.washingtonpost.com/news/the-switch/wp/2016/01/05/hackers-caused-a-blackout-for-the-first-time-researchers-say/ (accessed May 27, 2016). Meanwhile, some massive power-grid outages, such as those reported in Brazil in 2005 and 2007, were initially described on CBS's *60 Minutes* on November 6, 2009, as having been caused by cyberattacks. See http://www.cbsnews.com/news/cyber-war-sabotaging-the-system-06-11-2009/ (accessed May 27, 2016). But these allegations were denied by Brazilian officials three days later. See Marcello Soares, "Brazilian Blackout Traced to Sooty Insulators, Not Hackers," *Wired*, November 9, 2009, https://www.wired.com/2009/11/brazil_blackout/ (accessed May 27, 2016).

2. Thus CIA director John O. Brennan remarked in an interview on national television that countries that have this effects-based capability do not appear to have the intention of using it at present, whereas those adversaries that would be delighted to carry out such devastating attacks do not appear to have the capability, for the moment. The latter deficiency is apparently what has led to the rise in state-sponsored hacktivism as the more technically feasible tactic. See Scott Pelley, "John Brennan: No End to Terrorism," CBS News, *60 Minutes*, February 14, 2016, http://www.cbsnews.com/news/cia-director-john-brennan-60-minutes-scott-pelley/.

3. Shane Harris, *@War: The Rise of the Military-Internet Complex* (New York: Houghton Mifflin Harcourt, 2014). See also the detailed and authoritative expose of "the launch of the world's first digital weapon," Stuxnet and account of operation Olympic Games by *Wired* correspondent Kim Zetter in *Countdown to Zero Day* (New York: Crown Books, 2014). Cybersecurity expert Marc Goodman offers a comprehensive and, frankly, frightening survey of the range of vulnerabilities and the types of hacking and related crimes that states, especially, are likely to consider launching against us. See Marc Goodman, *Future Crimes* (New York: Doubleday, 2015).

4. This is a statement summarizing the Department of Defense cyber security strategy upon its release to the public in 2011. Quoted in the *Wall Street Journal*, it was at the time attributed to "an unnamed military official" and has been widely quoted since. See, for example, Bianca Bosker, "Pentagon Considers Cyber Attacks to Be Acts of War: WSJ," *Huffington Post*, May 31, 2011, http://www.huffingtonpost.com/2011/05/31/pentagon-cyber-attack-act-of-war_n_869014.html (accessed May 27, 2016).

5. Christopher Kims argues that, starting with the recent hack of the adultery facilitation site Ashley Madison—currently still of unknown provenance or purpose—big-data brokers and the IOT have made us unwilling accomplices in our increased vulnerability to cyberattacks. See Christopher Kims, "The Hacked Data Broker? Be Very Afraid," *Wall Street Journal*, September 8, 2015, B1, B4.

6. A new book by Russian dissident scholars Andrei Soldatov and Irina Borogan argues that the security breaches and revelations unleashed by Edward Snowden have unwittingly strengthened the hand of Russian president Vladimir Putin in his efforts to sow fear and gain full control of social media in Russia, ironically, on the grounds that the average citizen's data is not safe from intrusion and spying by the Americans. See Andrei Soldatov and Irina Borogan, *The Red Web* (Philadelphia: Public Affairs, 2015).

7. Dave Eggers, *The Circle* (New York: Afred A. Knopf, 2013).
8. See, for example, David Kleidman, "The Tragedy of John Allen and the Petraeus Scandal," *Daily Beast*, March 5, 2013, http://www.thedailybeast.com/newsweek/2013/03/04/the-tragedy-of-john-allen-the-petraeus-scandal.html (accessed April 22, 2013).
9. See http://www.nato.int/cps/en/natolive/topics_68368.htm (accessed May 27, 2016); and Todor Tagarev, *Building Integrity and Reducing Corruption in Defence: A Compendium of Best Practices* (Geneva: Geneva Centre for the Democratic Control of Armed Forces, 2010).
10. See Yuri Akdeniz, "Anonymity, Democracy, and Cyberspace," *Social Research: An International Quarterly* 69 (2002): 223–237; and B. Johnson, "Is There a Difference between Privacy and Anonymity?," *The Guardian*, June 14, 2007, http://www.guardian.co.uk/technology/2007/jun/14/guardianweeklytechnologysection.
11. Harvard University computer scientist Harry Lewis offers a somewhat more sanguine and positive account of the role of anonymity in cyberspace than I, though arguing also for limitations. See Harry Lewis, "Anonymity and Reason," *Privacy in the Modern Age*, ed. Marc Rotenberg, Jeramie Horwitz, and Julia Scott (New York: New Press, 2015), 104–111.
12. *Wikipedia*, the online encyclopedia, offers a complete account of Ellsberg and the "Pentagon Papers" incident, http://en.wikipedia.org/wiki/Daniel_Ellsberg.
13. A community of like-minded democracies that have agreed not to spy on one another and to collaborate in intelligence gathering and to share intelligence data that since WWII has been dubbed the Five Eyes.
14. This last seems to be the summary opinion of Marc Ambinder and D. B. Grady in *Deep State: Inside the Government Secrecy Industry* (Hoboken, NJ: John Wiley and Sons, 2013). This is the latest example of a deep-seated public ambivalence about secrecy and clandestine operations generally, which are viewed with extreme suspicion when carried out by government agencies, even if undertaken for the public welfare under strict supervision. The demand for government transparency does not, apparently, carry over into nongovernmental arenas, since a lack of transparency is taken as tantamount to respecting privacy. But this is hopelessly muddled. Secrecy is not always wrong, but is always subject to what I term a "hermeneutic of suspicion" when carried out as a policy, regardless of who does it. I discuss the problem of government secrecy, the public's confusion over it, and how to better understand and deal with it at some length in the concluding chapter of *Anthropologists in Arms: The Ethics of Military Anthropology* (Lanham, MD: AltaMira Press, 2009).

CHAPTER 7

NSA Management Directive #424

Anticipatory National Self-Defense

In light of the urgent need for more effective security and protection from state-sponsored hacktivist attacks, how should we now regard the massive big-data collection and surveillance programs which, we recently discovered, our US security agencies engaged in without our knowledge or consent? Ought we to view them with suspicion, as further episodes in a long history of state abuses of power? Or should we realize in hindsight that these agencies and their personnel were attempting, on our behalf, albeit covertly, to put in place some of these urgently needed security measures to protect us? And if so, should at least some of them be retained?

In this chapter, I defend these ongoing covert security operations—*not* their excessive secrecy, but their underlying purpose, function, and structure. I view them by and large as lawful exercises of responsible executive power in pursuit of a robust program of national anticipatory self-defense against state-sponsored hacktivism. To make this case, I first address the charge that the NSA surveillance program is nothing more than another instance of antiterrorist mission creep (like the Patriot Act itself, which authorizes these activities). I also address the concerns that this surveillance represents simply an illicit expansion of government power whose aim is the abrogation of individual privacy. It seems to me that the matter is far graver than these descriptions of routine bureaucratic overreach and government oppression suggest.

I defend the view that the NSA surveillance and data-mining programs represent a deliberate, thoughtfully conceived, yet morally problematic program by US security and intelligence forces of *preventive self-defense*, against terrorism, surely, but against a number of other threats as well, including infrastructure sabotage, crippling state and corporate espionage, and even, to the degree it is legally permitted, against the commission of serious international and domestic Internet crime, both in the United States and abroad. That characterization does not, however, serve by itself as a blanket justification for the program. Beyond the morally problematic nature of anticipatory or preventive self-defense itself, one must also consider whether the program is effective, judged from a variety of legitimate critical perspectives, including but not limited to its scope and costs. And, of course, one must decide whether the costs in terms of individual liberty and personal privacy are worth the level of security they may be found to purchase.

By describing the intent and the technical details behind this NSA surveillance program, I hope to establish that, whatever its flaws and excesses, it was never intended to be, nor did it ever resemble, an operation of Stasi-like surveillance of American citizens or of innocent persons elsewhere in the world, though that is exactly how these actions were at first portrayed by the press and a critical public. What this program represented instead was an ambitious attempt to establish and secretly carry out an effective program of preventive self-defense, of not only American citizens, but also, to a lesser degree, the citizens and polities of our allied nations (at the very least, our Five Eyes allies) against a variety of forms of cyberattack. Once again, such a characterization alone certainly does not justify the program, but it may help correct the impression of what it signified, and will hopefully turn the debate in a constructive direction toward the policies that underlie this strategic objective.

PREVENTIVE WAR

First, I take it as largely settled opinion that Stuxnet and Olympic Games constituted, beyond question, a program of preventive war—anticipatory self-defense against the prospects of an Iranian nuclear threat in the foreseeable future. If so, Edward Snowden's revelations of massive ongoing telephony and data surveillance by the NSA re-engages the same controversy over the morality of preventive war that was first enjoined during the administration of President George W. Bush in justifying the American-led intervention in Iraq.[1] Any attempt either to justify or criticize the NSA program thus first requires recognizing that it represented from its outset a novel form of this resurgent doctrine in the just war tradition: namely, that when faced with a very definite and gathering threat, a nation or society is *entitled to defend itself by any legitimate means possible, even before the first blows against it are struck or even imminent.* This, it seems to me, is the dimension that has been missing from public discussions of the Snowden affair, and which places that affair squarely in the context of this book.

It is against that wider backdrop that we should interpret the international press reports published by *The Guardian* and other news media beginning in June 2013. These news media carried a series of reports detailing a range of surveillance activities carried out by the NSA in the United States and abroad. This program had been undertaken with the full cooperation of our Five Eyes partners. Snowden decided by himself that these secret surveillence activities were morally reprehensible violations of individual rights of privacy.

The generic working features of the program were relatively clearly outlined in a heretofore secret memorandum, "NSA Management Directive #424." This document contains all that Snowden's stolen and disclosed files have thus far largely revealed, albeit in bits and pieces. Specifically, this includes PRiSM (revealed in June 2013), XKeyscore (revealed in July 2013), and, somewhat later, the Enterprise Knowledge System and the data-chaining program Treasure Map, coupled with the extent and scope of data collection of various types throughout this period.[2]

"Mainway" is the code name of a massive data storage unit near completion in the vicinity of Bluffdale, Utah, in which the NSA has been storing some two billion "record events"[3] a day since 2010. When fully functional, as Snowden's public disclosure of "NSA Management Directive #424" reveals, the capacity of the Utah site will exceed ten times that amount daily—that is, twenty billion records). These record events can, in principle, include logs of telephone, Skype, and cellphone calls, tweets, Facebook posts, emails, Internet-site visits, GPS coordinates, and so forth, although some forms of these kinds of data are relatively more easy to collect than others, and the collection of all is subject to a variety of fairly complex legal regimes and accountability measures. This kind of massive big-data collection has frequently been characterized as the amassing of an enormously large haystack, within which intelligence and law enforcement agencies under current US law are entitled to search for a very few, legally distinct needles.

The Enterprise Knowledge System consists of a variety of relational databases that are legal subsets of this haystack (such as PRiSM), together with analytical tools and risk-analysis, or data-chaining software programs (XKeyscore and Treasure Map). Collectively, this "system" constitutes the means by which the enormous trove of so-called metadata is parsed, subdivided, and finally mined or analyzed in accordance with the various legal regimes and presidential directives that govern the permissible use of the information.

Section 215 of the Patriot Act (2004), for example, authorizes the collection of telephony records of domestic communications, which are held for a period not exceeding ninety days. Only the FBI is authorized to examine these data, and only with an approved warrant granted by a court upon presentation of evidence pertaining to the suspicion of domestic wrongdoing. Section 702 of the Foreign Intelligence and Surveillance Act,[4] by contrast, empowers the NSA to collect records from nine major Internet service providers regarding emails, Internet telephone calls, and other information that passes through the physical infrastructure of the Internet that is located on US soil.

Section 702 is actually a powerful signal intelligence authorization tool, inasmuch as (owing to the historical irony of its origins, cited in the introduction) virtually all of the Internet infrastructure worldwide is connected to systems within the continental borders of the United States, so that virtually all Internet traffic eventually passes across US borders. Those telephony data involving a US citizen are subject to the same constraints of examination as are data described in Section 215 of the Patriot Act, while those communications occurring strictly between non-US citizens are *not* subject to legal protections and may be treated as signal intelligence subject to analysis. Finally, Presidential Directive 12333 has long authorized the NSA to collect signal intelligence anywhere outside the continental United States in pursuit of national security. Data so obtained are not subject to these domestic legal protections.[5]

"Data-chaining," as the generic procedure of big-data analysis is sometimes characterized, is the linking up into a variety of patterns this enormous welter of otherwise seemingly random, obscure, discrete, and usually trivial and inconsequential "record events." The result is a kind of topographical mapping of patterns of movement and communication that filters out or excludes the metadata of most of us—unless that data can be gathered up into a pattern that is interesting or suspicious. The result might be compared to the kind of whiteboard that investigators create to help them solve a crime, connecting the various clues and pieces of data—except that this whiteboard would encompass a degree of detail and a diversity and quantity of data that would vastly exceed the capacities of human investigators.

The weakness of a whiteboard analogy, however, is that in surveillance operations, these data are assembled *prior to* rather than after the commission of a crime or act of terrorism or sabotage. This constitutes the kind of preventive self-defense that is permitted under domestic law in certain restricted situations to foil criminal conspiracies, but which is outlawed under international law in the case of interstate conflict.

XKeyscore and Treasure Map are analytical programs that review the connections and attempt to discern meaningful patterns within them. Treasure Map displays the data in patterns resembling a constellation or mandala of intricate communication nodes, while XKeyscore assigns a resultant risk-analysis score (vaguely analogous to the quantitative risk analysis offered in a FICO credit score), which in principle can be calculated for each and every node in the constellation. These patterns, and their respective scores, help analysts discern where and what sorts of communicative activity represent potentially suspicious correlations and connections of data clusters, rather than merely of discrete individuals. Just as a FICO score can be computed by a credit bureau through the gathering and analyzing of a wide array of otherwise disparate data concerning our economic "health" and financial transactions, so a score assigned by XKeyscore offers a quantitative measure of what might be termed the "degree of suspiciousness" or the "surveillance-worthiness" of patterns of underlying connections that might be spotted on the initial data-chain analysis. That score may ultimately help human analysts identify probable cause for a closer scrutiny of any of the nonrandom patterns of interpersonal communication discerned in the otherwise discrete, mathematically driven data-mining of many individuals' otherwise random and irrelevant record events.

XKeyscore has been inaccurately described in some accounts as a spying and surveillance tool that would allow an individual operator, such as Snowden, to sit at his desk, figuratively speaking, and without a search warrant, tap into anyone's phone calls, given only an email address. But that is a substantial mis-characterization, and agency officials flatly denied that Snowden, as a low-level employee, could ever have done such a thing.

What XKeyscore actually does do is something else entirely: it analyzes keyboard strokes and communication patterns at the speed of light and flags any that are suspicious for follow-up by a human SIGINT operator. If the signals (emails, etc.) emanate from or are sent to an American, the SIGINT operator would need to obtain a FISA court clearance or a domestic search warrant to do any substantial follow-up on the content of the communications or to directly surveill any individual's real-time online activities. All of the foregoing information and more regarding the covert signal intelligence operation known as the Enterprise Knowledge System is now more or less readily (and reasonably accurately) available online.

As morally problematic as this policy and these activities may seem, if we consider the recent tragic terrorist attacks—the Boston Marathon bombing (April 15, 2013), the Paris nightclub and soccer stadium attacks (November 2015), and the bombing of the offices of the humorist magazine *Charlie Hebdo* (January 7, 2015)—big-data surveillance *might* have helped to detect and deter all three. At the very least, these constitute clear contexts in which citizens generally opposed both to massive surveillance and to the general concept of preventive self-defense suddenly found themselves clamoring for more of both.

INITIAL PUBLIC RESPONSE

As mentioned, however, the scope and ambition of this effort elicited immediate comparisons with Stasi surveillance programs in East Germany.[6] Certainly, that comparison was foremost in the public reaction to Snowden's revelations within Germany itself, a culture that remains understandably sensitive about such matters in the aftermath of abusive internal intelligence gathering under both the Nazi and the East German Communist regimes. I do not find these specific comparisons very accurate or convincing. The underlying policy of relying on massive data collection and cyber surveillance as a form of anticipatory or preventive national self-defense nonetheless highlights two very critical, and as yet poorly understood, features of cyber conflict in general that are worthy of attention and concern.

First, in law and ethics we distinguish clearly between domestic law enforcement and its monopoly on the use of force under a rule of law, and international armed conflict, during which domestic laws and the rule of law itself are often seriously eroded. A critical feature of cyber conflict generally, as we have seen, is that it has seriously blurred the distinctions between what were once different and distinguishable levels of activity and conflict. In the case of serious cybercrime and cyberespionage, however, we are increasingly straying into an area in which nations can, with increasing plausibility, declare these to be the equivalent of an armed attack by another state. In particular, with increasing plausibility and legal verisimilitude, such charges can be lodged against states that willingly harbor or tolerate terrorists or international criminal organizations within their borders.

A second, even more important difference from traditional conflict is that the pursuit of cyber strategy and the employment of cyber weapons and tactics have been largely under the control of intelligence agencies and personnel, whose rules of engagement are vastly different from those of conventional military combatants or of agents of domestic law enforcement. As we saw earlier, spying and espionage activities do not typically rise to the level of a threat or use of force under international law, let alone of armed conflict between states, but many do constitute criminal acts under the domestic law of the jurisdictions within which they take place.

Conventional war, by contrast, is understood to occur within zones of combat in which the conventional rule of law has broken down, and to which only the international law of armed conflict applies. This latter legal regime is far more tolerant than domestic law regarding the permission to pursue conflict with deadly force (as Jeff McMahan and David Rodin have both observed).[7] The law of armed conflict does, however, encompass certain basic moral principles—noncombatant immunity and proportionality, for example—that do not arise as constraints in the pursuit of espionage. Likewise, in domestic law enforcement, unrestricted surveillance, not to mention the use of force, falls under strict legal regimes with accountability, oversight, and at least some degree of transparency, including (most importantly) challenges and adversarial review of the policies and procedures pursued. Few if any of these international or domestic legal constraints, however, apply in the case of espionage, surveillance, or covert action.

As we have seen, the emergence of relentless and unrestricted cyber conflict over the past decade has seriously eroded all of these firewalls against governmental overreach. Thus far, this fundamental distinction regarding rules of engagement has not been fully acknowledged, let alone well understood. Cyberwar, as we learned, is nothing less than unrestricted warfare carried out by spies and espionage agents—that is, by persons who might not think themselves bound by ordinary legal restraints—rather than by conventional combatants trained in the law of armed conflict. Unrestricted warfare is not legally permissible or morally justifiable in the conventional case, but it is routine practice among agents of espionage, especially those engaged in state-sponsored hacktivism. In cyber conflict, and in planning for it, many of the weapons and tactics are specifically designed to operate against civilians and civilian noncombatant targets, a feature that, as we noted, is illegal and decidedly immoral in the conventional case.

THE DILEMMA OF EDWARD SNOWDEN

Now let us turn to the NSA contractor who stole these data and programs in order to "blow the whistle" on covert signal intelligence activities by the US government. Whatever else one might say concerning the legality, morality, and prudence of his actions, Edward Snowden is fundamentally correct in his statements regarding the notions of publicity and informed consent, which together constitute the hallmark of democratic public policy. In order to be morally justifiable, any strategy or policy involving the body politic must be *one to which it would voluntarily assent when fully informed about it*. The American public was not informed about these activities, and that, in essence, was Snowden's reason for leaking the documents, as he told the *New York Times* in an interview in October following the release of the files:

> So long as there's broad support amongst a people, it can be argued there's a level of legitimacy even to the most invasive and morally wrong program, as it was an informed and willing decision … However, programs that are implemented in secret, out of public oversight, lack that legitimacy, and that's a problem. It also represents a dangerous normalization of "governing in the dark," where decisions with enormous public impact occur without any public input.[8]

What, however, does being fully informed mean when it comes to surveillance? Much of the literature on informed consent dwells on the problematic nature of voluntary consent, given the inequalities in power between those asking for that consent and those expected to grant it, the uncertain epistemic features of information about the contents of a policy, and the risks associated with pursuing it. Physicians, for example, routinely object that laypersons cannot voluntarily consent to treatment because they are often unable to appreciate the risks and costs, vis-à-vis the benefits, of complicated medical procedures, and are in any case frequently so traumatized by their illness or physical vulnerability as to be willing to consent to almost anything.[9] In other areas of scientific inquiry, as in anthropological field research, many researchers resist or reject the policy of informed consent, mistakenly believing that they will be obliged to have their research subject "sign a release form of some kind" (what we might term "procedural informed consent"). Even more often, the policy of informed consent is resisted over concerns that the subjects of a study, once fully informed about it, will view it as an unwarranted intrusion into their cultural privacy and withhold their permission; or, perhaps even worse, that they will cease to act naturally and instead start to "perform" for the external observer, thus ruining the authenticity of any field data collected.[10]

What position should we therefore adopt regarding the prospects of giving collective informed consent to a policy of cyber surveillance whose technological sophistication and scope stagger the imagination, and whose implications neither we nor those implementing the policy can possibly foresee?

Not only do we (that is, the collective body politic) lack the technological sophistication to fully appreciate all the dimensions involved in the workings of this policy, but, just as in the instance of anthropological field work, we may need to be deliberately blind to some of the features of our own surveillance, lest we (the protected) and those seeking to harm us (criminals, terrorists, agents of adversarial nations) begin to alter our respective behaviors in response.

There is an approach embodied in a number of generally accepted and morally justified practices that may offer some insight into this current cyber dilemma. We can draw an analogy between the present circumstances in cyberspace and a variety of practices in other domains that seem to entail secret and clandestine elements but at the same time exhibit respect for individual privacy and confidentiality. Examples include patients being asked to participate in double-blind medical experiments; undercover agents working as part of a domestic police effort to apprehend criminals (such as drug dealers) or to prevent the fomenting of criminal conspiracies; tenure deliberations and blind peer review in academic institutions engaged in the pursuit of scientific research; and confidential agreements among heads of state in the pursuit of policies clearly in their respective public's interests.

Another, obviously more problematic, example is the practice of espionage agents of rival states engaging in HUMINT (intelligence gathered by interpersonal contact) and SIGINT (intelligence gathered by the interception of signals) activities, which fall outside the normal bounds of law and morality.

GOVERNMENT DECEPTION AND PUBLIC TRUST

Sadly, it is hard to imagine at present what could ever undo the damage that has been done to the public's trust in the US government as a result Snowden's disclosure that it has been engaged in secret policies, supervised and overseen, in turn, by secret laws and secret courts. Nonetheless, examining some analogies may help to inform the public discussion, which Snowden has said he hoped to encourage, concerning policies that might seem "evasive and morally wrong."

As just noted, the key issue in these disparate analogies is informed consent. Following these examples, the NSA surveillance program (like double-blind medical studies) could—and, I believe, should—seek to inform, and to obtain voluntary consent from the subjects of security surveillance, making it clear that they must be willing to remain ignorant of certain features of the program for the sake of its effectiveness. That is, certain procedural details in all of the purportedly analogous instances will remain secret, *but the general operations* (undercover police work, big-data surveillance, and so on) should be disclosed, and the nature of the risks to privacy and other basic rights generally entailed should be fully divulged to the affected parties, or to those on whose behalf the policies are being carried out.[11]

Such activity constitutes the kind of anticipatory self-defense that is permitted under domestic law in certain restricted situations to foil criminal conspiracies, but which is outlawed under international law in the case of interstate conflict. Yet this effort is directed more at the new kinds of interstate conflict described heretofore, than it is against domestic crime. We will return to this ticklish point in a moment.

DEFENDING NATIONAL BOUNDARIES AND PERSONAL LIBERTIES

The intent of the state (or, more specifically, its security and intelligence organizations) in conducting surveillance seems of paramount importance in judging the ethics of the surveillance policies. In the present case, we encounter a clear conflict between the well-established and accepted (though not universally) norm—that is, privacy—and the alleged benefits that come from violating that norm through the mining of metadata by the NSA.

As I have repeatedly noted, much of the world's Internet traffic travels through what are euphemistically termed "pipes and switches" that lie geographically within the United States. Hence, very much as an air traffic controller monitors airplane traffic, the United States is in a position to monitor and survey not only its own Internet traffic but that of the entire world. This gives a whole new meaning to the sometimes cynical characterization of America as "the world's policeman," and it also runs hard against a recalcitrant feature of the international cyber community itself: its anarchist and libertarian streak. So the outrage, both domestic and international, over the revelations that the NSA was monitoring so great a quantity of electronic communications has been palpable. One might take this as strong evidence that from a philosophical perspective the norm of privacy is widely valued as an important right, a kind of exercise of individual autonomy that ought to be strongly protected, even though, when hard-pressed, neither constitutional lawyers nor scholars of moral philosophy and jurisprudence can clearly define, let alone agree on, exactly in what this right substantively consists.[12]

Defenders of the practices of email packet sniffing and metadata mining more generally, however, reply that there is a second important norm: the security of citizens in a democracy that is devoted to respecting and protecting their rights. That is to say, there may be a legitimate tension or conflict between the long-standing and widely accepted norm of privacy—one that functions with special vigor in the cyber domain—with a second, and at least as important norm: namely, that ordinary citizens minding their own business, who have done nothing wrong, do not deserve to be unduly subject to grave but avoidable risks of harm. I will term this the "security norm." Security of life, person, and property is one of the most basic and fundamental of human rights, and it is one of the chief functions of just and minimally rights-respecting governments to ensure that all citizens enjoy it.[13]

The tension between these two norms is hardly new or unfamiliar. It was, after all, one of the Founding Fathers, Benjamin Franklin, who observed that a people who sacrificed privacy (liberty) for the sake of security would end up with little of either. But Franklin was not referring to security in the deeper sense discussed here. Instead, he was denouncing a cowardly and risk-aversive desire to preserve the political status quo at all costs, instead of standing up for justice and basic human rights.

In our own time, violations of privacy are often regarded not merely as intrusion on personal liberty but also as an ominous foreboding of totalitarianism. Hence, the thinking goes, if the United States currently monitors the patterns of email traffic among foreign nationals in an effort to combat terrorism and criminal conspiracies, what is to prevent it on some future occasion from opening and reading those emails, or actually listening to those telephone conversations? And what is to prevent it from moving from intrusion for security purposes to the suppression of all free speech and action for political purposes?

Citizens in a rights-respecting and rule-governed nation might reply that the degree of plausibility and severity of the threat justifies their collective response to it. As with the formation of the Transportation Security Administration in the United States in the aftermath of 9/11, or as in the 1950s civil-defense campaigns throughout Europe and North America against the threat of thermonuclear war, citizens would likely be willing to accept considerable inconvenience and limitations on their freedom and privacy, if the threat of harm were severe enough—Ben Franklin's warnings notwithstanding. Americans, in particular, would also be well instructed to recall the threats to liberty and privacy that the US government perpe-trated decades earlier in response to potential or imagined threats, such as J. Edgar Hoover's FBI wiretapping and McCarthyism.

STATE NORMS FOR RESPECTING SOVEREIGNTY
AND ATTAINING SECURITY

This is not an impossible puzzle to solve, and responding to a threat per-ceived to be grave need not degenerate into the kind of fear and hyste-ria that fostered those abuses of government power in the United States during the 1950s and 1960s. What is required to guard against the hyste-ria and abuses is, of course, *due process and, in particular, robust adversarial review*. As noted earlier, some transparency—that is, admitting that sur-veillance actions are taking place, justifying them, and clearly stating who is exercising accountability and oversight, if not precisely how it is being exercised—is desirable to prevent arbitrary abuses of privilege.

It is also of important to distinguish between types of intentions. For all China's denunciation of the NSA's activities,[14] the US government, unlike the government of China, has made no attempt—or even harbored any intent—to "lock down" the Internet, control dissent, or pry into the personal lives and beliefs those who disagree with its policies in an effort to control their political expression. Whatever it is, or may become, the United States is not now, nor is it realistically likely to morph into, a closed and repressed society like that of North Korea or even a quasi-democratic theocracy like Iran. It is neither fair nor particularly efficacious, then, to judge its behavior by the political standard set through the domestic poli-cies of far more repressive governments.

In particular, it is a serious mistake to draw a parallel between the past behaviors of corrupt or authoritarian regimes and the future intentions and behaviors of basically democratic and minimally rights-respecting ones. To compare the US actions to those of China regarding data control, as some have done, is completely wrongheaded. *The intent of the Chinese government is not to protect individuals from harm but to control them against their will.* The intent of the US government is precisely not to control or intrude on individuals' private lives but to exercise its legitimate responsibility to pro-tect citizens from an unreasonable threat of harm, particularly from the new threats now persistently posed by state-sponsored hacktivism.

Given this critical distinction, we need now, in the same spirit in which we examined previous forms of conventional and cyber conflict, to con-sider emergent norms that might prove appropriate to the governance of espionage and surveillance, which is itself designed to prevent criminal conspiracies or outright warfare and which aims purely at attribution and denial of anonymity rather than invasions of individual privacy. Such activities by a citizen's own government would be characterized as morally permissible if and only if

- the focus of the *surveillance is limited* insofar as possible to legitimate security objectives and military targets, and the sole purpose is to prevent armed attack or its equivalent;
- the *harm threatened is genuine* and reasonably well-defined, and there exists legally defined probable cause for surveillance;
- there is *suitable transparency, oversight, and accountability* for the program of surveillance, with full adversarial review of the legal permissions ultimately granted;
- the individual privacy of third parties and bystanders is not infringed, and no harm is done to civilians or their property; and,
- most particularly, *the broad scope and reach of surveillance efforts are known to and approved by the public*, on behalf of and for the security of whom such surveillance is undertaken (informed consent).

In the case of massive classified surveillance efforts, however, this last condition might seem too enormous to be a feasible undertaking. No doubt the political leaders who gave their consent to pursuing the secret policy thought so. But imagine that the director of national intelligence or the director of the NSA—in the numerous speeches that both they and other government representatives gave in the years leading up to the Snowden disclosure—had simply divulged the bare outlines of the policy. The precise details, including the scope of surveillance and the specific algorithms and programs used in data-mining and detective data-chaining, would not need to have been disclosed.

Instead, they could have made a simple, frank statement to American citizens and citizens of allied countries that the intelligence services of these states were cooperating to monitor the patterns of telephone and electronic communication in the cyber domain in an effort to discern and prevent criminal and terrorist conspiracies from coming to fruition. Further, what could have been fully disclosed was a procedure for providing accountability and oversight to the process.

In other respects, the foregoing caveats hardly comprise a complete or sufficient list of guiding precepts, but I do believe they encompass some of the lessons that we have learned from the Snowden fiasco that should now be woven into the revision of our master narrative on ethics and cybersecurity.

It would be an abuse of the legal permission defined above, for example, for a human cyber warrior to listen in to Skype conversations between private adults who are not engaged in any crime or to read their emails for amusement, let alone to impede their free activity or interfere with their political rights of free expression. In the next chapter, I will try to portray such activity as a fundamental betrayal of "professional ethics" as well—that is, an abrogation of some of what must now come to be seen as the central moral principles defining a new kind of military profession: the cyber warrior. Meanwhile, that such things were allegedly permitted to occur and that the general outline of the program itself was not acknowledged by the political establishment have done serious harm to the public's trust in the security agencies of its government and must now be urgently and quickly repaired.

This can be done, however, only by adhering in the future to basic principles of sound security as outlined previously, including the adherence of administrators of such programs to a basic code of conduct that will serve to guide and limit their actions to justifiable objectives. We will examine the case for, and the possible content of such a self-governing, regulatory code of conduct in conclusion.

NOTES

1. The Deen K. Chatterjee, ed., *Gathering Threat: Essays on Preventive and Preemptive War* (New York: Cambridge University Press, 2013).
2. See George R. Lucas, Jr., "NSA Management Directive # 424: Secrecy and Privacy in the Aftermath of Snowden," *Journal of Ethics and International Affairs* 28, no. 1 (2014): 29–38.
3. I use this designator specifically, since the relative obscurity of otherwise public events of these sorts has been found to have a unique status in domestic United States law, even while specific kinds, such as telephone call logs (luds) were deemed to be in the public domain with no presupposition of privacy attached, according to a much-invoked 1979 Supreme Court ruling on telecommunications subject to police search and seizure.
4. The Foreign Intelligence and Surveillance Act of 1978 sought, in the aftermath of revelations of abusive intelligence practices by United States agencies abroad, to establish appropriate congressional and judicial oversight of these, while allowing for appropriate levels of secrecy. The act established the so-called FISA courts specifically to provide confidential judicial review of federal intelligence agencies. The 1978 act was modified in 2006 and 2008 to accord with provisions of the 2001 Patriot Act to permit gathering and analysis of telephony metadata with appropriate oversight in order to provide insight into the workings of foreign

terrorist organizations. See https://it.ojp.gov/PrivacyLiberty/authorities/statutes/1286 (accessed February 18, 2016).

5. This is an enormous, complex, and highly contested subject, and my summary should be subject to interpretation and careful review in light of extensive documents and discussions of NSA texts and enabling legislation available from the website of the American University in Cairo: http://www.aucegypt.edu/gapp/cairoreview/pages/articleDetails.aspx?aid=468 (accessed May 28, 2014).

6. This surveillance, and its impact on both the surveilled and the surveillance personnel, was detailed in the moving and troubling German film *The Lives of Others* (*Das Leben der Anderen*, 2006).

7. The relative tolerance of the use of deadly force in international law for purposes labeled as "self-defense" is criticized on a number of grounds by David Rodin, in *War and Self-Defense* (Oxford: Oxford University Press, 2002); and in Jeff McMahan, *Killing in War* (Oxford: Oxford University Press, 2009).

8. James Risen, "Snowden Says He Took No Secret Files to Russia," *New York Times*, October 17, 2013, http://www.nytimes.com/2013/10/18/world/snowden-says-he-took-no-secret-files-to-russia.html (accessed February 16, 2016).

9. A controversy arose recently over lack of informed consent by subjects in a 1950s study of an experimental treatment for prostate cancer funded by the National Institutes of Health at Columbia University; the subjects were homeless men from the Bowery neighborhood of New York City. See Gina Kolata, "Decades Later, Condemnation for a Skid Row Cancer Study," October 17, 2013, http://www.nytimes.com/2013/10/18/health/medical-experiments-conducted-on-bowery-alcoholics-in-1950s.html (accessed April 27, 2016).

10. G. R. Lucas, Jr., *Anthropologists in Arms: The Ethics of Military Anthropology* (Lanham, MD: AltaMira Press, 2009), e.g., chap. 6.

11. This was among the conclusions of the internationally distinguished assembly of legal scholars, moral philosophers, and public policy authorities who convened at the University of Pennsylvania's Center for Ethics and the Rule of Law, on November 22–23, 2013, as mentioned in the introduction. The speaker that day was the then deputy director of the NSA, and among the participants was the lead lawyer in an American Civil Liberties Union suit against the NSA.

12. Several excellent accounts of the origins, role, and current legal understanding of this norm are offered in the essays in *Privacy in the Modern Age*, ed. Marc Rotenberg, Julia Horwitz, and Jeramie Scott (New York: New Press, 2015).

13. One such defense of the security versus privacy norm is Daniel J. Solove, "The End of Privacy," *Scientific American*, September 2008, 101–106, http://www.nature.com/scientificamerican/journal/v299/n3/full/scientificamerican0908-100.html.

14. David E. Sanger, "Differences on Cybertheft Complicate China Talks," *New York Times*, July 10, 2013, http://www.nytimes.com/2013/07/11/world/asia/differences-on-cybertheft-complicate-china-talks.html.

Conclusion

Toward a "Code of Ethics" for Cyber Warriors

Our discussions of cyber conflict, law, ethics, and significant moral issues of privacy and anonymity have intentionally been structured to illustrate the fundamental approaches to moral reasoning that have been elicited through our analysis. That is, this book is intended to be a synoptic, inclusive, and comprehensive master narrative of these issues and experiences—a summative account that incorporates all the details of various rival accounts into a coherent narrative designed to make sense out of confusion, integrate the salient features of rival interpretations, resolve disputes, and point the way forward toward greater law, order, and security for all in the cyber domain.

As cautioned, however, this means that this narrative, even if complete and accurate, needs to be updated constantly and rewritten in the face of new events and novel circumstances. One of those novel circumstances is the tendency of powerful state entities to back away from conflicts that constitute an effects-based equivalent to conventional war, and to defy apocalyptic predictions in this regard by turning instead to what I have euphemistically described as "mischief" in the form of state-sponsored hacktivism. Accordingly, we have considered the emerging moral norms of responsible state behavior that might reasonably be imposed on these activities, as well as upon efforts by victim states to combat them.

Some of the latter efforts—including the ambitious, robust, offensive efforts at preemptive self-defense by the NSA revealed by Edward Snowden—have raised ethical concerns among wide portions of the public that is presumably being protected under this covert umbrella of security. This has led to criticism and increasing mistrust between those citizens and their government (as well as to embarrassment and political difficulties with citizens of allied nations abroad). If we reject the more sinister accounts of Snowden's motives and instead accept his account of why he did what he did, how do we summarize the dilemma his behavior presents?

I suggested in the opening pages of this book that we would be unable to deny that Snowden had engaged in deception, betrayed his fellow workers and his employer, stolen data and files that were the property of the US government, and leaked his government's proprietary secrets to the public (including to enemies of the United States). In so doing, he violated the oath of loyalty he had sworn and contractual agreements to which he had given his voluntary promise and consent when he signed a contract to work with top-secret, classified materials in a government setting. He does not deny that he did all these presumptively terrible things, as judged from a moral perspective, purposively. And so—like all those who wage war, use deadly force against other human beings, lie, cheat, and steal—Mr. Snowden must be called to account for his actions.

Fortunately for Mr. Snowden, and for those who believe that his illegal actions were morally justified, he is able to avail himself (or we can do so on his behalf) of precisely the same pattern of moral reasoning that we carefully reviewed in these other contexts, especially in the declaring of war and the waging of armed conflict. That is, his behavior constitutes an example of *making oneself a grave exception to prevailing moral norms* that prohibit doing what he did. We, the public threatened by his betrayal, sitting in collective judgment on his actions, now

- demand at minimum that he had significant, compelling reasons for his action (just cause);
- need to examine his intentions in deliberately setting aside these moral norms and breaking the law, and demand at least that his actions were not purely personal and self-serving but oriented toward the public's welfare (right intention); and
- inquire whether and to what extent he first availed himself of other, less dramatic and damaging alternatives before engaging in these morally prohibited and illegal forms of behavior (last resort).

We cross-examine the behavior of self-proclaimed whistleblowers like Edward Snowden, just as we are supposed to cross-examine our own and others' behavior when we propose to undertake something we are clearly, and beyond any question otherwise enjoined not to do: lie, steal, kill, betray the trust of the members of our community, break the law, or wage war, for example. And when the sole authority competent to make this final judgment, a jury of peers (legitimate authority), convenes to consider these circumstances and arguments, one final consideration that will weigh heavily for or against Mr. Snowden's actions is the question: How much damage did his actions inflict on the public, especially when compared to the damage he claimed was being inflicted upon them by the secret and covert actions he revealed (proportionality)?

At the time of this writing—more than two years after those initial revelations—the hypothetical jury of peers is still out. The public remains deeply divided over whether Snowden's actions constituted legitimate whistleblowing or whether they are tantamount to treason.

It should hardly be surprising that the former director and the general counsel (chief legal adviser) for the NSA, upon their own departures from office (under a cloud of suspicion for having authorized or carried out the alleged governmental abuse), remained furious at Snowden, demanding that he be extradited, returned to the United States, and tried as a traitor. Nor is it surprising that a large segment of the public, including a number of prominent political leaders, still believes that Snowden is a hero and that the government's data-collection and surveillance programs should be reigned in or halted altogether.

An interesting minority view, however, was expressed by the outgoing deputy director of NSA, who, while remaining upset at Snowden for the damage he caused, thought it might be appropriate to grant him amnesty, or punish him less harshly, because though culpable, *he might have made an honest mistake.*

Snowden claimed that, while working as a contractor at NSA, he had discovered a massive campaign of illegal surveillance of American citizens. NSA staff responded that all the actvities in which the agency was engaged were authorized under existing domestic law and subject to congressional oversight and judicial review. Individuals who were willing to comment for the record, moreover, indicated either that the behavior Snowden alleged was not even possible within their programs of surveillance and data collection or, even if it were possible, such internal surveillance of American citizens was strictly prohibited by agency regulations, and not a goal of their intelligence activities.

These issues are still hotly disputed, and it will likely take several more years to resolve them. In the meantime, the NSA has been deeply scarred, and its efforts to conduct significant signal intelligence have been severely compromised. One can speculate, in the face of limited reporting on the subject, that the public suspicion and charges of misconduct have badly damaged morale within the agency,[1] especially considering that many individual agents believe themselves instead to be actively engaged in securing the public's safety and security.

If Snowden made a mistake in stealing and releasing information about the Enterprise Knowledge System to the public, what sort of mistake is it alleged to have been? I suspect all readers will agree that it is not a "mistake" for an employee to take considerable personal risks to reveal dangerous and illegal wrongdoing to members of the public whose welfare is thereby put at risk. Such actions would be heroic, rather than condemnable.

Snowden could, however, have been mistaken about the nature of the actions he revealed. He could also have been mistaken *in the way he revealed those activities to the public.* This could only be true, however, if there are "canons" of prescribed procedure that any whistleblower must follow. Thus, Snowden could either have been wrong about what the NSA program was doing or correct in his judgment but did not follow the proper procedure for calling public attention to it.

None of this has ever fully been clarified in the public debate on Snowden. I would now argue that both kinds of mistakes were made. First, a young, inexperienced contract employee (Snowden was not yet thirty years old and had been working for the NSA less than six months when he fled) at the very least misunderstood what he observed. He perhaps saw the prospects or possibility of illegal "internal" surveillance within the parameters of his workplace, and assumed that others were conducting such surveillance, or maybe he even witnessed agency employees engaging in or discussing the prospects for such unauthorized surveillance and assumed it was both ongoing and also illegal.

What neither Snowden nor his defenders have fully grasped is the claim made in this book that NSA's project, whatever its flaws or weaknesses, was being operated as something else entirely: a program of proactive, anticipatory self-defense against ongoing attempts by adversaries of the United States to engage in state-sponsored hacktivism. Subsequent admissions by the governments and intelligence agencies of our closest allies that they, too, carry out such activities and share the results with each other and with us, confirm that this kind of preemptive self-defense against cyberattacks is the *new norm of responsible state behavior,* emerging in the wake of widespread acts and threats of hacktivist attacks carried out by the cyber forces of enemy states and adversaries.

This is important because such a classification of the NSA big-data collection and analysis program changes both the nature and severity of Snowden's just cause for whistleblowing. If, instead of Nazi- or Stasi-style surveillance, the NSA was trying to protect those very same citizens from harm, then there is much less justification, or none whatever, for blowing the whistle on it. Moreover, the damage to the public's safety and welfare of doing so is not compensated proportionately by the goods accruing through the protection of either their personal privacy or anonymity. In that case, a mistaken judgment about what was at stake leads, in turn, to a violation of the kind of due process or proper procedure for whistleblowing itself.

This appears to have been what happened. It is difficult to review the record of Snowden's revelations, together with the subsequent public record of analysis and interviews with key government and public stakeholders, and objectively conclude anything else.

It is quite easy to see, in contrast, how a new employee might be misled and mistaken and could lead a habitually and quite properly suspicious and adversarial element in a press (which is fully familiar with the history of past government abuse and misconduct in this regard), in turn, to suspect government wrongdoing in this case. But not only has no actual case of wrongdoing or abuse (apart from general criticisms of big-data collection and meta-data analysis in principle)[2] been produced, but the officials and government agents cross-examined by congressional investigators and reporters have been unanimous and consistent in their accounts of, in essence, bending over backward to carry out these programs in full compliance with relevant law and with the fullest respect for citizens' rights and prerogatives.

The sole moral error (and it was a grave error, indeed!) with which I would charge relevant government agencies and their spokesmen is their habitual, entrenched penchant for excessive secrecy. Such spokesmen as General Keith Alexander and Vice Admiral Bernard McCullough frequently told that public that—while they themselves believed that more stringent security measures were needed in the cyber domain—the agencies they supervised were *not* enacting such measures, out of a concern for citizens' personal privacy.

They and other public servants, in effect, lied to the public. They did so, allegedly, to hide their activities from our adversaries in cyberspace. But as I have repeatedly remarked ever since, those rogue actors were aware of the measures being taken against them—the general outline of them, at least. We had nothing to fear by confirming that America and its intelligence allies were engaged in a robust program of preventive defense against their attacks. I believe much less harm would have been done to both national security and public trust had those same officials simply reassured the public that they were engaged, to the full extent permitted by law, in providing for American security, while at the same time fully respecting the individual liberty, privacy, and dignity of every citizen. They could have reminded the public, moreover, of the constitutional safeguards then in place to ensure the protection of those individual liberties and rights, and perhaps even invited them to subject those institutions (such as the FISA courts and the congressional oversight committees) to further examination and review, to assure Americans that they could be comfortable with what was being done on their behalf. This might well have led some members of the public to advocate for strengthening the robustness of adversarial review of both the courts and the congressional committees, thereby revealing and addressing this weakness in the system of oversight without spawning more mistrust of federal institutions.

Rather than being a side story to global cyber conflict, moreover, *the Snowden affair goes to the heart of the moral challenges it poses.* These moral challenges, in turn, involve far more than simply the driving tension between public security and personal privacy. They involve also the ability of the general public to trust their fellow citizens to protect both security and their privacy in good faith, rather than covertly attempting to subvert both.

A "CODE OF ETHICS" FOR CYBER WARRIORS

What might have occurred, instead, had Snowden, as part of his orientation to his new workplace, been confronted with a shared conception of the Good in a professional sense, in the form of a code of ethics that every intelligence agent learned and is asked to affirm (in addition to the oath of loyalty to the Constitution already required of all federal employees)? Had such a code of the cyber warrior been promulgated, and had it contained some of the provisions we have previously derived and considered, especially regarding the importance of respecting citizens' privacy and acting in accordance with the informed consent of the governed, it is hard to see how even a young, inexperienced, new employee could have formed such dramatic misconceptions of what was being undertaken in his workplace.

What, indeed, might have been the result had Vice Admiral Bernard McCullough or General Keith Alexander and General Michael Hayden been subjected to the same moral orientation regime as Snowden? The political and military leaders of most allied nations would understandably bristle at the suggestion that their ethics were somehow deficient and in need of remediation. But that, unfortunately, is because most of these leaders possess an understanding of ethics that is hardly more sophisticated than that of Mr. Snowden—or, for that matter, the rank-and-file citizen of this or any country. All labor under what we labeled "folk morality," the unwieldy conglomeration of false or misleading beliefs about what ethics is and what it demands. They think in terms of simple legal compliance, a regime of external regulations, or vacuous exhortations to be persons of character and integrity who can be merely counted on not to succumb to the temptations of gifts such as Lady Gaga tickets, the services of a prostitute, or the latest electronic gadet, offered by an unscrupulous government contractor. They do not think deeply enough of what it means to be engaged in trying to protect a vulnerable population that is deeply conflicted about the concerns we have discussed, while misrepresenting their efforts to that same public deliberately, in an excessive show of secrecy. If ethics is, finally, about maturity of judgment and strategic thinking about one's goals and objectives, and how to take the proper paths to achieve these, and not about simple compliance with guidelines more suited to the guidance of small children than world leaders, it is likely that the Snowden affair would have turned out much, much differently.

This proposal might strike some as naïve and ill-conceived. But it is difficult to work for years alongside members of the uniformed military services and civilians in the Department of Defense, as I have, and not come to admire their widespread dedication to duty and public service. They may be no abler than the general public to articulate these ideals, but they frequently express strong intuitions about the Right and the Good, as well as the elements of these embodied in the core values of democratic and rights-respecting states, to which they have pledged their lives, personal honor, and allegiance.

What a written code of ethics does for such people—and indeed, for all of us, as their clients and beneficiaries—is to capture, in hortatory and inspirational prose, a clear formulation of these goals and aspirations. Moreover, as we have seen in our examination of emergent moral norms, the ideals of best practice and the limitations on acceptable practice arise from the deliberations and experience of members of the community of practice themselves, and reflect their shared values, to which they *voluntarily hold themselves accountable*.

How, confronted with such an orientation and education in the purpose and goals of intelligence and security personnel, could Snowden or anyone else go so completely wrong in forming an impression of their sincerity and devotion to duty and to public service? This is especially true if the proposed code of the cyber warrior contains explicit reference to the twin importance of public security, on one hand, and to the individual citizen's rights to liberty and privacy, on the other. The code would explicitly commit the cyber warrior and defender of national security to respect the latter in the course of defending the former.

This is hardly a new proposal. Computer scientist Dorothy Denning, who now devotes her career to educating and preparing the new cyber warriors, began a discussion of the relevant precepts constraining permissible conduct of conflict in cyberspace more than a decade ago.[3] Matthew Beard, a thoughtful young Australian scholar and ethicist, has devoted his own recent research to exploring just what such a code would entail, with reference to the traditional code of the warrior about which Shannon E. French wrote, likewise over a decade ago.[4] Beard addresses a point of confusion in Denning's earlier proposals, however, noting controversially that true cyber warriors would not *themselves* deliberately engage in hacktivism per se; conversely, hacktivists (whether individuals or state-sponsored teams) are no more true cyber warriors than terrorists or participants in mob violence qualify as conventional warriors.[5]

This is an intriguing claim, inasmuch as it goes to the heart of what a true reflective dialogue concerning what sorts of morally permissible and impermissible acts would serve to define the parameters of a professional code of ethics for such individuals. Beard's point is moral consistency—an issue that frequently arose during discussions of the ethics of legitimate warriors engaged in irregular warfare as well. Moral consistency inherently demands that the legitimate warrior not engage in the kinds of activity from which he or she is simultaneously committed to protecting the public. That is, no more than police are permitted to engage in criminal acts in order to combat crime are legitimate combatants in irregular wars permitted to deliberately commit atrocities against civilians. By extension therefore, cyber warriors would not arbitrarily hack civilian targets or engage in the other kinds of activities associated with state-sponsored hacktivism. Instead, *their role is to protect victims from such attacks.*[6]

Beard cites other examples of moral prohibitions that would be self-imposed as a matter of the "warrior's honor," as much as or more than through law or federal regulation: for example, the prohibition against abusing one's position of trust as a cyber warrior to violate a subject's privacy for personal gain or amusement. These kinds of proposals are illustrative, but by no means exhaustive. Rather, they point the way toward *the kinds of deliberations that those legitimately engaged in cybersecurity should have among themselves* about the legal permissibility and moral probity of their tactics.

Prior to writing this book, my career was focused more generally on moral education and on preparing military personnel to understand and willingly embrace the uniquely moral dimensions of their public service. It seems to me incumbent now, when faced with the new and disruptive innovations of state-sponsored hacktivism, that we encourage and assist military and civilian intelligence operatives to explore the moral values that undergird their own public service, and to *codify these values in a clear expression of their moral vision and mission.* Such clarification, guidance, and efforts at professional self-regulation are urgently required in the face of the widespread confusion that cyber conflict has fostered. It is my profound hope that this book will aid in beginning that process of self-reflection and dedication to the high purpose of public service that cybersecurity professionals, engaged in defense of their nation and fellow citizens, have so long exhibited in the practice of their profession.

NOTES

1. A Reuters News Service interview with the incoming NSA director, Admiral Mike Rodgers, stated, "Morale among the NSA's tens of thousands of employees has taken a hit, and Rogers said many people in the agency found it both uncomfortable and perplexing to be under public scrutiny." See "NSA's Future Rests on Admiral Rogers' Shoulders," Reuters News Service, May 19, 2014, available from Voice of America, http://www.voanews.com/content/nsas-future-rests-on-admiral-rogers-shoulders/1917485.html (accessed September 15, 2015).
2. The key, still unanswered, question in this respect is not whether the programs of surveillance and data collection were illegal (they were not), or immoral (they were not), or abused by those who carried them out (there is absolutely no concrete evidence of this). Instead, the question is whether they were effective, and effective to a degree that warranted the enormous investment of personnel and funding in carrying them out. Is it, finally, effective to look for a needles in a haystack by first collecting the entire haystack? That, it seems to me, is a far more urgent and important question to study and answer.
3. Dorothy Denning, "Cyberwarriors: Activists and Terrorists Turn to Cyberspace," *Harvard International Review* 23 (2001): 70–75.
4. Shannon E. French, *The Code of the Warrior: Warrior Codes, Past and Present* (Lanham, MD: Rowman and Littlefield, 2004).
5. An earlier generation of cyber warriors, and their teachers, such as Denning and Schwartau, wondered if it would be necessary for government security agents to adopt the tactics of their adversaries, and even whether it would be necessary for individuals either to learn how to protect themselves or to hire private experts to do so. Such speculations find historical parallel in the frontier arming of individuals for self-defense in the early history of the United States, as well as in hiring of private security agents (Wells Fargo, Brinks) to provide security for vital social institutions. But eventually, such security on the frontier was deemed an "inherently governmental" function and subsumed within the institutions of civil society (police, courts, and the like).

    We seem to face such a choice in the present in the cyber domain, and I am clearly advocating for the training of a government sector, accountable to citizens, whose members are charged with this provision of security as an "inherently governmental" function, complete with a recognized code of conduct governing their behavior.
6. See Matthew Beard, "Beyond Tallinn: The Code of the Cyber Warrior?," in *Binary Bullets: The Ethics of Cyber Warfare*, ed. Fritz Allhoff, Adam Henschke, and Bradley Jay Strawser (New York: Oxford University Press, 2016): 139–156.

REFERENCES

Akdeniz, Yuri. 2002. "Anonymity, Democracy, and Cyberspace." *Social Research: An International Quarterly* 69: 223–237.

Allhoff, Fritz, Henscke, Adam, and Strawser, Bradley J., eds. 2016. *Binary Bullets: The Ethics of Cyber Warfare*. Oxford: Oxford University Press.

Ambinder, Marc, and Grady, D. B. 2015. *Deep State: Inside the Government Secrecy Industry*. Hoboken, NJ: John Wiley and Sons.

Arquilla, John. 1999. "Ethics and Information Warfare." In *The Changing Role of Information in Warfare*, edited by Z. Khalilzad, J. White, and A. Marshall, 379–401. Santa Monica, CA: Rand Corporation.

Arquilla, John. 2010. "Conflict, Security, and Computer Ethics." In *The Cambridge Handbook of Information and Computer Ethics*, edited by Luciano Floridi, 133–149. New York: Cambridge University Press.

Arquilla, John. 2012. "Cyber War Is Already upon Us." *Foreign Policy*, March–April, http://www.foreignpolicy.com/articles/2012/02/27/cyberwar_is_already_upon_us.

Arquilla, John, and Ronfeldt, David. 1993. "Cyberwar Is Coming!" *Comparative Strategy* 12 (2): 141–165.

Arquilla, John, and Ronfeldt, David. 2001. *Networks and Netwars: The Future of Terror, Crime, and Militancy*. Santa Monica, CA: Rand Corporation.

Baier, Kurt. 1958. *The Moral Point of View*. Ithaca, NY: Cornell University Press.

Balendra, Natasha T. 2008. "Defining Armed Conflict." *Cardoza Law Review* 29 (6): 2461–2516.

Barrett, Edward. 2013. "Warfare in a New Domain: The Ethics of Military Cyber Operations." *Journal of Military Ethics* 12 (1): 4–17.

Beard, Matthew. 2013. "The Code of the Cyber Warrior." MA thesis, Notre Dame University of Australia. Paper presented at "Cyberwar, Cybercrime and Cyberdefence: Mapping the Ethical Terrain." Hosted by the Center for Applied Philosophy and Practical Ethics. Charles Sturt University and the National Security College, Canberra, AU, August 5–6, 2013. https://soundcloud.com/unda-cfes/the-code-of-the-cyberwarrior.

Beard, Matthew. 2016. "Beyond Tallinn: The Code of the Cyber Warrior?" In *Binary Bullets: The Ethics of Cyber Warfare*, edited by Fritz Allhoff, Adam Henschke, and Bradley Jay Strawser. New York: Oxford University Press.

Betts, Alexander, and Orchard, Phillip, eds. 2014. *Implementation in World Politics: How International Norms Change Practice*. Oxford: Oxford University Press.

Bowdon, Mark. 2011. *Worm: The First Digital World War*. New York: Atlantic Monthly Press.

Brenner, Joel. 2011. *America the Vulnerable: Inside the New Threat Matrix of Digital Espionage, Crime, and Warfare*. New York: Penguin Press.

Brenner, Joel. 2013. "N.S.A.: Not (so) Secret Anymore." Blog entry, December 10, http://joelbrenner.com/blog/. Accessed March 14, 2014.

Breyer, Stephen. 2015. *The Court and the World: American Law and the New Global Realities*. New York: Alfred K. Knopf.

Calhoun, Craig, ed. 1992. *Habermas and the Public Sphere*. Cambridge, MA: MIT Press.

Carr, Jeffrey. 2011. *Inside Cyber Warfare: Mapping the Cyber Underworld*. 2nd ed. Sebastapol, CA: O'Reilly Media.

Council of Europe. 2001. "Convention on Cybercrime." Treaty No. 185, Council of Europe, Treaty Office, Budapest, November 23. http://conventions.coe.int/Treaty/EN/Treaties/html/185.htm. Accessed March 14, 2014.

Chatterjee, Deen K., ed. 2013. *The Ethics of Preventive War*. New York: Cambridge University Press.

Clarke, Richard A., and Knake, Robert K. 2010. *Cyber War: The Next Threat to National Security and What to Do about It*. New York: HarperCollins.

Clausewitz, Carl von. (1830) 1976. *On War*. Edited and translated and by Michael Howard and Peter Paret. Princeton, NJ: Princeton University Press.

Coleman, Stephen. 2015. "Even Dirtier Hands in War: Considering Walzer's Supreme Emergency Argument." *Research in Ethical Issues in Organizations* 13: 61–73.

Cook, James. 2010. "'Cyberation' and Just War Doctrine: A Response to Randall Dipert." *Journal of Military Ethics* 9 (4): 411–423.

Cook, James. 2015. "Just War under CyberGaia." In *The Routledge Handbook of Military Ethics*, edited by George Lucas, 421–431. London: Routledge.

Cook, Martin L. 2007. "Michael Walzer's Concept of Supreme Emergency." *Journal of Military Ethics* 6 (2): 138–151.

Copp, David. 2015. "Explaining Normativity." *Proceedings and Addresses of the American Philosophical Association* 89 (November): 48–73.

Curtis, S. 2012. "UK Faces Weekly Cyber Attacks." *Techworld* online, April 24. http://news.techworld.com/security/3353135/uk-businesses-face-weekly-cyber-attacks—report. Accessed March 15, 2014.

Denning, Dorothy E. 1998. *Information Warfare and Security*. Boston: Addison-Wesley.

Denning, Dorothy E. 2001. "Cyberwarriors." *Harvard International Review* 23: 70–75.

Denning, Dorothy E. 2007. "The Ethics of Cyber Conflict." In *Handbook of Information and Computer Ethics*, edited by K. E. Himma and H. T. Tavani, 407–428. New York: John Wiley and Sons. Available online at: http://faculty.nps.edu/dedennin/publications/Ethics%20of%20Cyber%20Conflict.pdf. Accessed March 14, 2014.

De Oliviera, Nythamar Fernandes. 2000. "The Critique of Public Reason Revisited: Kant as Arbiter between Rawls and Habermas." *Veritas* 45 (4): 583–606.

Dipert, Randall R. 2010. "The Ethics of Cyber Warfare." *Journal of Military Ethics* 9 (4): 384–410.

Dipert, Randall R. 2013. "Other Than Internet (OTI) Cyberwarfare: Challenges for Ethics, Law, and Policy." *Journal of Military Ethics* 12 (1): 34–53.

Dipert, Randall R. 2013. "The Essential Features for an Ontology for Cyberwarfare." In *Conflict and Cooperation in Cyberspace*, edited by P. A. Yannakogeorgos and A. B. Lowther, 35–48. Boca Raton, FL: Taylor & Francis.

DoD. 2011. US Department of Defense Strategy for Operating in Cyberspace. Washington, DC: Department of Defense, July 1. http://www.defense.gov/news/d20110714cyber.pdf. Accessed March 15, 2014.

DoS. 2011. "International Strategy for Cyberspace: Prosperity, Security and Openness in a Networked World." Report by the Office of the President. Washington DC, May 1. http://www.whitehouse.gov/sites/default/files/rss_viewer/international_ strategy_for_cyberspace.pdf. Accessed March 15, 2014.

Dunlap, Charles J. 2011. "Perspectives for Cyber Strategists on Law for Cyberwar." *Strategic Studies Quarterly* 5 (1): 81–99.

Eberle, Christopher. 2013. "Just War and Cyber War." *Journal of Military Ethics* 12 (1): 54–67.

Eggers, Dave. 2013. *The Circle*. New York: Alfred A. Knopf.

Fabre, Cecile. 2012. *Cosmopolitan War*. Oxford: Oxford University Press.

Fabre, Cecile, and Lazar, Seth, eds. 2014. *The Morality of Defensive War*. Oxford: Oxford University Press.

Finnemore, Martha, and Sikkink, Kathryn. 1998. "International Norm Dynamics and Political Change." *International Organization* 52 (4): 887–917.

Floridi, Luciano, and Taddeus, Mariarosaria, eds. 2014. *The Ethics of Information Warfare*. Amsterdam: Springer.

French, Shannon E. 2004. *The Code of the Warrior: Exploring Warrior Values Past and Present*. Lanham, MD: Rowman and Littlefield.

Gibbard, Allan. 2003. *Thinking How to Live*. Cambridge, MA: Harvard University Press.

Gibson, William. 1984. *Neuromancer*. New York: Ace Books.

Gjelten, Tom. 2010. "Extending the Law of War to Cyberspace." *Morning Edition*, National Public Radio, September 22. http://www.npr.org/templates/story/ story.php?storyId=130023318. Accessed March 15, 2014.

Goldman, Jan, ed. 2005/2009. *The Ethics of Spying: A Reader for the Intelligence Professional*. Vols. 1 and 2. Lanham, MD: Scarecrow Press.

Goodman, Marc. 2015. *Future Crimes*. New York: Doubleday.

Graham, David E. 2010. "Cyber Threats and the Law of War." *Journal of National Security Law* 4 (1): 87–102.

Greenberg, Andy. 2012. *This Machine Kills Secrets*. London: Penguin.

Gross, Michael L. 2014. *The Ethics of Insurgency: A Critical Guide to Just Guerilla Warfare*. New York: Cambridge University Press.

Gross, Michael, and Meisels, Tami. 2016. *Soft War: The Ethics of Unarmed Conflict*. Cambridge: Cambridge University Press.

Habermas, Jürgen. 1991. *The Structural Transformation of the Public Sphere*. Translated by Thomas Burger. Cambridge, MA: MIT Press.

Hardin, Garrett. 1968. "The Tragedy of the Commons." *Science* 162 (3859): 1243–1248.

Hare, Richard M. 1952. *The Language of Morals*. Oxford: Clarendon.

Harris, Shane. 2014. *@War: The Rise of the Military-Internet Complex*. New York: Houghton Mifflin Harcourt.

Hurka, Thomas. 2005. "Proportionality in the Morality of War." *Philosophy and Public Affairs* 33 (1): 34–66.

Jenkins, Ryan. 2013. "Is Stuxnet Physical? Does It Matter?" *Journal of Military Ethics* 12 (1): 68–79.

Johnson, James Turner. 2014. *Sovereignty*. Washington, DC: Georgetown University Press.

Jonson, Albert, and Toulmin, Stephen. 1990. *The Abuse of Casuistry*. Berkeley: University of California Press.

Klabbers, Jan, and Piiparinin, Tuoko, eds. 2014. *Normative Pluralism and International Law: Exploring Global Governance*. Cambridge: Cambridge University Press.

Knappenberger, Brian. 2012. Writer, director, producer. *We Are Legion: The Story of the Hacktivists*. DVD. Download available at http://wearelegionthedocumentary.com/. Accessed February 17, 2016.

Koepsell, David R. 2003. *The Ontology of Cyber Space*. Peru, IL: Open Court Publishing.

Korsgaard, Christine. 1996. *The Sources of Normativity*. Cambridge: Cambridge University Press.

Lewis, Harry. 2015. "Anonymity and Reason." *Privacy in the Modern Age*, edited by Marc Rotenberg, Jeramie Horwitz, and Julia Scott, 104–111. New York: New Press.

Liang, Q., and Xiangsui, W. 1999. *Unrestricted Warfare: Warfare without Boundaries*. Los Angeles: Pan American Publishing. Originally published in Beijing by PLA Literature and Arts Publishing House. English translation selections are available at http://www.cryptome.org/cuw.htm. Accessed March 14, 2014.

Libicki, Martin C. 2007. *Conquest in Cyberspace: National Security and Information Warfare*. New York: Cambridge University Press.

Libiciki, Martin C. 2009. *Cyberdeterrence and Cyberwar*. Santa Monica, CA: Rand Corporation.

Libicki, Martin C. 1995. *What Is Information Warfare?* Washington, DC: National Defense University, Institute for National Strategic Studies.

Lucas, George R., Jr., 2009. *Anthropologists in Arms: The Ethics of Military Anthropology*. Lanham, MD: Alta Mira Press.

Lucas, George R., Jr. 2013a. "Can There Be an Ethical Cyberwar?" In *Conflict and Cooperation in Cyberspace*, edited by Panayotis A. Yannakogeorgos and Adam B. Lowther, 195–210. Boca Raton, FL: Taylor & Francis.

Lucas, George R., Jr. 2013b. "*Jus in Silico*: Moral Restrictions on the Use of Cyber Warfare." In *The Routledge Handbook of War and Ethics*, edited by Fritz Allhoff, Nicholas G. Evans, and Adam Henschke, 367–380. New York: Routledge.

Lucas, George R., Jr. 2013c. "Emerging Norms for Cyber Warfare." Keynote address. "Conference on Ethics and Cyber Security." Center for Applied Philosophy and Practical Ethics, Australian National and Charles Sturt Universities, Canberra, AU: August 5–6, 2013. http://philevents.org/event/show/11114.

Lucas, George R., Jr. 2013d. "Navigation, Aviation, 'Cyberation:' Developing New Rules of the Road for the Cyber Domain." Inaugural Public Security Lecture, National Security College, Australian National University, Canberra, AU: August 7, 2013. http://www.youtube.com/watch?v=cs7RXAPzG84.

Lucas, George R., Jr. 2013e. "Privacy, Anonymity, and Cyber Security." *Amsterdam Law Forum* 5 (2): 107–114.

Lucas, George R., Jr. 2014a. "Permissible Preventive Cyber Warfare." In *The Ethics of Information Warfare*, edited by Luciano Floridi and Mariarosaria Taddeo, 73–82. Amsterdam: Springer.

Lucas, George R., Jr. 2014b. "NSA Management Directive #424: Secrecy and Privacy in the Aftermath of Snowden." *Journal of Ethics and International Affairs* 28 (1): 29–38.

Lucas, George R., Jr. 2014c. "State-Sponsored Hacktivism and the Advent of 'Soft' War." *Ethics and Armed Forces* 2: 16–23.

Lucas, George R., Jr. 2014d. "Automated Warfare." *Stanford Law and Policy Review* 25 (2): 317–339.

Lucas, George R., Jr. 2014e. "Ethics and Cyber Conflict: A Review of Recent Work." *Journal of Military Ethics* 13 (1): 20–31.

Lucas, George R., Jr. 2015a. "War." In *The Bloomsbury Companion to Political Philosophy*, edited by Andrew Fiala, 109–126. London: Bloomsbury.

Lucas, George R., Jr. 2015b. *Military Ethics: What Everyone Needs to Know.* Oxford: Oxford University Press.

Lucas, George R., Jr., and David Whetham. 2015. "The Relevance of the Just War Tradition to Cyber Warfare." In *Cyber Warfare: A Multidisciplinary Analysis*, edited by James A. Green, 160–173. London: Routledge.

MacIntyre, Alasdair. 1981. *After Virtue.* South Bend, IN: University of Notre Dame Press.

MacIntyre, Alasdair. 1988. *Whose Justice? Which Rationality?* South Bend, IN: University of Notre Dame Press.

MacIntyre, Alasdair. 1990. *First Principles, Final Ends, and Contemporary Philosophical Issues.* Milwaukee, WI: Marquette University Press.

MacIntyre, Alasdair. 2009. "Intractable Moral Disagreements." In *Intractable Disputes about the Natural Law: Alasdair MacIntyre and Critics*, edited by Lawrence Cunningham. Notre Dame, IN: University of Notre Dame Press, 1–52.

McMahan, Jeff. 2009. *Killing in War.* New York: Oxford University Press.

Müller, Harald, and Wunderlich, Carmen, eds. 2013. *Norm Dynamics in Multilateral Arms Control: Interests, Conflicts, and Justice.* Athens: University of Georgia Press.

Nye, Joseph. 2004. *Soft Power: The Means to Success in World Politics.* New York: Public Affairs Press.

Ohlin, Jens David, Govern, Kevin, and Finkelstein, Claire, eds. 2015. *Cyberwar: Law and Ethics for Virtual Conflicts.* New York: Oxford University Press.

O'Meara, Richard M. 2014. *Governing Military Technologies in the 21st Century: Ethics and Operations.* New York: Palgrave Macmillan.

O'Neill, Onora. 1986. "The Public Use of Reason." *Political Theory* 14 (4): 523–551.

Owens, William A., Dam, Kenneth W., and Lin, Herbert L. 2009. *Technology, Policy, Law, and Ethics Regarding U.S. Acquisition and Use of Cyberattack Capabilities.* Washington, DC: National Research Council and American Academy of Sciences, 2009.

Perry, David. 2009. *Partly Cloudy: The Ethics of Espionage, Covert Action, and Interrogation.* Lanham, MD: Scarecrow Press.

Postma, Peter B. 2015. "Regulating Lethal Autonomous Robots in Unconventional Warfare." *University of St. Thomas Law Journal* 11 (2): 300–330.

Price, Richard. 2008. "Moral Limit and Possibility in World Politics." *International Organization* 62 (2): 191–220.

Rid, Thomas. 2011. "Cyber War Will Not Take Place." *Journal of Strategic Studies* 35 (1): 5–32.

Rid, Thomas. 2012. "Think Again: Cyberwar." *Foreign Policy* online, March–April. http://www.foreignpolicy.com/articles/2012/02/27/cyberwar. Accessed March 14, 2014.

Rid, Thomas. 2013. *Cyber War Will Not Take Place.* London: C Hurst & Amp.

Rodin, David. 2002. *War and Self-Defense.* Oxford: Oxford University Press.

Rodin, David, and Shue, Henry, eds. 2008. *Just and Unjust Warriors: The Moral and Legal Status of Soldiers.* Oxford: Oxford University Press.

Rotenberg, Marc, Horwitz, Julia, and Scott, Jeramie, eds. 2015. *Privacy in the Modern Age.* New York: New Press.

Rowe, Neil C. 2007. "War Crimes from Cyberweapons." *Journal of Information Warfare* 6 (3): 5–25.

Rowe, Neil C. 2008. "Ethics of Cyber War Attacks." In *Cyber Warfare and Cyber Terrorism*, edited by L. J. Janczewski and A. M. Colarik, 105–111. Hershey, PA: Information Science Reference.

Rowe, Neil C. 2010. "The Ethics of Cyberweapons in Warfare." *Journal of Techoethics* 1 (1): 20–31. http://www.igi-global.com/article/ethics-cyberweapons-warfare/ 39122. Accessed March 14, 2014.

Rowe, Neil C. 2011. "Toward Reversible Cyber Attacks." In *Leading Issues in Information Warfare and Security Research*, edited by J. Ryan, 145–158. Reading, PA: Academic Publishing.

Rowe, Neil C. 2013. "Perfidy in Cyberwarfare." *The Routledge Handbook of War and Ethics*, edited by Fritz Allhoff, Nicholas G. Evans, and Adam Henschke, 393–404. London: Routledge.

Sanger, David E. 2013. "Differences on Cybertheft Complicate China Talks." *New York Times* website, July 10. www.nytimes.com/2013/07/11/world/asia/differences-on-cybertheft-complicate-china-talks.html. Accessed March 14, 2014.

Sanger, David E. 2012. *Confront and Conceal: Obama's Secret Wars and Surprising Use of American Power*. New York: Crown Books.

Sanger, David E., and Schmitt, E. 2012. "Cyber Attacks Are Up, National Security Chief Says." *New York Times*, July 27.

Scanlon, Thomas M. 2014. *Being Realistic about Reasons*. Oxford: Oxford University Press.

Scheid, Don E. 2014. *The Ethics of Armed Humanitarian Intervention*. Cambridge: Cambridge University Press.

Schmitt, Michael N. 1999. "Computer Network Attack and the Use of Force in International Law: Thoughts on a Normative Framework." *Columbia Journal of Transnational Law* 37: 885–937. http://heinonline.org/HOL/LandingPage?col lection=journals&handle=hein.journals/cjtl37&div=39&id=&page=. Accessed March 15, 2014.

Schmitt, Michael N. 2002. "Wired Warfare: Computer Network Attack and *Jus In Bello*." *International Review of the Red Cross* 84 (846): 365–399. http://www.icrc. org/eng/assets/files/other/365_400_schmitt.pdf. Accessed March 14, 2014.

Schmitt, Michael N. 2011. "Cyber Operations and the *Jus in Bello*: Key Issues." *U.S. Naval War College International Law Studies* 87 (August): 89–110.

Schmitt, Michael N., and O'Donnell, Brian T., eds. 2002. *Computer Network Attack and International Law*. International Law Studies 76. Newport, RI: US Naval War College.

Schwartau, Winn. 2000. *Cybershock*. New York: Thunder's Mouth Press.

Singer, Peter, and Friedman, Allan. 2014. *Cybersecurity and Cyberwar: What Everyone Needs to Know*. New York: Oxford University Press.

Soldatov, Andrei, and Borogan, Irina. 2015. *The Red Web*. Philadelphia: Public Affairs.

Solove, Daniel J. 2008. "The End of Privacy." *Scientific American*, September, 101–106.

Spaak, Torben. 2003. "Legal Positivism, Law's Normativity, and the Normative Force of Legal Justification." *Ratio Juris* 16 (4): 469–485.

Tagarev, Todor. 2010. *Building Integrity and Reducing Corruption in Defence: A Compendium of Best Practices*. Geneva: Geneva Centre for the Democratic Control of Armed Forces.

The Tallinn Manual on the International Law Applicable to Cyber Warfare: Prepared by the International Groups of Experts at the Invitation of the NATO Cooperative Cyber Defense Center of Excellence. 2012. Edited by Michael N. Schmitt. Cambridge: Cambridge University Press, 2013. Online version available at https://www. ccdcoe.org/249.html. Accessed March 14, 2014.

Taylor, R. 2011. "Australia Warns on Cyber Attacks." Reuters News Service, May 30. http://www.reuters.com/article/2011/05/30/us-australia-cyber-idUSTRE74T0 KH20110530. Accessed March 15, 2014.

Tiki, Eneken, Kaska, Kadri, and Vihul, Liis. 2010. *International Cyber Incidents: Legal Considerations*. Tallinn: Cooperative Cyber Defence Center of Excellence.

Tripodi, Paolo, and Wolfendale, Jessica, eds. 2011. *New Wars and New Soldiers*. London: Ashgate.

Vitoria, Francisco de. 1991. *Vitoria: Political Writings*. Edited by Anthony Pagden and Jeremy Lawrance. Cambridge: Cambridge University Press.

Walzer, Michael. 1977. *Just and Unjust Wars*. New York: Basic Books.

Whitehead, Alfred North. 1925. *Science and the Modern World*. New York: Macmillan.

Yannakogeorgos, Panayotis A. 2013. "The Prospects for Cyber Deterrence: American Sponsorship of Global Norms." In *Conflict and Cooperation in Cyberspace: The Challenge to National Security*, edited by Panayotis A. Yannakogeorgos and Adam B. Lowther, 49–80. Boca Raton, FL: Taylor & Francis.

Yannakogeorgos, Panayotis A., and Lowther, Adam B., eds. 2013. *Conflict and Cooperation in Cyberspace*. Boca Raton, FL: Taylor & Francis.

Zetter, Kim. 2014. *Countdown to Zero Day*. New York: Crown Books.

INDEX

Belmont convention, 106n10
Bentham, Jeremy, 84n43
best practice
  in cyberconflict, 118–119
  derivation of, 46, 112, 122n8,
    163, 192
  versus law, 112
  versus morals, 46, 92
  as norms, 46, 111, 122n8, 163
Bhagavad Gita, 97
bomb, logic, 31n16
bombers, suicide, 23
bot
  definition of, 11n5
botnet
  definition of, 11n5
  uses of, 20
Building Integrity (NATO program), 134

Canada
  as intelligence ally, 139, 143, 144
casus belli
  cybercrime as, 63
causation, principle of, 43
CCC. *See* Convention on Cyber
  Crime (CCC)
China. *See also* People's Liberation Army
  cyberattacks by, 5, 75
  cyber capability of, 24, 75
  cyberespionage by, 5, 19, 75–76,
    78, 153
  just war theory in, 97–98
  and norms of state behavior, 120
  and *Tallinn Manual*, 44
civil disobedience
  whistleblowing as, 48
civilians
  cybersecurity for, 131–133
  cyberthreats against, 4, 5, 6, 24, 26–27,
    34, 59, 61, 117, 118, 131, 148
  prohibition against attacks on, 65, 74,
    103, 114, 118, 148, 154, 164
Clarke, Richard A., 5, 6, 24–25
Clausewitz, Carl von
  definition of war by, 23, 29, 118
  and ethics in war, 37–38
collateral damage
  from cyberattack, 3, 59, 103, 118–119
  from exemption, 46
Confikker (worm), 30n6

conflict. *See also* armed conflict;
  cyberconflict. *See also under* war;
  warfare
  development of laws governing, 85
  unrestricted, 24–27, 28, 85–86
Convention on Cyber Crime (CCC), 6
conventional warfare. *See* warfare,
  conventional
Cook, James, 42, 43
Cooperative Cyber Defence Centre of
  Excellence (CCD COE), 64
Council of Europe
  and cyber crime, 58
covert operations. *See* espionage
crime
  as *casus belli*, 63
  cyberactivity as, 147–148
  versus war, 9
cunning of history, 105n8, 128–129
cunning of nature, 93–94
  function of, 94–95
Cutting Sword of Justice, 10
cyber
  etymology of, 16
cyber Armageddon
  possibility of, 27–28
cyberattack
  countermeasures to, 70, 95–96, 119,
    130–131
  as irregular warfare, 23–24, 25–26,
    118, 147
  protection against, 130–131
cyberbullying, 13n10
cyber conflict
  assessing threat from, 16–17, 114–115
  attribution problem in, 43, 117
  best practice in, 118–119
  versus cyberwar, 125–126
  deception in, 66
  emerging norms for dealing with,
    114, 121n4
  as equivalent to armed attack, 25–26,
    114–115, 118–119
  ethics in, 85–86, 95–98, 114, 118
  goals of, 95
  how to behave in, 42, 95–96
  and international law, 38, 85, 96
  justification for, 102
  master narrative of, 114–119, 125–126
  morality in, 86–87

moral principles in, 96
as not war, 57–58
oversight of, 38, 39
and rights versus security, 74–75
in unrestricted warfare, 25, 85–86
and *Talinn Manual*, 39, 69–70
as war, 57, 69–70, 115–116
cybercrime
as *casus belli*, 63
classification as, 6
emerging norms for dealing with, 115
as espionage, 6
history of, 20
international cooperation in
combating, 58
motives for, 8–9, 20
Stuxnet as, 70–71
as war, 147
cyber domain
anonymity in, 49, 73, 151–152
borderless nature of, 87
as a commons, 120–121n1
criminal law in, 73–74
definition of, 17
international law applied to, 73, 75
as lawless frontier, 75, 85–86,
151–152, 165n5
malevolent misbehavior in, 19–20
morality applied to, 48–49, 90,
93, 120
moral relativism in, 93
resistance to regulation of, 73, 110
sectors of vulnerability in, 130–131
state of nature in, 88–89
cyberespionage
as act of war, 68, 147
by China, 5, 24–25
physical damage by, 68
response to, 95–96
under *Talinn Manual*, 67–68
Cyber Fighters of Izz ad-Din al-Qassam,
10, 130
cyber–ontological paradox, 62
cybersecurity. *See also* security
and anonymity, 135
obstacles to, 131–132
and privacy, 8, 25, 27–28, 129–130,
131–133, 135, 137–139
ways to enhance, 132–133
cyberspace, 16

description of, 17
development of military
capabilities in, 24
ethics versus folk morality
in, 85–104
extent of, 17
global norms for, 112
malevolent misbehavior in, 19–20
norms for behavior in, 121n4
political sabotage in, 20
transactions in, 18
cybersurveillance
and anonymity, 135
containment of, 119, 133
informed consent to, 148–150
and irregular warfare, 24
mission creep in, 142
as preventive self-defense, 142–143
public response to, 147–148
cybertheft
by China, 5
of patents and trade secrets, 5
cyber vandalism, 19–20
*Cyberwar: Law and Ethics for Virtual
Conflicts* (Ohlin et al.), 42
cyberwarfare, 33–35
versus cyber conflict, 125–126
definition of, 6
distributed denial of service as, 4–5
emergent norms in, 46–47,
109–120
ethics of, 40–41, 118, 164
etymology of, 7, 16
examples of, 6–7, 115–116
experience with, 114–115
hacking as, 6, 64
under just war theory, 40–41, 96
and international law, 96
as other than war, 42
perfidy in, 65, 66
potential for authorization of, by UN
Security Council, 64
potential outcomes of, 7
ruses in, 65, 66
threat of, 27–28
as unrestricted warfare, 26, 148
cyberwarriors
moral code for, 104, 157–165
as vigilantes, 164
Cyberwarriors for Freedom, 20

cyber weapons. *See also* warfare,
  irregular
  accessibility of, 27
  versus conventional weapons, 43, 58
  definition of, 7–8
  under international law of armed
    conflict, 60, 61, 96
  legality of, 26
  morality of, 26
  Stuxnet as, 3
  under *Talinn Manual*, 60–61

Darkode.com, 25, 31n17, 58
dark web, 25, 31n17
data chaining, 145–146, 147
data mining, 142–143, 147
  and privacy, 151, 152
  purpose of, 142–143
DDoS. *See* distributed denial of service
Denning, Dorothy, 7, 163–164
Dipert, Randall, 16, 41
discrimination. *See* principle of
  distinction
distinction. *See* principle of distinction
distributed denial of service (DDoS), 20
  as act of war, 5, 117
  in Estonia, 4–5, 20, 43, 64,
    115–116, 117
  by Iran, 109
  in Ossetia, 116
domains of experience, 17
doxing
  definition of, 5, 13n10
  etymology of, 13n10
drone pilots
  as unconventional forces, 34
drones
  attacks by, 24
due process
  and surveillance, 137, 153
  and whistleblowing, 161
Duqu (virus), 79n9

economy of force. *See* principle of
  economy of force
"Eight Points for Attention" (Mao), 98
Ellsberg, Daniel, 49, 99, 136–137
emergent norms. *See* norms, emergent
email
  Internet pathway of, 18, 151

packet-sniffing, 133, 137
  privacy of, versus mail privacy, 137
  verifying authenticity of, 18, 137
Emile (Rousseau), 93–94
Enterprise Knowledge System, 11,
  130, 144
  contents of, 144–145
epistemological crisis, x, xi
espionage
  versus conventional warfare, 34, 148
  cybercrime as, 6
  definition of, 6, 13n14
  emergent norms in, 153–154
  oversight governing, 35
  purpose of, 34
  rules of engagement for, 26, 76, 148
  state-sponsored hacktivism as, 61
Estonia distributed denial of service, 4–
  5, 20, 43, 115–116
  appropriate responses to, 69–71,
    72, 117
  attribution problem in, 4, 20, 30n7,
    54n23, 72, 116, 117, 124n17,
  importance of, 64
  and international law, 68–72
  perpetrators of, 20
  and *Talinn Manual*, 69–70
ethics. *See also under* moral; morality
  in cyber conflict, 35–40, 40–41,
    95–98, 103
  in cyberspace, 85–104
  for cyberwarriors, 104, 157–165
  definition of, 91, 163
  emergent norms in, 46, 85
  exemptions in, 45, 48
  versus folk morality, 85, 88–91
  and international relations, 37–38
  and just war theory, 42–44
  lack of consensus on, 35
  and law, 40–41, 43, 147
  versus morality, 91, 111, 114
  and sound strategy, xi
  of Stuxnet, 59–60
  universality of, 111
  violations of, 155, 164
  and war, 37–38
ethics, professional, 111, 162–165
  under cyberwarfare, 34–35, 103–104,
    155, 164
  lack of understanding of, 162–163

as self-governance, 95, 97, 98, 111,
    162, 164–165
    military, 97, 101–102,
        103–104, 107n12
    universality of, 95
    violations of, 155
"Ethics of Cyber Warfare" (Dipert), 41
exception. *See* morality of exceptions
exemption. *See* morality of exceptions

fallacy, naturalistic, 46
Federal Bureau of Investigation (FBI)
    cyber operations of, 25
Finkelstein, Claire, 1
Five Eyes, 139, 143, 144
Flame (surveillance software), 10–11
folk morality, 35–40
    in cyberspace, 85–104
    definition of, 35
    versus ethics, 85, 88–91, 162–163
    examples of, 36, 88
    moral realism in, 88
    moral relativism in, 89
    problems with, 35–36
    and professional ethics, 162–163
Foreign Intelligence and Surveillance Act
    (FISA) (1978), 145, 155n4
Franklin, Benjamin, 152
freedom of expression
    and cybersurveillance, 27, 136,
        153, 155
    and hacktivism, 21
    Sony Pictures hacking as, 5–6
French, Shannon E., 164

Gandhi, Mahatma, 99
"General Orders #100," 102, 107n12
Geneva Convention
    Additional Protocol of 1977, 58–59
    origins of, 107n12
Georgia
    cyberattacks on, 118
Gibson, William, 16
Global Positioning System (GPS), 17
Golden Rule
    universality of, 90
Good, 56n36
    in cyber domain, 93, 129
    nature of, 56n36
    in professions, 95, 105–106n9, 163

possibility of achieving, 92–93, 95
shared conception of, 75, 86, 92–95,
    162, 163
good governance, 40,
    features of, 52n15
government
    abuse of power by, 153, 161
    deception by, 49, 150–151
    hacktivism by, 5, 19, 70, 72, 75–76
    public trust in, 150–151,
        157–158, 163
    secrecy in, 161
    vulnerability of, to cyberthreat, 131
GPS (Global Positioning System), 17
Graham, David, 63

hacking
    of Sony Pictures, 5–6, 28
hacktivism, 20–21
    definition of, 6
    justification for, 22
    political goals of, 21
    and transparency, 21
    and vigilantism, 21
    and whistleblowing, 21
hacktivism, state-sponsored, 8–9, 10
    advantage of physical distance in, 62
    attribution problem in, 61–62, 117
    definition of, 20
    as espionage, 61
    as equivalent to armed conflict, 58
    in Estonia, 4–5, 20, 43, 64, 115–116
    examples of, 20
    and law of armed conflict, 61–64, 78
    threat from, 27–28
    as warfare, 27–29, 33, 64
hacktivist, 20–21
    political goals of, 21
    ways of being, 21–22
Hadith
    jus in bello in, 98
Hardin, Garrett, 110
Hare, Richard M., 56n36
Hegel, Georg Wilhelm Friedrich, 105n8
Helsinki Congress, 107n10
Hobbes, Thomas, 9
    and rights versus security, 49, 73, 91,
        92–93, 94
Hoover, J. Edgar, 152–153
human nature, 93–94

human rights
  law, 37, 39, 87
  universality of, 36, 37, 39, 87, 91,
    111, 152
humanitarian intervention
  and just war theory, 41
  as other than war, 33, 42
humanitarian law
  command responsibility in, 43–44
  distinction in, 43–44
  foundation of, 107n12
  and just war tradition, 43–44, 77–78
  military necessity in, 43–44
  principles of, 43–44, 102
  proportionality in, 43–44
Hume, David, 56n36, 122n8

improvised explosive devices (IEDs), 23
India
  just war theory in, 97
industry
  vulnerability of, to cyberthreat, 131
information warfare. *See* cyberwarfare
informed consent
  to medical experiments, 150
  and Natural Security Agency, 150–151
  potential abuses of, 155
  problematic nature of, 148–149
  resistance to, 149–150
  to surveillance, 148–149, 154
Inglis, Chris, 1, 10
Innocence of Muslims, The, 10
insurgency
  legitimate authority in, 100, 101
intelligence. *See also under* espionage
  agencies, purpose of, 34
  agencies, rules of engagement for, 26,
    147–148, 150
  ethics, 34–35
  operations, oversight governing, 35
International Committee of the Red
    Cross, 43
International Convention on Cybercrime
    (2001), 58, 63
international humanitarian law. *See*
    humanitarian law
international law
  acts of war under, 115
  armed conflict under, 69
  and China, 5

and cyber conflict, 35, 38–40, 43, 57,
  73–76 77
and cyber weapons, 96
and espionage, 6, 26, 147–148
and the Estonian cyberattacks, 68–72
and Iran, 3
and irregular warfare, 35
and just war theory, 41, 44, 77–78
moral principles in, 26, 32n19
nature of, 32n18, 109, 120
and preventive self-defense,
  146–147, 151
positivism in, 77
state focus of, 87, 102, 109, 112
and state-sponsored hacktivism,
  9, 61–64
and Stuxnet, 58–61
and the *Tallinn Manual*, 64–68
international law enforcement
  cooperation in, 58, 62–63
international law of armed conflict. *See*
  law of armed conflict
international relations
  and ethics, 37–38
  norms in, 112, 125n5
Internet. *See also under* cyber
  crime, 25
  extent of, 17
  pathway of email in, 18
  verifying authenticity in, 18
Internet of Things, 17
  security of, 17, 128–129
Interview, The, 5–6
Iran
  response of, to Stuxnet, 10–11, 109
  state-sponsored hacktivism by,
    10–11, 109
  and Stuxnet, 3, 116, 118
Islam
  and just war theory, 98
Islamic State
  as legitimate authority, 101
  moral realism under, 37
Israel
  cybersupport for bombing raid by, 116
  as developer of Stuxnet, 3, 118
ius gentium (customary law), 39, 112

jus ad bellum
  and collective security, 65

and cyber conflict, 42–43, 65
definition of, 74, 97
history of, 74, 97
moral principles in, 99–100
oversight of, 97
and self-defense, 65
in *Tallinn Manual*, 65
and use of force, 65, 74
jus gentium, 102
jus in bello
and cyber conflict, 42–43
definition of, 74, 97
history of, 74, 97
and military ethics, 101–102
oversight of, 97
jus in silico, 102–104
just cause. *See* principle of just cause
just war reasoning, 42, 97–98
just war theory
challenges to, 44
cultural bias in, 44
cyberwarfare under, 40–41, 96, 103
and ethics, 42–44
history of, 97–98
and international law, 77–78
and legitimate authority, 100–101
and morality of exceptions, 98–101
purpose of, 42, 44
relevance of, to cyberwarfare, 41
supreme emergency in, 45, 55n32
just war tradition
conflict under, 96–97, 100
cyberwarfare under, 40–41
and international law, 43–44, 77–78
and preventive self-defense, 143–144
purpose of, 42

Kant, Immanuel
cunning of nature in, 93–94
and emergent norms, 47, 93–94
perpetual strife in, 94
Kim Jong-un, 5, 109
King, Martin Luther, Jr., 99
Korea, North. *See* North Korea
Kuhn, Thomas, x

land domain, 17
Langner, Ralph, 3
last resort. *See* principle of last resort
law

versus best practice, 112
and conduct, 39–40
of cyber conflict versus cyber war,
125–126
and cyberwarfare, 41
emergent norms in, 46, 85,
110–111, 114
and ethics, 40–41, 43, 147
normative force of, 39–40
versus norms, 112–113
positivism in, 76–77, 84n43
and surveillance, 148
law of armed conflict
attribution in, 43
in conventional warfare, 26, 60, 148
and cyber conflict, 37–38, 61, 68, 74, 103
cyberweapons under, 60
and ethics, 37–38
foundation of, 107n12
moral equality of soldiers under, 44
moral principles in, 87, 102, 148
relevance of, to cyberwarfare, 41
rules of, for using weapons, 58–59, 60
of the sea, 41
space, 41
state focus of, 87
and Stuxnet, 58–61
law, international. *See* international law
legitimate authority. *See* principle of
legitimate authority
liberty
government threat to, 152–153
and just war reasoning, 98
protection of, 151–153
right to, 36–37
versus security, 25, 49, 73, 74–75,
88–89, 91, 92–93, 94, 110, 152
Libicki, Martin C., 7
Lieber, Franz, 102, 107n12
Lieber Code, 102, 107n12
Locke, John, 91
Lockheed Martin
cybertheft from, 5
logic bomb, 31n16
LulzSec, 20, 21

Machiavelli, Niccolò
and ethics, 37–38
MacIntyre, Alasdair, x, xi
and emergent norms, 47

Rousseau, Jean-Jacques
 human nature in, 93–94
rules of engagement
 for cyberwarfare, 35, 66–67, 147–148
 for espionage, 26, 147–148
 for irregular warfare, 33–34, 35
Russian Federation
 cyberconflict by, 78, 116, 118
 and Estonian distributed denial of
  service, 4, 20, 115–116, 117
 and norms of state behavior, 120
 and *Talinn Manual*, 44

sabotage, 115
Sabu, 21
Schmitt, Michael, 42, 64
sea domain, 17
security
 versus anonymity, 49
 of information, 131
 Internet crime as threat to, 25, 131
 of Internet of Things, 17, 128–129
 versus liberty and privacy, 25, 27–28,
  49, 73, 74–75, 88–89, 91, 92–93,
  94, 110, 129–131, 152
 national, 151–153
 packet-sniffing for, 133, 152
 right to, 152
 software for, 132
 ways to enhance, 132–133
self-defense, anticipatory, 142–155
 and *jus ad bellum*, 65
 permissible, 129–130, 143–144,
  145–146
 state-sponsored hacktivism as, 128
 Stuxnet as, 60–61, 72, 118, 119
 surveillance as, 139, 142–143, 150–
  151, 157–158, 160
 under *Talinn Manual*, 68
 utility of, 147
Shanghai Unit 61384
 cyberthefts by, 5
shashou-jian (Chinese doctrine of
 unconventional warfare), 24
Silver Rule, 90
Snowden, Edward
 accountability of, 157–158
 dilemma of, 148–150
 and moral principles, 158–159,
  161–162

public response to, 147–148
 violations of morality by, 48, 158–159
 whistleblowing by, 1–2, 11, 21, 99,
  130, 143, 157–160
social contract theory
 versus moral realism, 88
Sony Pictures
 hacking of, by North Korea, 5–6,
  13n10, 28
space domain, 17
spear phishing, 18–19
spies. *See also* espionage
 classification of activities of, 6, 26, 28
 compared with warriors, 34
 constraints on, 34, 138, 148
 and cyberwar, 26, 62, 63, 138, 148
spoofing
 definition of, 14n25
 by Iran, 10
state of nature (Hobbes), 9
 in cyber domain, 88–89
 versus moral realism, 88
state-sponsored hacktivism
 accountability for, 127
 and anonymity, 125–139
 attribution of, 127
 by China, 5, 153
 civilian targets of, 4–5, 20, 43,
  115–116, 148
 definition of, 9
 and emergent norms, 126–128,
  157–158
 by North Korea, 5–6
 and privacy, 125–139
 response to, 4, 10–11, 64, 68, 69–71,
  72, 95–96, 109, 115–116, 117,
  127–128
 as self-defense, 128, 148, 153, 160
 as unarmed conflict, 8, 128–129
 by United States, 11
 weapons of, 19, 20, 30n6, 31n16,
  79n9, 127
strategy
 and ethics, xi
Stuxnet, 116
 as act of war, 3–4, 6, 60–61, 68, 70–71,
  117, 143
 developers of, 3
 discovery of, 3
 escape of, 3